Wittgenstein and Contemporary Philosophy of Language

For Lucy

Wittgenstein and Contemporary Philosophy of Language

Bede Rundle

Basil Blackwell

First published 1990

Basil Blackwell Ltd
108 Cowley Road, Oxford, OX4 1JF, UK

Basil Blackwell, Inc.
3 Cambridge Center
Cambridge, Massachusetts 02142, USA

British Library Cataloguing in Publication Data

A CIP catalogue record for this book is available from the British Library.

Library of Congress Cataloging in Publication Data

Rundle, Bede.
Wittgenstein and contemporary philosophy of language / Bede Rundle.
p. cm.
Includes bibliographical references.
ISBN 0-631-17198-3
1. Wittgenstein, Ludwig, 1889–1951 – Contributions in philosophy of language. 2. Languages–Philosophy. 3. Meaning (Philosophy) 4. Wittgenstein, Ludwig, 1889–1951 – Contributions in concept of meaning in philosophy. 5. Wittgenstein, Ludwig, 1889–1951 – Contributions in concept of truth. 6. Truth. I. Title.
B3376.W564R86 1990
121'.68'092–dc20 89-28191
CIP

Typeset in 10/12pt Sabon by Ponting–Green Publishing Services, London
Printed in Great Britain by Billing & Sons Ltd, Worcester

Contents

Abbreviations

AWL	*Wittgenstein's Lectures, Cambridge 1932–1935, from the notes of Alice Ambrose and Margaret MacDonald*
BB	*The Blue and Brown Books*
CV	*Culture and Value*
LA	*Lectures and Conversations on Aesthestics, Psychology and Religious Belief*
LFM	*Wittgenstein's Lectures on the Foundations of Mathematics, Cambridge, 1939*
LW I	*Last writings on the Philosophy of Psychology*, Vol. I
LWL	*Wittgenstein's Lectures, Cambridge 1930–1932, from the notes of John King and Desmond Lee*
M	*Wittgenstein's Lectures in 1930–1933, in G.E. Moore, Philosophical Papers*
MS	Unpublished material cited in the von Wright catalogue (*Wittgenstein*)
OC	*On Certainty*
PG	*Philosophical Grammar*
PI	*Philosophical Investigations*
PR	*Philosophical Remarks*
RFM	*Remarks on the Foundation of Mathematics*
RPP I	*Remarks on the Philosophy of Psychology*, Vol. I
RPP II	*Remarks on the Philosophy of Psychology*, Vol. II
TLP	*Tractatus Logico-Philosphicus*
WVC	*Wittgenstein and the Vienna Circle*
Z	*Zettel*

Preface

The more Wittgenstein's later philosophy is expounded and debated, the more compelling his views are found to be. In some areas, the philosophy of mathematics being the most notable, misinterpretations continue to stand in the way of acceptance, but by and large positions which initially struck many as outlandish are now being seen more clearly for what they are, and being seen to be importantly right. By contrast, the more that comes from the pens of those who derive their inspiration from Frege and subsequent work in formal semantics, the more the inadequacies in this approach are exposed. This tradition has one outstanding achievement to its credit, the systematization of propositional and predicate logic, but as time goes by with nothing more than programmatic suggestions being advanced, the idea that the concepts which have proved fruitful here will shed light on issues in the philosophy of language becomes increasingly implausible.

I do not for a moment offer these observations as reflecting a general consensus, but to some extent their disputability is unimportant, since, while they represent my general outlook, the argument of this book takes me to a position which is as close to that rejected as it is to Wittgenstein. There is nothing in the following pages which deserves to be called a 'theory' of meaning, but system and pattern are identified in a way that is congenial to those who have such a theory as their goal, and on the main topic – the analysis of meaning – the account which takes shape has more in common with the primitive picture which Wittgenstein criticizes than it has with the doctrine of meaning as use, so more in common with the kind of semantics which accords with the approach which I regard as misconceived. However, while it is agreeable to find points of convergence, overall it is more likely that the ideas elaborated here will find favour with supporters neither of formal semantics nor of Wittgenstein. The *rapprochement* with the former is only at a very general level, with respect to aims rather than to detailed method. There is no question of looking to formal logic and the concepts which it can currently handle to provide a model for an understanding of natural language, and the argument of this book will make this as clear as it makes apparent the deficiencies in the Wittgensteinian alternative.

The attempt to grapple with meaning brings inevitable entanglement in other issues in the philosophy of language, some of which I have tried to deal with in my earlier *Grammar in Philosophy*, where much of the argument of the present work is prefigured. Questions of ontology, for instance, are discussed there at length, along with facts, modality, and the behaviour of words in indirect speech, and inadequacies in the current treatment of other topics may in some cases be remedied by having recourse to the fuller treatment in that volume. Some of the material presented here has already made an appearance in print, and I am grateful to the editors of *Mind* and *Philosophical Investigations* for allowing republication in the present form. Those who have a better grasp of Wittgenstein's thought than I may be displeased at the treatment meted out to him in the following pages. They may join me in expressing gratitude to Peter Hacker for the many occasions on which he has expounded and defended Wittgenstein to me with skill and scholarship; without his efforts even greater violence would no doubt have been done, both to the subtleties of Wittgenstein's thought and to the truth generally.

Bede Rundle
Trinity College, Oxford
July 1989

1

Meaning and Use

The thesis that meaning is use holds out the promise of enlightenment on two major fronts: the public character of use takes us out of the realm of the mental, with its attendant subjectivity, while the generality of use offers release from such restrictive models as that of name and bearer, opening up the way for an investigation of meaning which extends to speech acts in all their variety. But there are uncertainties, both in regard to the place of the thesis in Wittgenstein's thought and to its correctness generally. These uncertainties will be our concern in this chapter, along with a preliminary consideration of other concepts which, either in league or in competition with use, may be thought to have a part to play in elucidating meaning.

1.1 Wittgenstein on meaning

Although it is commonly associated with Wittgenstein, the injunction, 'Don't ask for the meaning; ask for the use', is evidently not to be met with in his published writings (cf. Hallett 1967, note 81, 203). Which is not to be wondered at, if, as is also commonly thought, Wittgenstein *identified* meaning and use. A reading of the opening passages of *Philosophical Investigations* is likely to leave us uncertain as to which of separation and identification better indicates Wittgenstein's position, though initially it appears to be the former that has the edge. Thus in §1 Augustine is represented as holding to a view of language which implies that with every word a meaning (*Bedeutung*) is correlated, this meaning being the object for which the word stands. This is perhaps to read overmuch into Augustine's claim that, as he heard words repeatedly used in their proper places in various sentences, he gradually learned to understand 'of what things they were signs' (*quarum rerum signa essent*). It may well be that no great significance should be attached to this use of the all-purpose 'things' (*res*) – less demanding, perhaps, than 'objects' – the emphasis, and the error, lying more with the supposed prelinguistic understanding which Augustine's reconstruction requires, as is clearer when the lines preceding the passage cited are taken into account. Still, as Wittgenstein suggests, it is true that one who describes language learning in this way is likely to be thinking primarily of nouns like 'table', 'chair', and 'bread', and of people's names, not of words like 'such', 'for', and 'yet'. Wittgenstein then asks us to think of another use of language – of certain transactions involving the word 'five' – which leads him to the question, 'But what is the meaning of the word "five"?', a question which is met with one of his rare explicit answers: 'No such thing was in question here, only how the word "five" is used.'

The opposition here between meaning and use may look as clear as could be, but it remains possible that 'meaning' is being taken in conjunction with the misconception which Wittgenstein wishes to attack, a possibility that is strongly suggested by the immediate continuation in §2: 'That *philosophical* concept of meaning has its place in a primitive idea of the way language functions' (my italics) – which does suggest that our ordinary concept may escape unscathed.

It is true that the very grammar of 'meaning' may encourage the false picture, and in his 1932 Cambridge Lectures Wittgenstein appears to express misgivings with our everyday notions:

> The ideas of meaning and sense are obsolete. Unless 'sense' is used in such sentences as 'This has no sense' or 'This has the same sense as that', we are not concerned with sense.
>
> (*AWL* 30; cf. *M* 258)

Again, in *Philosophical Grammar* he remarks that the concept of meaning adopted in his philosophical discussions originates in a primitive philosophy of language, noting that the German word for 'meaning' comes from the word for 'pointing' (*PG* §19; cf. *RPP* I, §551). However, around the same time he is also reported as saying, 'To say that a word has meaning does not imply that it *stands for* or *represents* a thing', the words 'and', 'not', and 'or' being cited as examples (*LWL* 45). And, after all, it is a contention of both the early and the later Wittgenstein that language is all right as it is, so that if objects are inappropriately annexed to our everyday word 'meaning', it will presumably be only because philosophers' misconceptions have put them there. Wittgenstein allows that a language can be imagined for which the description given by Augustine is right; it is just that this is not the pattern for understanding every system of communication (*PI* §§2–3). Compare the following observation from his *Last Writings on the Philosophy of Psychology* (Vol. I, §332):

> 'Meaning' is a primitive concept. The form: 'The word means *this*' belongs to it; that is, the explanation of a meaning by pointing. This works well in certain circumstances and with certain words. But as soon as the concept is expanded to include other words difficulties arise.

While there may be no rejection of our ordinary notions, it remains true that part of the reason for preferring 'use' to 'meaning' is to be found in the consideration that the former is less likely to invite the kind of misconstrual that Wittgenstein is out to repudiate. In the 1934–5 lectures he identifies two misunderstandings for which the latter is held responsible: '"Meaning" is thought to stand for (1) something to which one can point, or (2) something in the mind' (*AWL* 151). It is not clear whether at this point he is totally rejecting these as possibilities, and in the *Lectures on the Foundations of Mathematics* they are tolerated alongside use as criteria of meaning (*LFM* 182), but on both occasions neither is allowed to have anything to offer with the likes of 'perhaps', 'two', and other words for which there is nothing picturable; the reality that corresponds to these words is merely that we have a use for them (ibid. 248–9). We may note that the conception which he extracts from Augustine is not in the first instance concerned with mental entities. The meaning of 'table' may be thought to be an object of sorts, but an object of a familiar concrete character, to be found in houses rather than heads. However, it is true that if we insist on extending this conception to the troublesome words like 'five' and 'or', a mentalistic account may prove hard to avoid, as Russell found: since nothing in the world answers to 'or', perhaps we should be looking to feelings of hesitation or indecision for its correlate (Russell 1940, chapter 5).

As we have seen, Wittgenstein allows that the meaning of a word may be explained by pointing, but even when we can speak of an object corresponding to a word, that object is not describable as the word's *meaning*. Not, at least, once use comes to its position of dominance in his thought. In the *Tractatus* he had roundly declared: 'The name means the object. The object is its meaning' (*TLP* 3.203). However, the meaning of the name 'Moore' is not a certain human body, for we do not say that the meaning sits on a sofa (*LWL* 62; cf. *AWL* 44, *PG* 63–4). On the contrary, the meaning of a word is 'part of language' (*LWL* 62), it is constituted by the place of the word in grammar (*PG* 59), by its role in the calculus (*PG* 63), and – his final formula – by its use in the language (*PG* 60).

On the other hand, as Wittgenstein realized, locating meaning so firmly within language may also provoke unease:

> It is a queer thing that, considering language as a game, the use of a word is internal to the game whereas its meaning seems to point to something outside the game. What seems to be indicated is that 'meaning' and 'use' are not equatable. But this is misleading.
>
> (*AWL* 48)

How exactly we are misled is not further elaborated, but there are also indications that Wittgenstein did not wish to go so far as to identify meaning and use. Just previously he had said:

> I have suggested substituting for 'meaning of a word', 'use of a word', because *use of a word* comprises a large part of what is meant by 'the meaning of a word'. Understanding a word will thus come to knowing its use, its applications.
>
> (*AWL* 48)

Is use, as far as words are concerned, and philosophical corruptions aside, just what meaning comes to? Or, since a large part is still less than the whole, is use perhaps merely the legacy of an obsolete notion of meaning? Again, speaking of contradictions, Wittgenstein confesses not to know whether we are to say they have a meaning, but he is clear that they do not have a use (*LFM* 223).

A measure of uncertainty persists into the later writings. The tentative formulation, 'if the meaning is the *use* we make of the word' (*PI* §138), suggests that he thought the equation at least disputable – cf. also *PI* §561 – and while there is no 'if' in the best-known passage presenting the equation, that equation is qualified:

> For a *large* class of cases - though not for all - in which we employ the word 'meaning', it can be explained thus: the meaning of a word is its use in the language.
>
> (ibid. §43)

Previously, use had been said to constitute a large part of meaning, presumably for any word. Here use is equated with meaning, but for a large class of cases only. Whether this class is taken to include all cases of word meaning is not clear. Certainly, the qualification given with 'the meaning of a *word*' can take care of uses of 'meaning' which fall outside the range of the explanation, as when natural phenomena are said to have meaning, so it would look to be words themselves that are to provide the exceptions – though for a different interpretation see Baker and Hacker 1980, 250.

Not unnaturally, Wittgenstein is led to speak of use as *determining* meaning (*PI* §139), and at more than one point he urges that we let the use of words *teach* us their meaning (ibid. 212, 220), both of which would appear to make better sense if we have something less than complete identity. On one occasion he remarks, 'Not every *use*, you want to say, is a meaning' (*LW* I, §289). This is of interest, not only for the possibility contemplated, but also for the clumsiness attending this occurrence of 'is', a clumsiness that is removed by substituting the more accurate 'determines'. Compare, too, the claim that the meaning of a statement is its method of verification, or the parallel observation that 'The sense of a question is the method of answering it' (*PR* 66). How *p* is shown to be true is doubtless intimately connected with the matter of what *p* means, but the latter is not literally a *method* of any kind.

While the meaning of, say, 'butterfly', may be given by a rule for its use, it likewise cannot be said to *be* that rule. Wittgenstein was alive to the incongruity in this identification (cf. *M* 258), but we might have doubts about *any* talk of rules in this connection. An uncritical invocation of rules is a feature of much current philosophy of language, the notion being one which, at best, is thoroughly overworked. And not simply in those cases where the fancifulness of the theorizing is evident, as with supposed rules of depth grammar; even at the more homely level where Wittgenstein operates there is generally a less misleading way of doing what he seeks to do by appeal to rules. A rule may antedate a practice, in which case we look to it for guidance, as the arbiter of correct procedure; but the practice may antedate the rule, and then the acceptability of the rule is judged by its fit with that practice. Linguistic rules are overwhelmingly of the second kind. Let me elaborate.

'The rules of grammar distinguish sense and nonsense', says Wittgenstein (*LWL* 47). Indeed they may, but that is not to say that they determine either. On the contrary, linguistic rules are typically only derivative: conformity with actual practice is fundamental to correctness, rather than accord with a rule, though the extent of the difference depends on whether the rule is one that prescribes or describes practice. Suppose we have a rule which disallows the combination of a psychological predicate, as 'dream' or 'forget', with a designation of a body. The sentence, 'His body forgot', could then be said to be nonsense because it violates this rule, but only in the uninteresting sense that it violates a rule aimed at proscribing a form of nonsense. The sentence is not nonsense simply because it violates a rule, but because it and similar sentences are nonsense the rule is describable as one that proscribes nonsense. Here I am thinking of the rule as given an injunctive form, as 'Do not . . . ', or 'You must . . . ', but suppose we take a formulation which comes closer to a description, as with the more narrowly grammatical rule: subject and verb invert after 'seldom' – so 'Seldom have I seen . . . ' rather than 'Seldom I have seen . . . '. Here the gap between violating the rule and being out of step with actual practice is narrower, but the latter remains the prime consideration, since whatever significance the rule has it has simply as codifying that practice, as providing a means of referring to it. It is no explanation of the character of *p* as *nonsense* to appeal to the violation of a rule, unless that rule is a (dispensable) description of the practice. On the other hand, there could be an authority that laid down by fiat what was to count as good English, since such character, unlike nonsense, is something that might be secured by stipulation.

Perhaps the most compelling reason for speaking of rules is provided by the possibility of appraising usage as correct or incorrect, so it is important to stress that such appraisals may be understood simply in terms of agreement or disagreement with the underlying pattern of usage which a rule epitomizes. That, more generally, correctness as accord with a rule may be secondary, is clear. A rule or recipe for wiring a plug or baking a cake is of no account unless it prescribes an appropriate way of going about the task, the notion of the correct practice or procedure being once more the notion that has priority. And has priority over the notion of a regularity as well: the right way of driving a golf ball is not necessarily the way generally adopted, the dominant regularity, but the way that stands the best chance of success. Even when the regularity gives rise to a rule, it cannot, of course, be said that the rule reduces to the regularity; the two are not of comparable types. What is true in the present instance is simply that the aim is to conform to the general practice, to speak as native speakers do, an aim which inevitably takes us to regularities of usage.

We may also note that, while talk of rules or of the practice which they aim to represent may come to much the same thing, it is only when a rule formulation exists that we can justify talk of applying or consulting, of misinterpreting or being guided by a rule, notions which come into their own with the teaching and speaking of a second language, but which have relatively little to do in describing how the native speaker comes to say what he says. Nor, when they lack the reality which a formulation confers, does it help to relocate rules in mind or brain, as part, perhaps, of our innate endowment; that does nothing to reinstate ways of speaking which require that we make sense of rules as guides to practice, as susceptible of misunderstanding, or indeed as having any kind of descriptive or normative role whatsoever. (Cf. Baker and Hacker 1984a, chapter 8, where this aberration of modern linguistics is criticized at length.)

Wittgenstein's ready talk of linguistic rules appears better suited to his earlier conception of language as a calculus, and indeed he acknowledges that, because they represent as regulated what is fluctuating, rules may mislead with respect to natural language (*PG* §36; *PI* §81). True, in *Philosophical Grammar* he states that 'we are interested in language as a procedure in accordance with explicit rules' (§32), but since we are also said merely to *envisage* language as a game played according to rules (ibid. §§26, 36), there need be no contradiction of the view, more apparent in his later writings, that the practice has priority: if *p* is nonsense, that is because usage has not conferred a sense upon it, rather than because there is a rule which proscribes it. Note, too, his observation that we do not learn to use words with the help of rules (*LW* I, §968). However, the impression is sometimes conveyed that he is prepared to take the case where a rule has been formulated as a model for language use generally. Consider *PI* §558, where he speaks of 'the rule which shews that the word "is" has different meanings', or *PI* 147, where, apropos 'not', it is stated that without certain rules the word has as yet no meaning, and if we change the rules, it now has another meaning. In so far as the explicit rule remains his model, it is surely one that misleads as much as it illuminates.

1.2 *Difficulties with meaning as use*

Given that neither use nor rules of use is a clear candidate for an identity with meaning, can we simply settle for the claim that use *determines* meaning? In his account of Wittgenstein's lectures in 1930–3, Moore reports him as saying that the meaning of a word is determined by the grammatical rules in accordance with which it is used (*M* 258). Wittgenstein apparently preferred to use the word 'determined', saying that you would be tempted to say that the meaning *was* a list of rules only if you persisted in thinking that to the word 'meaning' an entity must correspond. But the observations are made with respect to grammatical rules, not to use, and the following remarks make it doubtful whether the refinement suggested is one that Wittgenstein would accept for the latter:

> If I stick to saying that the meaning is given by the use, then I cannot use an expression in a different way without changing the meaning. But it is then misleading to say, 'The expression *must* have a different meaning if used differently.' It is merely that it *has* a different meaning – the different use *is* the different meaning.
>
> (*LFM* 192)

On the other hand, emphatic though it may be, Wittgenstein's purposes do not always require that he press this dubious equation. Thus, one of his major concerns is to combat the thought that the meaning of an expression is a mental accompaniment to that expression (*AWL* 3, 49–50, 78–9; *BB* 65), an image or idea from which the use flows or can be derived (*AWL* 50–1, 86–7). His counter is in part to reverse this priority, to give use precedence over anything that might go on in our heads, a reversal which demands that sameness of use should bring with it sameness in meaning, but not that every difference in the former be reflected in the latter. If a divergent understanding of an expression is something that must always be capable of showing itself in the way a speaker uses that expression, if agreement in use entails agreement as to meaning, if all the information about meaning is extractable from the use, then differences in the images or experiences that may accompany the word drop out as irrelevant, a conclusion which requires that meaning be exhaustively determined by use, whilst leaving it open whether we are dealing with the limiting case where use and what use determines are one and the same (cf. *RPP* I, §212).

I doubt that, in general, Wittgenstein would wish to be held to anything more definite than the claim that much the same ground is covered by *use* as by *meaning*, though less misleadingly by the former. But whether or not he came to think of the two as the same, or as close as makes no difference, I suggest that we can go no further than this relation of determination – understood logically, not causally. Questions of meaning do appear to be, invariably, questions of use, but the converse does not hold: the use of a word, but not its meaning, can be fashionable, ill-advised, or unjustified; it can be encouraged or prohibited, accompanied by gestures, occasion disputes, and reveal something about the speaker. Not so its meaning. So great are the differences in the behaviour of the two, we might find it puzzling that their identity should ever be advanced, even only tentatively, but a different grammar does not, of course, mean that substitution of the one term for the other is always ruled out, and the occasions when either may be employed are sufficiently numerous for the supposition of an identity not to be immediately recognizable as nonsense. Thus, because to learn the use is to learn the meaning, we find Wittgenstein saying:

> . . . A meaning of a word is a kind of employment of it.
> For it is what we learn when the word is incorporated into our language.
>
> (OC §61)

In the light of the reason offered the identity may look irresistible, but no more is strictly warranted than is given by our more cautious formula.

That 'use' enjoys a broader application is further apparent in the ways in which the term may be expanded: we have what a word is used of, when, by whom, and to what end, and differences in meaning are not always brought in tow by differences in these respects. The case for sameness of meaning co-existing with a difference in use is sometimes argued on the basis of pairs like 'foot' and 'paw', or 'cut' and 'mow'. The words in each pair supposedly mean the same, but 'foot' is used of human beings, 'paw' not, and 'mow' is used with respect to cutting grass, but not to cutting hair. I do not find this appeal persuasive. To take an example as favourable as any, consider the various collective nouns – *bevy*, *pride*, *gaggle*, *shoal*, *covey* – which characterize collections of creatures, though not the same range of creatures in any two cases. The common thread of meaning is sufficiently to the fore to make us feel that most members of this easily extended list are redundant. However, we do not want a principle that would allow two terms to collapse into synonymy whenever there was a third term, as 'collection', whose applicability was guaranteed by that of each; and, indeed, however contrived the distinction between, say, a flock of quails and one of partridges, the differentiating conditions with which 'bevy' and 'covey' are thus associated are such as to go with a difference in meaning: despite the sameness at the level of *flock*, *collection*, or *gathering*, a difference remains in what each of the terms is applied to.

In this instance, differences in use preclude a single meaning through involving differences in application. The difficulty arises when there is no such involvement, as with the pair 'lift' and 'elevator', terms typically used on opposite sides of the Atlantic. A trivial divergence, no doubt, but one that qualifies as a difference in use, yet, like variation in frequency of use, does not issue in a difference in meaning.

Wittgenstein was, perhaps, aware of this difficulty. Shortly before remarking, 'Not every *use*, you want to say, is a meaning', he had written:

> One doesn't say, for instance, that 'walk' and 'walks' have different meanings.
>
> They mean exactly the same thing, we would tell someone; namely, *this* – and then we would demonstrate walking to him.
>
> (*LW* I, §274)

It is not clear that we should say without qualification that 'walk' and 'walks' are the same in meaning, but what is of greater interest to our present concern is that we have here a difference in use which, for Wittgenstein, is consistent with sameness of meaning, a sameness which, moreover, is apparently shown by the common extralinguistic reference.

A more general basis for setting aside irrelevant differences in use is suggested by a possible interpretation of *PI* §43. It is difficult to tell just what exceptions Wittgenstein had in mind when he said that in a large class of cases, though not for all, the meaning of a word could be explained as its use in the language. The natural

thought is that the equation of meaning with use is taken to fail in some cases, but could it be the phrase 'in the language' that requires exceptions to be admitted? The reason for this qualification could be to ensure that use is envisaged at the right level of generality. It is a matter of the use as described by grammar, so of features that are central to the given word, not of anything and everything that comes in under the broader heading. Cf. *PG* §23, where the observations are juxtaposed:

> The use of a word in the language is its meaning.
> Grammar describes the use of words in the language.

However, while proper names are thought of by Wittgenstein as having meaning, their meaning is presumably to be explained at a local rather than at a global level, with reference to particular individuals, or to a particular person's conception of a given individual, rather than in such a way as would define anything as general as a use in the language. To speak of the meaning of 'Robinson' as being its use is dubious on more than one count, but at all events it must be a matter of use on the part of a subgroup of speakers, not use in the language at large.

This interpretation is not one that I offer with any confidence, but it has at least this much support: specifying the use in the language of '*N*' can illuminate general character as a *name*, but this generality will have to be sacrificed, the qualification 'in the language' dropped, if, as Wittgenstein implies at *PI* §79, a name may have a multitude of meanings; furthermore, the way the topic is taken up in the immediate continuation of §43 – 'And the *meaning* of a name is sometimes explained by pointing to its *bearer*' – suggests a possible connection with the grounds for introducing that qualification.

The example of 'lift' and 'elevator' appears to secure a difference between use and meaning in an uninteresting way, but it does point to the need for a restriction on the former that looks to be important: very crudely, it is only a divergence with respect to what the words are used *of* that threatens a difference in meaning; other differences, such as those on the side of the *users*, are not germane. Overlapping the latter we have the whole range of *tonal* differences which separate a standard word from its poetic, archaic, learned, dialectal, or slang equivalents, as 'over' and 'o'er', 'clot' and 'thrombosis', or

'child' and 'bairn'. Distinctions in use abound with such pairs, but without assuring a difference in meaning.

Perhaps Wittgenstein, too, would wish to see 'use' further circumscribed; certainly, if use as *function* is too broad, use as *application* comes closer to what is wanted. However, if any chance of a match with 'meaning' requires a restriction along the lines just indicated, we have not got away from the kind of semantic notion considered central by one who takes a word-world relation to be at the heart of meaning – just the kind of conception that the appeal to use may be hoped to discourage. To take this point a stage further, consider the word 'but', which, when it joins two clauses, can be said to signal or signify a contrast between these. In this form we have not provided a specification of use, but while that is easy enough to remedy – 'the word is used to signal a certain contrast' – it is far from clear that the resulting invocation of 'use' is of any great moment. It does draw attention to the purpose or intention into which the word may enter, but the bulk of the work is done by the further qualification, the qualification which indicates what precisely the word is used to *do*, and which, it would appear, is closer to 'mean' than is 'use' itself. This is an important objection, since it indicates not merely that use, as the broader notion, has to be restricted if it is to fall in step with meaning, but that the restriction may prove to convey the substance of the latter – and indeed in such traditional terms as *signify*, *signal*, *designate, convey*, and *indicate* – in which case the significance of the possibility of invoking use is considerably diminished.

I present this objection as showing that *use* may not have the advantages initially supposed, but of course much depends on what is claimed for the particular expansions. The way in which these semantic terms make an appearance might even be regarded as a consideration in favour of use, though Wittgenstein would demur if no more than the traditional battery of terms, presenting for the most part variations on the notion of reference, is allowed. However, while, for instance, 'what *w* is used of' has no application to words such as 'yet', the way this scheme, like others of a referential character, is so often, so clearly, and so non-accidentally relevant does encourage the search for related formulae to cope with the less amenable expressions.

Here we may note the following. Take a relatively straightforward word, such as 'sunset'. What we might think to *do* with this word will be very much dependent upon the fact that it is associated with

one phenomenon rather than another – just the point of focus when our concern is to distinguish a term from its near synonyms. Indeed, that it is the word for the daily disappearance of the sun below the horizon far outweighs any other aspect of its use as far as its meaning is concerned. Not only does this dimension have priority; if it is lacking entirely, there is some difficulty in seeing how the word can function *as* a word. After all, what does a word have that equips it for a linguistic use beyond its symbolic or representational status? As a mere sound or mark on paper there is otherwise not much to a word that a use might hope to exploit, nothing that gives it any advantage over a meaningless noise. Wittgenstein is reported as saying that when we say 'and' has a meaning, 'what we mean is that it works in a sentence and is not just a flourish' (*LWL* 43). The difficulty is to see how this can be worked up into a satisfactory elucidation of 'and' without assigning the word *any* role that might be characterized in these traditional terms – as when I spoke of 'but' as signalling or signifying a contrast. Successful use of a tool is dependent upon its having a character which suits it to a purpose; if the analogy extends to words, we can ask what it is about 'and' and 'but' that enables these to do their very different jobs in the way that the construction of saw or hammer equips each for its use. Even if the requisite character of 'and' is determined by its use, the point still holds: such character appears to be presupposed by those numerous uses which depend on meaning.

Such terms as 'symbolic' and 'representational' may, and no doubt should, occasion disquiet. *Representing* may be associated with the idea of being a substitute for something, and that is hardly the role of a word. As Wittgenstein puts it, a picture may be a substitute for a person – when one would rather see him but must make do with the picture – but 'the sign on the map is not a substitute for the object that it means' (*RPP* I, §207). However, the notion of representing is not one that Wittgenstein wishes to proscribe in this connection – it is precisely because of their representational role that samples can be reckoned part of language (*PI* §50) – and while 'represent' may move towards 'stand in for' – Wittgenstein in the *Tractatus*, and even in *Philosophical Grammar*, took the German *vertreten* this way (*TLP* 3.22; *PG* §46) – a more apposite equivalent is given by 'stand for'. Even more generally, we have the notion of a word as a word *for* something. True, it is far from evident how this, or *standing for*, can be realized with respect to a word like 'and', and further elucidation is required to show that we have to do here with a real possibility. I shall approach this question by indicating how we may be too readily satisfied by an account of the use of 'and', an example which will also serve to introduce the topic of *truth*, one of the main contenders for the role of key concept in explaining meaning.

1.3 Meaning and truth

The relevance of truth in this connection comes out in the systematic way whereby variations in meaning at the level of the word issue in variations in possible truth values at the level of the sentence. A difference in meaning between 'salt' and 'pepper' is, essentially, a difference in what goes by the names, but this at once founds the possibility of a difference in the distribution of truth values with respect to propositions in which now one, now the other, occurs. The notion of truth is also naturally invoked if anything like the account of meaning just implied for these two nouns is to be extended more generally. Since co-extensive terms are not invariably synonymous, it is not quite right to say that the identity of 'salt' *qua* meaningful term is just a matter of the particular fashion in which it divides up the world, just a matter of what it is true of, what not. But while we should expect this reference to truth to be retained in a more accurate account, the formula seems, at first sight, not even relevant to a word like 'too', say, as this occurs in 'These shoes are too small'. However, because it joins with a term, 'small', which does have application in the required way, 'too' can be brought into the scheme, its specific meaning emerging in just that restriction of application which its incorporation within the larger phrase induces. Quite generally, the pattern of explanation appropriate to a verbal phrase can be passed on to any term that modifies the truth condition associated with that phrase.

What that pattern embraces is considerable. Not only single words, as 'small', 'unexpectedly', or 'soon', but larger phrases, as 'while you were out' or 'in spite of his illusions'. Thus, the truth-based account of the predicate in 'He was resting' is extendible to a qualification such as 'all afternoon', in so far as the latter makes for a restriction of the condition associated with the predicate in a way that is a direct function of its meaning: the temporal phrase clearly contributes to the truth value of the whole, which is false – its negation true – when 'all afternoon' does not give the correct temporal measure. The same holds for the clause added in 'He was resting while you were out.' This makes a contribution at the same point, and the availability of a negation bearing upon the clause enables us to speak of the falsity of the whole when that condition fails.

This, in outline, is the appeal of truth in explaining meaning: a linguistic form capable of truth and falsity provides a framework in which the individual word can be seen to make a contribution that is a direct function of its particular meaning, even though we may be able to make no sense of the word as marking some kind of extralinguistic character when it occurs in isolation, without the benefit of a surrounding linguistic context. In short, with truth we are offered the means of keeping a broadly Augustinian conception of language in the running. And, of course, truth's applicability does not end with the single clause, but the scheme is further extended by giving a truth-functional account of the various conjunctions which, like 'if' and 'or', play a pivotal part in the recursions which generate the larger units of language.

If we bring such a sentence as 'He thought it was Monday' under this pattern of explanation, '. . . thought it was Monday' being a predicate which may be truly or falsely affirmed of a designated individual, we shall be looking at the words from a different perspective from one which would seek to represent 'He thought . . .' as a function which takes sentences as arguments, and which finds this particular phrase problematic through not being truth-functional; that is, the truth value of 'He thought that *p*' is not a function of the truth value of *p*. Clearly, if our concern is with meaning generally, the notion of a truth-conditional explanation will be of greater applicability than that of a truth-functional explanation.

While there are many words for which truth is of uncertain relevance, the conjunction 'and' appears to be supremely well-suited to an account that is not merely truth-conditional, but more narrowly truth-functional as well. This, I suggest, is an illusion, but before indicating why, we shall consider what might be reckoned the simplest form of definition for the word in its use with clauses. Suppose we try to clarify 'and' by saying that it is used to conjoin. Since conjunctions as a class have that role, we might improve on this by saying *merely* conjoin, a description which at least looks to have the generality needed to accommodate the range of words and phrases which 'and' brings together. However, this generality may now be excessive, since the word is not used to unite just any two sentences that might naturally succeed one another. We may follow 'Where have you been?' by 'I've been waiting for ages', but not form the compound sentence, 'Where have you been and I have been waiting for ages'; similarly, 'Watch out! Those bricks could fall!', but not 'Watch out and those bricks could fall!'; and 'John was disappointed. He had expected a much better response', but not (with rare exceptions) 'John was disappointed and he had expected a much better response.'

If q is to be joined to p by 'and', it must exhibit a degree of homogeneity, both syntactic and semantic, with p; it must make sense as offering an addition to p, as when the two clauses can be regarded as exemplifying a common theme, or when q describes an event which follows upon an event specified in p. Failure of the requisite relation is most marked when there is not even agreement as to sentence type – though not all such combinations, as assertion plus question, are ruled out – but even with homogeneity in this respect the necessary unity may be lacking, as the last example illustrates. Far from being indifferent to what it conjoins, 'and' forces what follows into the pattern set by what precedes. That imposition is acceptable with 'John was disappointed and his friends were upset', but with 'John was disappointed and he had expected a much better response', use of the conjunction has the effect of putting the two clauses on a par, as if they were advanced together simply as instances of truths. That of course is possible, and it could also be that their unity resides in the way they jointly answer a question, but it is more likely that the second clause is offered in explanation of the first, in which case it does not have the like status that 'and' would imply.

An account of 'and' which merely states that it is used to conjoin will not do, but this is secondary to the matter of homogeneity in the two clauses. After all, what is 'conjoin' to mean here? It is not merely that the word provides a sound or shape to bridge groups of words, written or spoken. That it could do without having any more significance than an 'er' or 'um' that fills a gap between spoken words, and which, if it has a meaning, has it more as a natural sign *of* rather than as a conventional sign *for* something. Again, if 'and' merely signified that what was being said was an addition to what had gone before – in the sense of merely another thing said, not a continuation of a theme – then it would serve little use, in that it would convey nothing that was not totally obvious.

'And' is not a mere noise, an acoustic coupling, but it has a meaning, and – in my view – a description of its use bears upon this only to the extent that it makes clear what the condition is with which the word is associated. Can we say, by way of such description, that we link words with 'and' when we think that they *are* linked, in theme? Or is it perhaps rather that we use 'and' when we want the words in question to be *seen* as thus linked? We noted how we might or might not wish to unite the clauses in 'John was disappointed and he had expected a much greater response', and we can make the point more clearly by invoking a comparison with 'but', which stands in exact contrast to 'and'. In '*p* but *q*' there is standardly a shift in direction which 'but' marks, whereas with 'and' a continuation of theme is signalled. So, 'I've got the time, but I haven't got the money' – not 'and' – but 'He is a dentist and his wife is also' – not 'but'. These, at least, are the forms that need no explanation; the conjunctions *can* join sentences where it is more readily seen how one might go either way. Compare 'He spends the term in Oxford and goes to London in vacations' with 'He spends the term in Oxford but goes to London in vacations.' With 'and' the theme common to both clauses – where the person resides – is acknowledged, while if we wish to highlight the contrast within this we shall turn to 'but'. Given the possibility of such alternatives, it may be thought preferable to characterize 'and' in terms of the second of the formulae suggested – and analogously for 'but' – rather than speak as if we had no choice in treating the relevant conditions as either comparable or contrastive. However, if the clauses are to be seen in either relation, this is because there is thought to be a real contrast or comparison which the conjunction can reflect.

None of this is brought out if we speak just in terms of a use to conjoin, but is an expanded account of use possible along the lines of 'use to extend the theme of the preceding clause'? It would seem not, since 'and' signifies that what follows has this character, rather than itself achieving such an extension. Likewise, a specification of the use of 'but' is inadequate so long as it does not make plain that the word is associated with a contrast, a shift in direction, in the clauses it conjoins. The same pattern extends readily enough to other conjunctions, as those classifiable as temporal or consequential. In all cases an adequate account of use must be elaborated to such a point that the relation signalled by the conjunction is made explicit. The schema, '*w* is the word for . . .', is not one that suits all words equally well, but whereas talk of the *use* of 'and' may take us off in a number of directions, 'and' is a word for a relation . . .' is already on course to arrive at the meaning of the conjunction.

What has become of truth? We shall consider later how the claim of this favoured notion to throw light on meaning is to be assessed, but it should be clear why it has played no part in our deliberations to date. Not only does a truth-conditional account simply pass over the conditions of continuity and contrast with which 'and' and 'but' are associated, thereby being totally uninformative on the question of their distinctive meanings; when the clauses are other than assertoric, it does not get off the ground at all, not even to the point of giving the illusion that their meanings have been explained. It is quite plain that any involvement of these conjunctions with truth is inessential, to be put down to the character of the conjoined clauses, and not to the conjunctions themselves. The account here offered, by contrast, is in no way embarrassed by combinations in which, for instance, imperatives and interrogatives figure. Furthermore, the failure of a term to behave as a term with 'sense', to 'contribute to truth conditions', need not present the slightest obstacle to seeing how its meaning might be grasped. 'But' is not used in *stating* a contrastive condition, but we are required merely to learn of its association with that condition, an association which does not presuppose any particular grammar for the word. Again, a term like 'the' is not usefully thought of as true of anything, but a child can come to understand it by learning of the condition in terms of which a definite descriptive phrase is used to single things out. The topic is another to which we shall return.

1.4 Tone

The notion of a tonal difference was introduced in terms of examples, as with 'over' and 'o'er'. This hardly makes plain in what such a difference consists, though even without further elucidation the phenomenon is seen to be one that puts a simple identification of meaning with use under pressure: the difference in tone between 'over' and 'o'er' goes with a difference in use, but the two forms are surely univocal.

The example of 'but' is worth pursuing further in this connection. I say that the word is used to signal a contrast, a shift in direction, but it may not always be clear what, in narrower terms, the contrast is between. If someone says, 'The jug is empty, but it is made of plastic', we may wonder: is it that the first clause confirms, whereas the second contradicts, what has been claimed? – e.g., 'That glass jug is empty.' Or does the first give a reason why the jug is suitable for some purpose, the second a reason why it is unsuitable?

In 'The Thought', Frege contends that with 'but' (*aber*) we intimate that what follows is in contrast with what would be expected in the light of what preceded. While this can accommodate 'He is ailing but contented', it will not do for 'Roger is in good health but his brother is seriously ill', where it is merely the contrast in what is said of the one person as against the other that attracts the 'but', with no suggestion of unexpectedness. Or again, with 'The house suffers from dry rot, but it is cheap', the second consideration is clearly *not* unexpected in the light of the first, the contrast between the good and the bad being what is likely to have dictated the choice of conjunction.

If we look for possible differences in truth value between '*p* and *q*' and '*p* but *q*' we shall be disappointed. We can accordingly say that the true/false poles here provide too gross a device with which to detect a difference in meaning, but Frege, for one, would not find this worrying. Identity of behaviour in respect of truth value shows, at least in this kind of example, agreement in 'sense', and this does not coincide with our 'meaning'. The latter also perhaps embraces *tone* or *colouring*; at all events, it is to that category that what differentiates 'but' from 'and' is assigned. That Frege has not demarcated his categories in the most useful way is suggested by the consequent grouping of this difference alongside that between 'steed' and 'horse', say, or more generally between poetic (archaic, slang, dialectal) words and their standard equivalents. Where tone is thought of as the kind of aura that may cling to poetic language, or to other forms where the medium is as important as the message, such a characterization of conjunctions is out of place – as if what were being communicated were essentially the same whether we said '*p* and *q*' or '*p* but *q*' or '*p* although *q*' or '*p* despite the fact that *q*' or '*p* whereas *q*', and so on, totally ignoring the precise relation that each conjunction conveys. The particular character of, say, a dialectal word, may be due to associations which the word has but of which the speaker is quite oblivious. In this respect the way 'but' has meaning is as with words which have no special tone, the shift in direction implied being of course in no way peripheral as far as the question of meaning is concerned, but constituting just that condition which any native speaker would intend to signal by his use of the word.

The tone distinctive of 'but' is for Frege a matter of a contrast merely suggested or hinted at, not explicitly asserted. However, the condition definitive of 'and' is equally one that is inexplicit. That is, 'and' heralds the extension or continuation of a theme, but, as with the contrast implied by 'but', we do not as much as *say* that the second clause continues the theme of the first. Similarly, if I assert 'The hall is full', I do not as much as say 'There is a hall', so on this way of looking at it the difference between 'the' and 'there is' is also a difference in tone. Not, surely, a use of the notion that has much to recommend it.

In *Last Writings* I, §726, Wittgenstein speaks of two words for 'sabre', *Sabel* and *Säbel*, as having a different 'atmosphere'. They have the same meaning, however, '*in so far* as both are names for the same kind of objects'. He then raises the question, 'But what is one to say here? *Do* they or *don't* they have the same meaning?', which he answers only to the extent of expressing his unwillingness to distinguish among kinds of meaning.

It is noteworthy that sameness on the side of the objects is here given its due without qualification. But how should Wittgenstein's question be answered? Granted, the stark alternatives posed give every appearance of a question envisaged as coming from the mouth of a misguided interlocutor, rather than from Wittgenstein; none the less, it may be that there is more to be said for coming down on one side rather than the other. Certainly, metaphor is one factor which makes clear that not all tonal differences are without repercussions on meaning. Colloquial language, and slang in particular, owes much of its flavour to the figures of speech which it deploys, often so as to suggest frivolity, flippancy, or irreverence. Thus 'sky pilot', (priest), 'drop a brick' (commit a *faux pas*), 'belly-ache' (grumble), 'breeze in' (enter), 'bowl over' (overwhelm), and so forth. Conversely, officialese and other forms of long-winded speech may convey pomposity: 'detrimental to the visual amenities of the locality' (unsightly), 'at this point of time' (now), 'having negative vulnerability to water entry' (waterproof).

The very way in which a figurative use draws upon a term which differs in meaning from the literal equivalent rules out strict synonymy with such pairs. Indeed, they will depend for their effect on there being a significant difference, as with a euphemism – 'departed' for 'dead' – or its opposite – 'coffin nail' for 'cigarette'.

Likewise, circumlocutions will have meaningful components not matched in the terser forms, so again we have only an approximation to sameness of meaning. More problematic are words and phrases which do not diverge from one another in these ways, as with 'mad' and 'gaga', 'truly' and 'verily', or 'dog' and 'bow-wow'. One common pattern here is the following. Although there will be occasions when the second member of these pairs in some way contrasts with its surrounding context, perhaps striking a discordant note, there are, or have been, contexts in which its use is quite unremarkable. In older speech there was nothing special about 'verily', but it was a standard equivalent of 'truly'. Similarly, in criminal parlance there need be nothing self-conscious about use of 'the nick'; in these circles it just is an accepted word for 'prison'. And perhaps there actually are people within the sound of Bow Bells who unaffectedly use 'apples and pears' for 'stairs', 'bo-peep' for 'sleep', and other instances of rhyming slang – though again we may have something like a figure of speech to complicate the comparison.

In their natural contexts, these various forms of non-standard speech may pass as the norm, so no special point is made by invoking them, no exploitation of the associations which they conjure up. Not so once we shift to a context where the word is not standardly used, for here it will stand out through its character as argot, as a regional term, or whatever, having a distinctive tone in so far as it is redolent of its original setting.

Consider now the question whether such associations require acknowledgement in an account of meaning. On the one hand, it is true that a person who is insensitive to a particular tone has failed to grasp an important aspect of the word, but it is more clearly an aspect of its use, rather than of its meaning, that eludes him. To defend constancy of meaning in a pair such as 'over' and 'o'er' we might hope to appeal to identical behaviour with respect to matters of truth, much as Wittgenstein acknowledges a single meaning for the two words for 'sabre' in so far as they are names for the same kind of object. Since, however, such a defence is (at best) available only with certain parts of speech – not with the pair 'yes' and 'aye', for instance – it would be desirable to have a more general approach. Here is one possibility.

In the standard use of a word, its use in contexts where it passes as the accepted term, an association of the kind in question will be in no way to the fore; perhaps it is not even something of which speakers are aware. Use of the word 'cobber' identifies the user as, in all likelihood, Australian, but the condition, 'user is Australian', will have no place in an account of the word's meaning, since where the word is standard that condition will not serve to differentiate any of its users. What, then, of the case where the word is used outside its natural setting, so where, relative to the context of its current use, it is felt to have a special tone? The speaker's choice of word will then call for explanation, and the intention behind its use is more than likely to connect with the associations which it brings to mind. If there is any chance of assigning these associations to the word's meaning, it will be with reference to uses of this latter kind. On the other hand, since this will be a special use, it would seem proper to exclude such associations, word meaning being a matter of what is *standardly* meant. We can trade on the associations to induce a certain belief in our audience, but that is to exploit the 'natural' meaning of the word: utterance of 'cobber' can be taken to mean 'naturally' that the speaker is Australian, and this is to be distinguished from properly linguistic meaning. Similarly, the regularity of the association of 'bye-byes' with the nursery can justify talk of a sign relation, but the way in which a word is a sign *of* something is different from the way it has meaning as a word, which is a matter more of its being a sign *for* something.

Needless to say, the topic of tone could be pursued further with profit, but this brief encounter suffices for the present purpose of improving upon Frege's treatment, and, more important, of giving a further example of the way meaning and use may part company. That is, the phenomenon of tone shows that not everything that can be reckoned to the use of a word deserves recognition in an account of its meaning. Can the tonal differences which argue a difference in use without one in meaning be handled by exploiting the fuller form, 'use in the language'? Possibly, but it is doubtful that this regularly yields the right answer: 'over' and 'o'er' have, over a certain range, a good claim to synonymy, but not to an identical use in the language.

2

Names and Ostension

Another possible separation of use and meaning arises with Wittgenstein's handling of the contention that the meaning of a word lies outside language. This is not a possibility he allows – 'the meaning must be entirely given, or determined, if you describe the language or its rules' (*LWL* 64) – though it may be thought he comes close to it when he speaks of a 'transitive' sense of 'meaning', the sense which applies when there exists something corresponding to the word – so with respect to 'red' rather than to 'and' (*LWL* 43, *BB* 161). Or again, with respect to 'walk' and 'walks', as in the observation already quoted: 'They mean exactly the same thing, we would tell someone; namely, *this* – and then we would demonstrate walking to him' (*LW* I, §274). However, 'red' does not require the existence of red things in order to have meaning, and while we may explain a word by pointing to something, what we point to is not the word's meaning.

This, at least, is Wittgenstein's claim, but it is far from clear that, as a thesis about words generally, it can be derived merely from a consideration of proper names, the example which he consistently invokes to this end. The topic is worth dwelling upon, since doubts about Wittgenstein's treatment of names ramify into doubts about his conception of meaning generally. Further questions relating to the complex of word, thing, and meaning will then be approached through a consideration of ostensive definition.

2.1 Proper names

The most obvious point to make against Wittgenstein is that a name like 'Moore' is simply not said to have a meaning in any relevant sense – i.e., etymology aside – though of course it has a use. We can certainly mean someone by 'Moore', but if asked what meaning the name had we should naturally reject the question with something like 'It doesn't have a meaning; it is just someone's name.' Why is it that proper names are thought to be in this respect unlike common nouns? The most striking difference relates to the demands made by the latter as regards answering features on the side of the persons or things to which they are applied, demands whose absence in the case of names makes for a seemingly arbitrary connection between name and bearer. In trying to decide whether to christen a child 'Peter' we do not have to ask whether the child has or will have what it takes to be named 'Peter', as opposed to 'Paul', say, and the Peters of this world may be united in respect only of this one attribute: they are all called 'Peter'. There are some constraints, e.g., with regard to gender in the case of first names, but even here a departure from the usual convention does not lead to misdescription; the particular role of 'Paul' as a name is not at risk if it is conferred upon a girl – it is just not its job to describe – whereas the use of a general term is such that there will be constraints of this kind whose violation its correct use cannot tolerate.

This is, however, far from being the end of the matter. The rejoinder which I describe as natural is surely correct in this instance, but it would not be right to say that names *never* have a meaning. Consider the following names of racehorses – all authentic: 'Emergency Plumber', 'Cool Enough', 'Bold Realm', 'Out of Hand', 'Seven Clubs' and 'All Agreed'. Improbable they may be, but they do function as names, and they do have meaning. Or again we have names of tunes and songs – 'Yesterday', 'Stardust' – names of books, films, plays, magazines – *Great Expectations*, *A Night at the Opera*, *The Rivals*, *Practical Computing*, and so on. Furthermore, not only is it unjustified to speak of *Practical Computing*, say, as an arbitrary title of a magazine, but there is an important respect in which names are not to be distinguished from other types of term on this score. What is arbitrary with a personal name like 'George' is its initial conferment, not its *re-application* once conferred. But the same holds for a name of a substance, such as 'uranium' – not a proper name – or for a general term, like 'parrot'. There was no compelling reason to dub the newly discovered element 'uranium', but once the name had become affixed, its re-application could not be deemed arbitrary.

In the light of these objections, our initial observations have to be modified. On the first point, what is of interest is that while a proper name may have a meaning, it is not determined as its bearer's name by the latter's characteristics. Knowing about a given horse, and having an understanding of such terms as 'filly', 'mare', and 'yearling', we may recognize that one of these descriptions is applicable. We do not in the same way appreciate that a horse's characteristics call for 'All Agreed' as its name in virtue of the meaning of this phrase, nor does it have a meaning which enables us to identify its bearer. It is not, then, that proper names perforce lack meaning. Rather, it is not because of any meaning it may have that we are required to accept '*N.N*' as a name of *N.N.* – though of course a name may, because of its meaning, be more or less apt, as with names of novels or films, where a central theme, event, or character is identified. The same observation provides an answer on the second point. The re-application of a name is clearly not an arbitrary matter; it is just that, even if a name has a meaning, it is not on this basis that it is recognized either as applying or as re-applying.

To see the underlying rationale for the difference between proper names and common nouns, consider further the use of the former. A name is conferred upon a person, planet, or play simply as being that individual person, etc.; it is not thought to substitute for some description which the individual is taken to satisfy. The point is not that individuals do not have unique properties. There are conditions necessary to being the individual in question – as being a human being – and further more specific conditions that are sufficient, as with date and place of birth, but *how* the name gets annexed to an individual is of no consequence, nor what the individuating condition is that a particular person happens to associate with a given name. It is the *identity* of an individual that matters for the use of a name, and the conditions that define the identity of a person are not derived from (an understanding of) his name. This is not to deny that the matter of identity may be problematic: we may have to decide just what changes are to be consistent with its being the same individual for purposes of using the name, and in some cases we may have to decide just what spatial parts are to be reckoned to that individual. For instance, does England embrace the Isle of Man? At all events, as long as there is no misunderstanding on the score of who or what the name is a name of, we have all that the particular role of names requires. The facts of identity which *A* associates with '*N.N.*' may not overlap with those associated by *B*, but provided it is a question of the same *N.N.*, there will not be a subsequent time at which *A* and *B* may find themselves talking about different individuals. With the common noun 'parrot', by contrast, a different conception of the conditions associated with the word may give rise to a difference in what is being spoken about.

A name, then, may have a meaning, but, as I say, that is not what qualifies it as the name of its bearer; to do what it does, viz. identify some person, place or thing, it does not need to compare in this respect with a common noun. With a noun we associate some repeatable condition, as that definitive of being a parrot, a pear, or whatever, an association that is necessary if we are to speak of things not yet encountered, since it is only exceptionally that the relevant range of individuals is actually presented to us, so that we might make clear the reference by ostension, as with a name. Of course, we may use a name without having met up with the bearer, but, special cases apart, the reference will be as determined by someone who did not arrive at knowledge thereof by proceeding from a condition given in advance – a condition which could be said to define the meaning of the name.

The association of proper names and common nouns with individuals and types respectively makes for the basic divide, but the distinction, and therewith the use of 'proper name', is not always clear, as names of days and months, for instance, reveal. Mass terms, such as 'uranium', come close to providing further illustrations. Such terms approximate to proper names if the 'individuals' in question are the various individual elements, substances, and so forth. At this abstract level the differences are not so much to the fore, but they emerge when the noun – or 'individual' – is related to particular instances – pieces, portions, slices. As with persons or things to which count nouns apply, so here we may wish to speak of any individual *amounts* which meet the condition for being uranium, and we can be said to be talking of some particular volume of matter – perhaps buried deep in the earth – in so far as it meets that condition; the reference can be to whatever bits happen to qualify, however far and wide they are scattered. Overall, 'uranium' compares more with a common noun than with a name. For a clear exemplification of the latter use we should want the term to be associated with a single lump of the substance. With such an association, the matter of identity would take over as the dominating concern, the features of uranium now definitive of the substance being of significance only in so far as they served to identify the lump as the original bearer of the name.

Does the Fregean notion of *sense* have a part to play in explaining the use of proper names? The notion is one that is embroiled in a number of bizarre theses – e.g., that in indirect speech a proper name stands for its sense – but it might be felt to have an innocent enough interpretation in the present connection. I claim that association of 'uranium', like 'parrot', with some general, constant, condition is necessary if these terms are to do what we ask of them – enable us to make pronouncements about creatures or lumps of matter as yet unencountered – whereas what we ask of a proper name requires no such association. Not only are any individuating conditions which we may link to a name like 'Polly' not repeated from one Polly to another, but a parrot's path through space and time generates indefinitely many individuating conditions, none of which has a better claim than any other to definitional status. However, that is not to deny that there will commonly be some feature or features that guide us in our application of a name, and it seems appropriate to bring in sense in connection with such conditions even if this association is not one that is made by speakers generally. Something of this character would seem to be what we have if we follow Wittgenstein in ascribing meaning to names, but we may also note a certain tension in this invocation of sense. On the one hand, if we succeed in specifying the sense of a personal name we should arrive at a condition that pinpoints a particular individual, that defines a criterion of identity for the bearer of the name – sense as determinative of reference. On the other hand, if sense is associated with 'mode of presentation', then a person's appearance is bound to loom large among the factors on which we are to fasten, and while a good pointer to identity, it is only by good fortune that this enables us to single out one person to the exclusion of all others – quite extraordinarily good fortune when we move from persons to parrots.

What is perhaps of greatest importance is that the notion of a term with sense is no substitute for that of a proper name. It is clearly no substitute if explained in terms of an association with a repeatable mode of presentation, allowing for duplicate individuals. If, on the other hand, we have a condition *C* necessary to being *N.N.*, that necessity can be granted without our having to allow that knowledge of the satisfaction of *C* by *N.N.* is indispensable to a mastery of the name. Replace '*N.N.*' by a specification of any such condition and we destroy the uniform relation of the name to the diverse conditions which might provide alternative bases for identifying someone as *N.N.* We may introduce the notion of sense in connection with such conditions, but even if 'sense' is in order where 'meaning' is not, the consideration remains that the use of a name transcends any such association.

This discussion of names confirms that the demands of meaning go beyond those of bare use. What is distinctive of a name is that its application is not mediated by an association with a commonly recognized condition on the side of the bearer, a condition which might define the name, whose specification might furnish an answer to the question, 'What is meant by "*N.N.*"?' As names of songs and stories show, it is not that there is never an answer to this question; just no answer that serves to specify a condition which the referent is required to satisfy. Inconsequential though it may seem, this divergence from descriptive terms defines an important constraint on accounts of meaning.

2.2 *Ostensive definition*

We have lost sight of the question which prompted the discussion of names, the question whether meaning is or is not within language. The view that it is not may be associated with a particular interpretation of ostensive definition: we may define a term *F* by pointing to a suitable instance and saying 'This is *F*', and what we thus single out is the meaning of *F*. We shall continue to defer until later chapters consideration of the points at issue with this way of speaking, but the preliminary topic of ostensive definition will now have our attention.

It is difficult to identify anything in Wittgenstein's writings that qualifies as an aspect of the Augustinian picture without at the same time identifying it as the target of his criticism. None the less, it would be wrong to portray this account of language as a total distortion in his eyes, the supposed error being more one of pressing a model beyond the bounds of its applicability. This observation is in place apropos ostensive definition, which is not only part and parcel of the Augustinian scheme, but is also crucial, in a positive way, to Wittgenstein's own conception of explanations of meaning.

In his later accounts of ostensive definition, Wittgenstein appears to be trying to balance two considerations. On the one hand, he wishes to lay bare the presuppositions of this form of explanation in a way that counts against attempts at endowing it with a privileged role: we misconceive its status if we think of it as providing language with a foundation. On the other hand, any out-and-out rejection of ostensive definition on the grounds that it is perpetually open to misunderstanding is not accepted as a telling objection.

To begin with the limitations, Wittgenstein maintains from the first that ostensive definition requires a degree of stage-setting. Correlating a word with an object does not of itself have any consequences, but we must commit ourselves to a rule of use (*LWL* 36), and what that rule is is not uniquely determined by this procedure: 'All the rules together give the meaning, and these are not fixed by giving an ostensive definition' (*AWL* 3). And, in the *Yellow Book*:

> An ostensive definition is not really a definition at all. Ostensive definition is one rule only for the use of a word. And one rule is not enough to give the meaning. For example, from 'This is sosh' you would not understand the use of the word 'sosh', though from 'This color is sosh' you would. That is, if a person is to learn the meaning of a word from such a definition he must already know what sort of thing it stands for. The word 'color' already fixes the use of 'sosh'. The ostensive definition is of use if you need to fill in only one blank.
>
> (*AWL* 45)

Later writings are more favourably disposed towards use of 'definition' in this connection, but the main point of the objection recurs, e.g., at *PI* §30, where he concludes: 'So one might say: the ostensive definition explains the use – the meaning – of the word when the overall role of the word in the language is clear.' However, as we shall see, the force of this objection is to some extent qualified by Wittgenstein's insistence that while ostensive definition *may* be misunderstood, it need not be. This is a common pattern of argument in the *Investigations*: the search for an infallible mark of some feature is indeed doomed to failure, but it is also declared to be unnecessary. He might, he suggests, explain the name 'Moses' as meaning 'the man, if such there was, who led the Israelites out of Egypt'. The terms of this explanation may in turn prompt further queries, queries to which there is no assignable end, but that does not disqualify the explanation: 'One might say: an explanation serves to remove or to avert a misunderstanding – one, that is, that would occur but for the explanation; not every one that I can imagine' (*PI* §87). And in the same paragraph: 'The sign-post is in order – if, under normal circumstances, it fulfils its purpose.' What matters is that an explanation should remove the doubts that *actually* arise.

Are there any words that are not susceptible of explanation by ostensive definition? In the 1930–2 lectures Wittgenstein offered the example of 'pal' as a word whose meaning cannot be thus conveyed (*LWL* 104), but for the most part he is extremely liberal in what he holds definable in this way: 'Now one can ostensively define a proper name, the name of a colour, the name of a material, a numeral, the name of a point of the compass, and so on' (*PI* §28). Although only names are instanced here, there is no reason to conceive of ostension so narrowly that it applies only to certain parts of speech, and elsewhere negation and disjunction are cited as suitable candidates (*PG* §25). Think, too, of the phrase 'all gone'; more challenging than the name of a colour, but a phrase that a child may learn early on, and one to which the notion of ostensive definition appears to have application.

This liberal conception of ostensive definition accords with Wittgenstein's demotion of other philosophical paradigms of explanation from their supposedly privileged position. A persistent philosophical contention is that words are satisfactorily explained only if given a definition in terms of genus and difference, of necessary and sufficient conditions for their application. However, whereas this is to impose a rigid, formalistic pattern upon our loosely structured usage, ostensive definition is more in harmony with actual practice. An understanding of 'red' can be manifested and conveyed by pointing to something and saying 'This is red'; this may be remote from the preferred philosophical form of definition, but you cannot ask for anything more than is given in our ordinary explanations, of which this is one, explanations which give *our* understanding – the only understanding there is – and for which in this instance there does not appear to be any real alternative. Once more, such an explanation is not shown to be defective by the fact that it can be misinterpreted, a possibility that cannot be ruled out with *any* form of explanation.

Whether the fit between ostensive definition and our understanding of language is as comfortable as this would suggest is a topic for the next two chapters. For the moment I wish merely to voice misgivings with Wittgenstein's defence of this style of definition. It is true that while ostensive definition may be misunderstood, it need not be, but this observation looks to be dangerously undiscriminating, being used as a leveller with respect to different forms of explanation when it may be that a scale of distinctions is required to do justice to the possibilities. Thus, it takes no account of the diversity among forms of explanation, or of variations within a single form, where there may be a considerable difference in the extent to which success can reasonably be expected. At *PI* 14 Wittgenstein imagines an attempt to explain 'modest' by pointing to an arrogant man and saying 'That man is *not* modest.' It is, he says, no argument against such a method of definition that it is ambiguous: 'Any definition can be misunderstood.' But the fair possibility of success in this instance contrasts with the merely chance expectation we should have if we tried to explain 'iceberg' or 'earthquake' by pointing at the objects in a room and saying 'This is not an iceberg (earthquake).' Here we may note that 'not modest' equates with 'immodest', having a degree of specificity comparable with that of 'modest' rather than with that of 'not an iceberg'.

Again, a word like 'red' is relatively unproblematic. If we are allowed to make use of ostensive definition on several occasions we can make colour the only constant, for practical purposes, thus reducing the chances of misinterpretation. On the other hand, it is difficult to see how even this extension could help with such terms as 'pensioner', 'tax demand', 'risk', or 'relic'. The example of colour terms is hardly typical, and it could be that Wittgenstein's general position suffers as a result of an excessive preoccupation with this limited case.

There are also terms for which the notion of confrontation with a sample becomes elusive, if not inoperable, e.g., with psychological verbs like 'know', 'hope', and 'understand'. However, whether ostensive definition risks being discredited in such cases depends on what is being claimed for it. If thought of as universally applicable, it runs that risk, but it is surely more reasonable to regard the procedure as coming up for possible criticism only when the notion of pointing at something makes sense; we may be generous in our interpretation of that notion, but even then it is hardly likely to apply with respect to most of those words which, like 'for', 'besides', and 'perhaps', spell trouble for the Augustinian scheme.

On the other hand, suppose it is decided to extend the scope of ostensive definition by weakening the requirement that there be a sample which one might single out, demanding, at the limit, no more than the use of words in the right circumstances. This latter may, of course, be all that a learner is exposed to that is of relevance to his acquisition of language, and if ostensive definition is broadened to take in this much it is hard to see what it might be unable to accommodate. For instance, those aspects of usage which fall under the 'grammar' of a word may be mapped out by the way the word is allowed in this combination, refused in that. Such patterns, which define the more subtle dimensions of use of such terms as psychological verbs, become appropriate material for ostensive definition as more liberally construed.

Wittgenstein's unwillingness to draw sharp boundaries might be thought likely to take him some distance in this direction, but given the large area of use or meaning which ostensive definition is taken to presuppose, it seems unlikely that he envisaged an extension of the notion to this all-embracing point. This brings us back to the seeming tension between the limitations of ostensive definition and the defence of the procedure which consists in pointing out that, while such a definition may be misunderstood, it need not be. If that defence is accepted, why is it that the definition can explain meaning *only* when the overall use of the word is understood – when, for instance, the word's role as a colour word is appreciated, but not its character as a word for just this colour? The general feature is not one that need be misinterpreted any more than the particular; in either case it could be that no misinterpretation even occurs to the learner.

This objection points up the unsuitability of some of the examples used by Wittgenstein to expose limitations in this form of definition, but when we turn to the deeper dimensions of use we find that the objection has less force. So, for instance, it might plausibly be said that in all cases of ostensive definition we assume that the learner knows what it is for the word to be a word *for* the characteristic or type of object in question. More particularly, the *kind* of referring that is proper to the category of word is taken for granted, rather than explained. Think here of the way indexicals work, as opposed to other types of referential term – and of the obstacles to defining 'I' by pointing to oneself, or 'you' by pointing to another. Think too how, in connection with private ostensive definition, the question *how* words refer to sensations is not even broached by the private language theorist, so that he pays insufficient attention to the fact that the application of 'pain', say, is mediated by behaviour. Compare the view cited, but not endorsed, at *PI* §264: '"Once you know *what* the word stands for, you understand it, you know its whole use."'

This aspect of use relates not so much to the interpretation of a word as sought by one who asks what it names or stands for – does it describe colour or shape? – as to what is comprised in its general grammatical role, and it would seem that no ostensive definition can stand a chance of success unless this fundamental aspect of use is already grasped by the learner. How, then, might such a grasp be acquired? Here Wittgenstein speaks in terms of ostensive teaching associated with a particular *training* (*PI* §6), and it does seem appropriate to make this shift when there is no assumption that the character of what is being done is appreciated, reserving talk of 'definition' for the more intellectual case – when, as he says, the learner can already speak. Whether 'slab' is understood as a description or as an order depends on the ostensive training with which the ostensive definition is associated. The latter operates at a level where, say, 'slab' is to be differentiated in meaning from 'block', but the common role of these words in the language game – their role in, say, giving orders – is not conveyed by any form of verbal explanation. Again, while something analogous to ostension may apply even with negation and disjunction, there is unlikely to be any question of definition. The parent may repeat 'No' to the child as a refusal, with some expectation that the message will eventually get across, but that is a matter more of training than of explaining.

Some uncertainty about Wittgenstein's intentions still perhaps remains, but it does appear that greater weight is to be attached to the reservations expressed about ostensive definition than to its rehabilitation. At all events, when such definition is construed in the less liberal way, we can readily grant that it has no essential role, that it is not required to provide language with a foundation. After all, we might not give children the benefit of *any* explanations or teaching, ostensive or otherwise, but simply leave it to them to pick up the language as best they could. And they could be successful.

To take an example of an 'internal' relation between concepts, a learner can expect to be told such things as 'It doesn't count as *lying* unless what is said is known by the speaker to be false', but this aspect of the word's grammar can become apparent without speakers having to stop to make the connection explicit. Given the host of such connections, explicitness in this respect is seen to be very much the exception; linguistic practice is, after all, prior to any reflections upon or explanations of it. So, the child gradually learns that ignorance that *p* is false is treated as a sufficient condition for an accusation of lying to be unwarranted, just as it learns that we say 'sang', not 'singed', but this is learning that does not demand correlative teaching. Indeed, in very many cases we may be quite unable to give any adequate explanation, verbal or ostensive, or our explanations may be so crude that, were they to be influential in dictating the child's usage, it would be denied a satisfactory grasp of the word. It is most fortunate that our rough and ready explanations find themselves overridden by the patterns of usage, much as the children of non-native speakers tend not to succumb to their parents' linguistic failings.

What of the normative element in meaning? There is no difficulty in imagining a society in which no use was made of *samples*, where people said such things as 'This is a hamster', but always as descriptions, never as explanations, as rules advanced in justification or criticism of uses of words. But would not the learner have at least to *treat* some pronouncements as if they were ostensive definitions, if he were to make any headway with learning the language? Not if that means accepting such descriptions as informed with an intention to instruct. Exposure to use of words in the right circumstances is certainly required, but the usage may be assimilated without the need for any reasoning in this way to conclusions about word meaning.

But explanations of words commonly specify what can and cannot be said, what is correct or permissible, and this is surely not just a matter of regularities? However, as intimated earlier, what can be said *can* be implicit in regularities of usage, prior to the formulation of a relevant rule. Think here of mistakes made by foreigners in speaking one's language. There are countless errors which a native speaker of English is never tempted to commit, since he is not subject to the distorting influence of another tongue. For instance, 'I drown' instead of 'I am drowning', 'I live here since ten years' for 'I have been living here for ten years', 'If he would have seen her' for 'If he had seen her', and so forth. Our avoidance of such errors does not depend on our having been introduced to rules which exclude them, yet their character as ill-formed is immediately recognizable; when we correct someone on such points we pass on knowledge of actual practice, but not, for the most part, explicit corrections which we have inherited.

If it is something we might dispense with altogether, what is the importance of ostensive definition? That it counts as a way of teaching should tell us something about meaning, and indeed the message that comes across as clearly as any is, surely, that a correlation of the word with something else is at the heart of what is learnable in this way. Objections to the efficacy of ostensive definition as an instrument of teaching, and defence of it against such objections, are of secondary importance in comparison with the background supposition that there is something of this character to be learned, even if this does not exhaust what is required for a grasp of meaning.

Indeed, is there not a case for saying that what can be learned must be learnable in something like this way? We can explain meaning by giving a synonym, but a more enlightening procedure is to make clear how circumstances of use suffice to determine meaning. Leaving aside the case where a word is introduced by paraphrase, there is mystery in the idea that a person should have a grasp of meaning – that a word should have a meaning to be grasped – if such circumstances, together with associated training, do not provide the wherewithal for understanding.

To make something of this possibility we may go back to the more general picture to which we are led by broadening ostensive definition to such a point that we end up thinking in terms simply of the use of words in appropriate circumstances. Let us ask how a child might come to an understanding of the word 'later', given that anything that might strictly qualify as ostensive instruction is not to be had. We want the child to know that it can have the biscuit, not now but *later*. The absence of anything relevant in the context for child or word to get a grip on may leave one repeating the word without any real hope of success: the child will doubtless conclude that it is not getting the biscuit now, but that is all. However, suppose we enlarge the conditions under consideration to take in both the statement containing 'later' and the subsequent time at which it is fulfilled. If at that time the child is able to recall that 'later' was used, it is in a position to put word and circumstance together – not necessarily reflectively – to come to a knowledge that if it is said that something will take place *later*, then while nothing may happen at the time of utterance, a subsequent happening can be expected. This looks trivial if put by saying that the child learns that when it is told that something will happen later, it can expect that event to happen later, but the point about the explanation is that it shows the learnability of the notion. Not only that, but shows it in a way that does not require imposing a restrictive grammatical framework upon the word, to make it out to be a name or other species of designator. We saw with 'and' and 'but' that we did not have to assume one grammar rather than another – in particular, a grammar congenial to truth – in order to see how a grasp of the meaning of either, in terms of a condition of homogeneity or heterogeneity, might be acquired. What we need by way of a word–world relation is, I suggest, no more than is necessary to show the satisfiability of this condition of learnability, where we are concerned not so much with indicating practical steps towards mastery of a word, but to make clear that there is indeed something to learn.

2.3 Signifying

The limitations which Wittgenstein sees in ostensive definition are also, to a large extent, associated with the idea of a word's *signifying* something, a term of some interest, in that its grammar better befits it than that of 'mean' to governing a grammatical object which serves to designate something. In §10 of the *Investigations* Wittgenstein addresses himself to the question of what the words of one of his imagined languages signify (*bezeichnen*). What is supposed to show what they signify, he responds, if not the kind of use they have? His questioner had supposed that we should explain meaning by invoking the formula, 'The word . . . signifies . . . '. Wittgenstein sees some use in speaking in these terms: we might differentiate 'slab' and 'block' by indicating the different objects to which each relates, and we might even speak of other signs as signifying numbers, rather than such objects – an interesting suggestion, in view of *PI* §1. However, while what sets 'slab' and 'block' apart can be approached in this way, the overall use of these words – including the kind of '*referring*' they involve – is supposed already known. Furthermore, to confine ourselves to what is offered by this formula is to ensure that we shall omit what makes for the distinctive character of a word type – of number words as against general terms, for instance. In short, far from elucidating meaning, the formula with *signifies* is silent on crucial differences between words, and in so far as there is anything of relevance in the notion, it will in any case be taken care of in an account of use. We are not being denied the notion, but it does nothing in the absence of the kinds of distinction that define the all-important differences between different parts of speech. Cf. *PI* §13: 'When we say: "Every word in language signifies something" we have so far said *nothing whatever*; unless we have explained exactly *what* distinction we wish to make.'

The force of this objection is to some extent diminished by the observation which follows, namely, that the contrast sought may be as provided by the kind of word 'without meaning' that occurs in Lewis Carroll's poems, or by words like 'Lilliburlero' in songs. That may put the contrast at just the level of generality desired. However, the objection remains that words of different grammatical types may differ *toto caelo*, so 'bat' as against 'but', or 'for' as against 'four', to such a point that it is hard to see how any common application of a notion like that of signifying could be other than uselessly general, or a gross distortion. What it comes to for 'but' will be a function specifically of the use of *that* word, or word type, not a recurrent notion which other word types involve, though supplement in different – and perhaps rather incidental – ways. Certainly, it would appear an absurd expectation that we should find just successive repetitions of the pattern presented by terms like 'table' and 'chair' and the things of which they are names. Furthermore, even though we may here speak more readily of a correlation between word and thing, that says nothing about how the word is to be used, but once more we are working up into a general account of meaning what is needed to fill only one possible lacuna in someone's knowledge, the assumption being that everything about what the word means is understood apart from what it stands for.

It looks as though it takes a drastically blinkered view of language to overlook the vast difference between 'since', 'by', 'very', 'several', 'anyone', and all the rest of the familiar motley. However, notwithstanding this variety, it has not been shown that 'signifies' is any less general than 'mean' itself. There may be a loss of information in going from a general account of use to a specification that encompasses no more than is conveyed by an instance of the formula, but the information may be information we can do without if the concern is with the central core of meaning of the word. This is especially likely if the force of an utterance is wrongly read into individual words. Take once more the example of 'slab'. It is true that in the simple language game with this and other words which Wittgenstein considers, appreciation of 'Slab!' as something to be acted upon is required along with knowledge of what the word more narrowly signifies. However, while this is true of 'Slab!'

as envisaged, it is hardly typical, individual words not in general being associated with a particular force, but lending themselves to incorporation within contexts having a variety of forces, as assertions, commands, expressions of wishes, and so forth. It is unfortunate that Wittgenstein fastened on the example of a one-word sentence, as this leads to a conflation of factors which are in general separable – a point that does not depend, we may note, on making 'Slab!' out to be elliptical.

Let us now take stock of our position. In so far as Wittgenstein's aim is therapeutic, to wean us off our illusions, to remove intellectual cramp, it may be of no account that, as has emerged throughout these first two chapters, meaning and use are not exact equivalents. Indeed, a mere approximation to 'meaning' could conceivably serve that end equally well – better, perhaps, than its replacement by a synonym, which might simply reproduce the original problems. Only 'might', however. It could be that 'use', while generally broader, agreed with 'meaning' over the area where they come into comparison, in which case its substitution could open our eyes to possibilities which concentration on the narrower term led us to overlook.

Wittgenstein does not in any event appear to have held unreservedly that the meaning of a word is simply its use in the language, but what is less controversial, whether or not it was his position, is the weaker claim that meaning is determined by use. Though weaker, this is enough for one of his major purposes, viz. to 'externalize' meaning, to combat a conception of it as a mental accompaniment to speech, an idea in the mind to which our words are answerable, an 'occult connection the mind makes between a word and a thing' and which '*contains* the whole usage of a word' (*BB* 73–4). In this context the importance of the appeal to use can hardly be over-estimated, even if it is an over-reaction to go so far as to assimilate meaning to it. However, in leaving open the possibility that meaning is narrower, even the weaker thesis exposes us to the risk that we shall have to restrict use by appeal to just the kinds of semantic notion that the shift from meaning might have been thought to dispense with, as when we speak in terms of what a word is used of, or again of what it is used to convey; in either case it is what is introduced in expanding the bare 'use' that does the work. This thesis still leaves much open, including the contention, at the heart of the Augustinian position, that what use determines is primarily an association of word and thing. Even 'use in the language', while protecting against the cruder irrelevances, does not of itself make clear what *use* is to comprise; certainly, it does not exclude the possibility that one of the traditional array of semantic notions might not after all prove central.

Much of the appeal of use derives from its divergence from meaning as regards the latter's relational character: the superficial grammar of 'mean' invites us to specify a *thing meant*, a task which, with so many words, appears impossible to carry out. However, the difficulties are not all on the side of meaning, but shortcomings in accounts of use suggest that we should not too readily allow the troublesome words to take us away from the pattern of explanation appropriate in the more tractable areas of the language. True, the formula '*x* means *y*' may be as much a recipe for frustration as for enlightenment, but something of a representational element, of a word as a sign for something, seems to remain important – what else is there that a linguistic act might exploit? – and the difficulties which words like 'such' and 'so' present can as well be regarded as constituting a challenge to the initial conception as a refutation of its applicability.

3

Family Resemblance

Wittgenstein's approach to philosophical problems can be called 'linguistic', not because of a preoccupation with the niceties of ordinary usage – to which he was largely indifferent – but because of the character of his method. Consider the way he seeks to achieve clarity in thinking about the mental. Knowing, understanding, meaning, remembering – these are not going to give up their secrets to one who attends more closely to the contents of his mind, who makes a more thorough study of the disclosures of introspection; what is required is not a phenomenological, but a grammatical investigation: does knowing have genuine duration? how do third-person and first-person uses of the verb compare? what contrasts give point to its use? (cf. Z §472ff.). On the other hand, we do not find Wittgenstein engaged in one pursuit that typifies much present-day linguistic philosophy, namely, the attempt to analyse a problematic term by distilling its character in a definition, as with the many refinements suggested for 'true and reasonable belief' in formulating necessary and sufficient conditions for knowledge. Not only would such a definition not serve Wittgenstein's ends, but he would query the presumption that a uniform characterization of our concept of knowledge can realistically be expected. Why he would raise this query, and what form he would suppose an explanation of meaning to call for, are issues we shall now take up.

3.1 Family resemblance and traditional definitions

A large part of Wittgenstein's attack on definition, as traditionally conceived, proceeds hand in hand with the exposition of an alternative account of concepts in terms of family resemblance. We might have thought that if *t* is a univocal term, then the objects which fall under it *must* share common properties; how could singularity of word meaning not be matched by uniformity in the answering objects? However, this *must* is countered with a possibility in which uniformity gives way to a network of overlapping similarities amongst items in the relevant range; the activities we call *games*, for instance, need have nothing in common in virtue of which they are thus describable, but the unity of the concept is founded in a whole series of criss-crossing similarities. Just as there may be no one feature or set of features common to all the members of a family, but a distribution in varying ways of facial characteristics, build, colouring, and so forth, that makes for the recognizability of a person as being a member of the family, so too we find this pattern with psychological concepts, as thinking and understanding, and even with formal concepts, as number and proposition.

The appeal to family resemblances may seem no more than is necessary to keep our explanations of meaning in contact with the actual workings of language. It is surely only a prejudice to suppose that things which receive a common description must present an unwavering uniformity of features; far more realistic, given the fluidity and diversity which the uses of words exhibit, to allow that a looser pattern of resemblances will be what answers to a single concept. However, while a distorted picture of language may be given by the essentialism which Wittgenstein seeks to combat, we meet with a number of uncertainties when we try to follow through his alternative, and it proves easier to find a model for the use of words that conforms to the position he rejects than to rescue the family resemblance approach from the difficulties with which it is in turn beset. In itself that is relatively unimportant; of greater moment are the repercussions for the more general issues with which the approach connects, and in particular the question of the degree to which the answer to a question of meaning may be hidden from speakers of the language.

It is a common supposition that explanations of meaning can be given, indeed are best given, by mapping words onto equivalent phrases to yield a definition *per genus et differentiam*, yet with the general run of words the applicability of this procedure is far from clear. Whether we can break down '*F*' into '*G* which is *H*' will depend not merely upon the appropriateness of this scheme, but also upon the resources of the language. There is no guarantee that the language will offer the wherewithal for such an analysis, and even when it does the relevance of the analysis may be questionable.

My dictionary defines 'limp' as 'a marked unevenness of gait, caused by some injury or defect', but what does my understanding of the word owe to this, or to any other definition? It is not something with which I in any sense *operate*, as if I were to translate into the expanded form when presented with the question whether someone had a limp, reverting to the original when matters had been decided in terms of the definition. As far as my understanding goes, the single word has priority over any such paraphrase; the latter would, after all, be formulated only after reflection upon the use of the former.

Definitions are like rules in their derivative character. It is perhaps not quite right to say that a word does not have a definition until one has been formulated, since 'has a definition' may mean only 'can be defined', but at all events, until a lexicographer or other authority has done his work there simply will not be a definition in anything more than this attenuated sense. You can draw a boundary, but so far perhaps, none has been drawn; and that is what definitions do.

In making this point I am relying on a use of 'definition' narrower than that employed in the phrase 'ostensive definition'. The idea of a verbal specification which delimits or demarcates the application of a term is very much part of our ordinary notion, so-called ostensive definition belonging under the broader heading of *explanations of meaning*. It is the relevance of definition more narrowly construed to our understanding of the general run of words that I am querying, though there is also the earlier point that acquisition of language does not await upon anyone offering any explanations at all. Not at least for the more basic items of our vocabulary. If the same cannot be said with respect to, say, technical terminology, then for the most part it will be the traditional form of definition that is needed.

Wittgenstein sees the provision of verbal equivalents of a word as playing only a small and inessential part in our everyday explanations of meaning. The consequent demotion of definitions is in line with the above observations, but a more distinctive aspect of the family resemblance account is the denial that, at least with some words, any definition in terms of necessary and sufficient conditions for the application of the word *can* be given. In fact it is not clear why associating a word *w* with a pattern of family resemblances should be inconsistent with giving *w* a definition in this traditional form. If *w* is susceptible of a family resemblance explanation, then it is no doubt required that such an account should also extend to the terms of any satisfactory definition, but it is not obvious that the form of the latter need exclude this possibility, any more than that it should exclude a degree of indeterminacy of sense: why should not a term *t* both mark a differentia in the definition and at the same time conform to the family resemblance scheme? Why should not *t*, whether for this or for some other reason, allow of borderline cases among the things falling under it, this character then being communicated to the definition as a whole? One of Wittgenstein's major aims is to rid us of the prejudice that our concepts must have rigid limits, well-defined boundaries. I have allowed that the idea of circumscribing or delimiting is one that is associated with the usual notion of definition, but that notion still leaves room for indeterminacy. There is, for instance, no question of going along with the absurd requirement that every possible application of a concept be determined in advance. Indeed, to speak of leaving room for indeterminacy suggests that we have a choice in the matter, when what should be stressed is that *no* form of definition is secure against this threat. It is a matter of degree only. We can have no cause to criticize a definition on the grounds that it excludes such character; we can merely take exception to an insistence that a satisfactory definition should reduce the degree of indeterminacy to zero.

Wittgenstein's discussion of 'game' reveals a belief that a specification of necessary and sufficient conditions may be unattainable in many cases. More emphatically, he occasionally intimates that family resemblance provides the *only* pattern:

> There is nothing identifiably in common to the states of affairs for which we use a word. There is only a number of overlapping resemblances. Our concepts are enormous families with various resemblances.
>
> (*AWL* 96)

However, a more important claim is that we do not *in fact* explain the meaning of, e.g., 'game', by detailing the common characteristics of games. What is crucial is that we *do* understand 'game', and that the explanation we receive is by way of example rather than verbal definition. This being so, then, as Wittgenstein says, 'giving examples of usages is not a second-best method of giving the meaning of a word' (*AWL* 96). Again:

> Here giving examples is not an *indirect* means of explaining – in default of a better. For any general definition can be misunderstood too. The point is that *this* is how we play the game. (I mean the language-game with the word 'game'.)
>
> (*PI* §71)

Supposing we did come up with a definition of 'game', it has still to be shown that this gives expression to our knowledge of what a game is (*AWL* 32). It may be that a game is as the definition would have it, yet the common feature which it isolates has nothing to do with what we mean by the word. On the contrary, whatever the purpose served by such a definition, it appears to be irrelevant to our actual understanding.

There are two theses which at this point appear fairly evenly balanced. On the one hand, we cannot accept without question that a feature which all games share is germane to the meaning of 'game'; on the other hand, pointing out that we often seek to explain a concept by exhibiting instances does not show that this practice actually counts for much in inculcating understanding. As mentioned earlier, our halting attempts at definition may fail lamentably to do justice to the subtleties of a word, though fortunately without ultimate detriment to the learner's understanding. A definition may point him in the right general direction, but the process of attunement to the word's nuances may be a gradual one, owing little to the explanation given. Similarly, presentation of samples may narrow down the possibilities, but the child's understanding may again be the result of what it manages to assimilate after exposure to the use of the word over a period of time, rather than what it takes away from an explicit lesson. Much, clearly, will depend on the word.

At all events, it remains to be seen whether the notion of family resemblance provides a key to an understanding of meaning when the appeal to definitions is unavailing. That appeal is misplaced if it implies that we typically work with definitions in a way that would require their actual formulation, and the consideration that a family resemblance account of meaning does away with such a demand counts in favour of that scheme. On the other hand, unless the role of dictionaries has been completely misunderstood, definitions are very much relevant to questions of meaning, and their relevance is something to which we must do justice.

3.2 The example of games

When Wittgenstein calls upon family resemblance to do what, in the less liberal scheme, had required a common property or cluster of properties, he is presumably not denying that games, say, have nothing at all in common, for they might all be described as 'activities'; rather, it is a matter of nothing in common that determines them all as games. So, two activities *a* and *b* may share a (further) pertinent feature, as also *b* and *c*, but *a* and *c* may have nothing in common in virtue of which they are games, yet for all that still be so describable. Perhaps we find that in some instances winning and losing, together with the exercise of skill, are to the fore, as with darts and tennis, but that skill has no place in certain other games, e.g., patience and roulette, while with some parlour games there is scope for skill but no winning or losing; e.g., a game where the participants have each to contribute a line towards making up a verse. This latter game might then have no characteristic that determined it as a game and which it shared with roulette.

That nothing more than such a chain of resemblances may, in Wittgenstein's eyes, link two games emerges clearly from the discussion in *PI* §66, taken in conjunction with the analogy in the following section, where it is suggested that the way in which kinds of number form a family can be likened to the disposition of fibres in a thread: no one fibre need run through the whole length of the thread, but there will be many overlapping fibres, and doubtless quite distinct fibres at either extremity. In the case both of numbers and of games it is in fact not easy to find considerations that are more than suggestive of this pattern – the features just cited are of course not the only ones relevant to being a game, nor is it evident that anything more than a small number of features need be considered. On the other hand, it might be countered that it is the *possibility* that is of primary interest, since acknowledging that games and numbers could conceivably conform to this pattern at least challenges the prejudice that demands a common property.

However, are we perhaps conceding too much in conceding even the possibility of this pattern? The open-endedness which on this account falls to the concept of *game* or of *number* may be judged an attractive feature of that account, but it is not obvious that it can be squared with the relatively determinate boundaries which, to all appearances, these concepts have. Thus, it is significant that while games do come in a variety of different forms, we are inclined to be quite definite in our exclusion of similar pursuits from the category. Skiing, for instance, is not a game, even if it could be the basis for one. True, the onus is not on Wittgenstein to explain why we draw the lines of application of 'game' as we do; usage could have gone a variety of different ways, but it just so happens that we exclude this and include that. On the other hand, if this and that are on a par as concerns possession of the kinds of feature thought to characterize the family resemblance concept, then there is a case to be answered. And there appears to be no shortage of resemblances of an apposite kind between skiing and acknowledged games – in terms of skill, competitiveness, exercise, amusement – no reason in Wittgenstein's terms why we should withhold the description 'game'. Similarly with mountaineering and weightlifting, and indeed with track and field events quite generally. It is true that sprinting and hurdling are numbered among the events at the Olympic or Commonwealth Games, but even this does not make for a sense in which either is deemed a game. Perhaps we have here a relic of an older, more general use, a label which it is convenient to retain even though it does not apply to the events individually.

When trying to show that winning and losing are not essential to the concept of a game, Wittgenstein appeals to the example of a child throwing a ball against a wall and catching it, but it is far from obvious that such a child *is* playing a game (*PI* §66). Mere playing, or playing around, is not necessarily playing a *game*; for that more by way of pattern or structure is required. This may be fairly minimal, as when the child says: the idea is to catch the ball three times in a row. But we want there to be some fixed objective, some aim that the child sets itself and which makes for a contrast with idle throwing. Again, children may be playing around with marbles, or just hopping about on one leg, but when one of them says, 'Let's have a game', we expect a more structured activity to ensue, with certain conditions specifying what is aimed at: you've got to try to knock the other player's marble out of a circle, for instance.

The objective of a game is something which the participants seek to attain acting in accordance with certain rules, a procedure not being deemed acceptable *just* in so far as it takes one closer to the objective. Furthermore, if the activity is only a game, the objective will be of an unserious and arbitrary character, not something there would be any point in pursuing outside the game. It is easy to give a description of golf which may make it seem remarkable that the sport should enjoy any following at all, but while spending hours trying to knock a small white ball into a series of holes may strike some as a futile pursuit, holing the ball in as few strokes as possible gains significance through becoming the focus of the players' endeavours, both success and the steps taken in the hope of achieving it providing a source of satisfaction, a rationale for the activity.

It is relevant to note a possible difference between a game and a contest. With a contest we have a direct manifestation of such attributes as speed and strength: a race is won by the fastest runner, a weightlifting competition is won by the person who lifts the heaviest weights. What is generally lacking here is the kind of framework which a game provides for the exercise of skills, and so forth – or just plain luck – the more arbitrary objective which these may be exploited to attain and which, indeed, commonly makes for an element of fun or amusement. Games can, of course, be deadly serious, in that winning can mean a lot to the players, but the objective will be one which, considered in itself, lies outside life's more serious goals, its unimportance in this respect making it something to which one's actions are appropriately directed for the sake of the fun that is offered. Such goals as health and happiness are pursued by whatever means we think will be effectual. Because they are of value in themselves, there is, moral considerations aside, no point in restricting ourselves to action in accordance with rules which might lessen the likelihood of success, rules which might have a place in a game just because in that context it is the attempt to gain the objective *all the while* abiding by the rules that makes for the challenge, the satisfaction, rather than the attainment of the objective *tout court*.

It seems indeed quite extraordinary that the rule-governed character common to games generally should not have been given its due by Wittgenstein. One explanation which might be ventured is that the German for 'game' – *Spiel* – is broader than the English term: the word is cognate with the verb for 'play' – *spielen* – so that, perhaps, one can speak of a game whenever one can speak of playing. However, in German as in English, the article in 'a game' makes demands not automatically met through the appositeness of the verb. Moreover, the suggestion does not help when Wittgenstein's discussion is carried on in terms of the English word, which he presumably understood well enough, and there is still the question why the activities at which you cannot be said to play, in English or in German, activities such as high-jumping or pole-vaulting, are not considered games, given what they have in common with these. Some of Wittgenstein's remarks would in fact suggest that he considered it obvious that games are rule-governed – 'if there are no rules there is no game' (*LWL* 48). On the other hand, he also asks, 'Why do you call primitive games without rules games?' (ibid. 101), and in general it seems he would regard the continuity between rule-governed games and merely playing about – and all the activities in between – as making it arbitrary to align 'game' with any subdivision of this spectrum of cases (cf. *AWL* 81).

At all events, if, as Wittgenstein urges, we actually look at games in all their variety – and set them against different but related activities – we are, I suggest, likely to be struck as much by the underlying unity as by the points of difference: games are rule-governed activities with an arbitrary and non-serious objective, an objective that is of little or no significance outside the game, but which we set ourselves to attain for the sake of the fun or other satisfaction that is to be derived from participation in the activity and/or attainment of the objective. This is not to deny that there can be borderline cases – think how quizzes as games and quizzes as contests shade into one another – nor extended uses of the term, but that is more a matter of there being central and peripheral cases, as when we speak of a game even though the objective is of a serious character. With a family resemblance concept, however, the pattern is different. There is a distribution of multifarious features throughout the range of games, but any activity so describable is just as much a game, and in the same sense, as any other.

3.3 Difficulties with family resemblance

It is the supposed consistency between the single concept of a game and the underlying pattern of family resemblance that is the greatest source of tension in this approach. Wittgenstein is in general disconcertingly ready to speak of a difference in meaning, practically any difference in use being allowed – as befits the assimilation of meaning to use – to make for a difference in the former; as if a multitude of meanings followed immediately, given no more than that the word or words encompassed many distinguishable things or circumstances. So, for instance, with respect to 'This is not green', or 'forgetting the meaning of a word' (*AWL* 120-1), with 'not', 'all', 'any', and 'some' (ibid. 116, 123), or with the word 'can', which is used in 'an infinite variety of cases', and whose uses 'form an enormously large family' (ibid. 94-5). With some of these early examples a family resemblance may be presented as a matter of a family of meanings, but the later writings for the most part reveal an opposing tendency. Where we might have expected Wittgenstein to associate a number of meanings with a word such as 'game' or 'number', we find him speaking of *the* concept of either (*PI* §§68, 70). There is a hint that he might be prepared to speak here of more than one meaning, in view of his claim that a word such as 'good' must have a family of meanings (*PI* §77), but the point appears to be directed to, e.g., terms of ethics and aesthetics, rather than to family resemblance concepts more generally, and in any case he clearly supposes that we have a single concept of 'good' in its ethical sense (*PG* 36). Furthermore, he shows no tendency to speak of subdivisions among the meanings of 'game' or of 'number' as a way of showing them to be such concepts, but the emphasis, particularly with 'game', appears to be precisely this: that games form a *single* family, that the unity of the concept is not at risk through resting on nothing more than a pattern of resemblances.

By supposing that 'game' has different senses we can of course allow that the activities that go by the name should come in as much variety as one might wish. Even with the requirement that the senses be related, the range spanned by the term can still be extensive. Not only can a proliferation of meanings cope with such diversity, but the possibility is not at odds with the more traditional scheme, since it could be that an analysis in terms of necessary and sufficient conditions corresponded to the word in each of its various senses. What makes Wittgenstein's account distinctive is his claim that the unity of a concept can be found in nothing more definite than a network of overlapping similarities, that we can have a word that is not simply ambiguous even though there may be nothing common to the various features which mark subdivisions among the things falling under that concept.

With this interpretation we have an account that is in no sense trivial. On the contrary, the difficulty lies in seeing how it could ever apply, for, if we had two games which really did have nothing of relevance in common, then we should surely be prepared to say without further ado that the common description could not apply to both univocally. It is not that we have various patterns of usage, resulting in family resemblance concepts in some cases, and in more uniform conditions in others; if a term behaved as Wittgenstein considers 'game' to behave, then, at least in the kind of case that sets this approach apart from others, we should simply have to ascribe more than one meaning to that term. It would be as with 'ball' in the very different phrases, 'ball of wool' and 'fancy-dress ball', the lack of anything relevant in common to balls of the two kinds ensuring straight off that the term has a different sense in application to either. This is, it is true, an instance where there is no chain of intermediate cases linking the two concepts, but if there were such a chain we could at best speak of *related* meanings – as indeed we might with respect to 'game' in the sense so far considered, and 'game' as used of wild animals. Even when there is a very close relation, a difference in meaning may be apparent. Think of the two uses of 'dog', one in which it is the generic term, and one in which it differentiates male from female. That we have two concepts is clear from the way 'Spot is not a dog', said with respect to a bitch, can be true or false, depending on how it is intended. The requirement for family resemblance is suspect because of the way it takes us towards the very kind of possibility on which a *difference* in meaning is founded.

The family resemblance scheme is not significantly improved if we make the weaker requirement that any two things subsumable under a given concept should have something in common, though not necessarily anything common to all instances, for this still allows that the rationale for applying the concept to one pair of things could, in terms of shared features, be quite different from that appropriate to another pair, so again treats the notion of sameness of meaning as if it did not have to go in step with sameness in the things to which the word is applied. Nor does it help to give the approach a more negative slant, not insisting that any particular concept conforms to the family resemblance pattern, but simply attacking the preconception that there *must* be something in common to items falling under a single univocal general term. There is nothing to fear from an attack which, if I am right, strains the concept of univocity to the point of incoherence.

It is important to bear in mind that different games are not to be thought so describable through being part of the same family, the same network of resemblances, for that is to give the same rationale for being a game to any two such activities – which is of course just what Wittgenstein is denying. So, for instance, it may be that we associate the term 'romantic' with a cluster of properties, so that two literary works may qualify for the epithet through presenting different items from the cluster. This would seem particularly likely if we compared, not one literary work with another, but a literary work and a musical composition. If the two features are realizations of a more general characterization – both express, in different ways, a longing for one's lost youth, let us say – we remain within the traditional scheme. If no such harmonization is possible, but we have to say: these just are two of the cluster of features which go to make for romantic character, then 'romantic' has a corresponding sense, betokening precisely that cluster, and again we remain at a distance from the family resemblance scheme. At *PI* §68 Wittgenstein apparently acknowledges that we could have such a concept of number, but claims that it would not square with our actual concept's lack of rigid limits. Again he is supposing that family resemblance is needed if we are to break out from the confines of a rigidly defined category, yet it is only when we enumerate the totality of instances – not when we generate the various subdivisions by differentiae in the definition – that we put a stop to the possibility of extending the range of the concept.

What of the suggestion that if *F* is a family resemblance concept, then *F*s will have nothing in common other than that they are *F*s? On its most natural interpretation, this may be true, it may be false, and either way it does not matter. Perhaps nothing is common to all the things that are *mine*; investigation will determine whether or not that is so, rather than the character of *being mine*. Here I am being charitable and ignoring what is *entailed* by applicability of the given term, as all games are classifiable as *activities*. More generally, it is difficult to avoid subsumption within a broader category, as represented by 'event', 'artefact', 'abstraction', and so forth, so if such generic terms are available, it will have to be the lack of a uniform differentia that thwarts the traditional scheme of definition. But why should 'game' be further 'decomposable'? Could it not be – and be what the suggestion under consideration implies – that nothing short of 'game' itself will serve to indicate what the various games have in common and which constitutes them as games? We can certainly allow that the language might not have provided for an accurate paraphrase of 'game', but even if our search for a definition should terminate at its starting point, that does not mean that a family resemblance is what justifies application of the term. It is a shared character, and not decomposability, that is to be opposed to mere resemblance, and such character is conceded if, on the strength of the shared univocal description, it is acknowledged that we can speak of something in common to all games, even if it can be said that they have nothing in common other than that they are games. Perhaps sour things likewise have nothing in common other than that they are sour; that does not place 'sour' in the category of family resemblance terms.

Might it not be that the uniform condition which we apparently demand for univocity is one that is in many cases only artificially contrived? So, we have a term 'game' that is applied initially to a circumscribed range of activities, and then extended to other activities which resemble these in certain respects. To maintain sameness of meaning we must have a correspondingly generalized reading of 'game', but the extension is one that we need not have made, and it is essentially a pattern of resemblances that underlies its application rather than the uniformity which would have been involved if there had been little or no room for a decision to bring these further activities under the given description. The term 'foot' provides an example of what I have in mind. This has a basic anatomical sense, but we also speak of a foot of a page, of a mountain, of a ladder, and so on. There is a correspondingly generalized reading as 'lowermost part', and if we wish to see the word as having a single meaning throughout it will be in some such terms that we explain it, but the reality might be said to be a series of resemblances rather than a strictly uniform feature.

This is not, however, the picture that Wittgenstein presents to us with 'game', but for that to apply we should have to have mountain and page sharing some feature, with a different feature uniting page and ladder, let us say. It is these irreducible differences that make it hard to think in terms of a single meaning: however much we broaden our reading of 'game', we do not find a level of generality at which such features as competition between players, amusement, and the exercise of skill, are drawn together. I should in fact maintain that 'foot' can be said to apply to page and ladder in the same sense, that there is nothing illusory in the use of the single term, no need to say that, strictly speaking, the articles do not compare in the relevant respect. Pages and ladders are admittedly very different, but given the highly general character of the condition, that is no obstacle to saying that each has, in the same sense, a lowermost part – just as we might say that each is old in the same sense. Of course, we are not obliged to speak of just one meaning of 'foot' in this use and in its anatomical use. Given the historical and psychological priority of the latter, it is natural to think of the former as an extended, albeit a related, use. But then once we differentiate senses in this way we depart from the family resemblance scheme.

By giving specific expansions of 'foot' as applied to a page and the same word as used of ladders, we can highlight the differences to the point that it looks foolish to speak of a single sense of the word, but the differences here count for nothing in the face of the availability of a characterization which, like 'lowermost part', is pitched at a suitable level of generality. Here we may recall how a special account of the meaning of 'good' has been thought required in view of the considerable differences amongst things which we call 'good', taken together with the word's apparent univocity. There is an ominous likeness between the arguments for family resemblance concepts and the reasoning which leads to a notion of 'evaluative' meaning. So, if we insist on specifying what 'good' comes to only in piecemeal fashion – 'a good fit' means 'a close fit', 'good weather' equates with 'fine weather', 'a good cure' comes to 'an effective cure', and so forth – then we may consider that no general description can stand a chance of matching 'good' in its various uses, and thus look to some other constancy – a common 'prescriptive' force – to explain why this one word can be used with respect to such different phenomena, why we are not forever in need of a new lesson to explain its use in respect of a new range of things. If, however, we cast our definition more broadly – e.g., a good *x* is an *x* that has what is wanted of an *x* – then we can bring the disparate characterizations under a common *descriptive* heading. A detailed consideration of what makes for a good piano may disclose nothing shared by a good coat, but a detailed consideration may obscure what the more general formula makes plain. Such a formula can also make plain why the word can be enlisted for the prescriptive use proposed, and in doing this show that such a use is not to be taken as filling the gap – in terms of a general characterization – which the supposed absence of a sufficiently general description was thought to leave open.

When we appear to be on the track of a family resemblance, we frequently meet with the following development. Consider the example of prepositions, often the most difficult parts of speech to master in learning a foreign language; their more literal uses may be grasped readily enough, but their further extension need not follow any clear principles. The preposition 'on', for instance, has certain spatial uses which we are inclined to think of as basic, but also a host of less concrete applications, as with 'on drugs', 'on purpose', 'on reflection', 'on good authority', and so forth, which may simply have to be learned case by case. Because we are to some extent presented with a family of analogous relations, with the differences not so sharp that we can speak of a series of different meanings, talk of family resemblance is attractive. On the other hand, in so far as there is no discernible thread running through some selection of the uses, we are obliged to give a piecemeal account of the word; the explanation, 'and others like these', may give no guide whatsoever to predicting further uses, but we are simply faced by the vagaries of idiom, with little sense of dealing even with variations on a single concept.

In the more favourable cases, where continuity is detectable, Wittgenstein's picture may, in fact, be too rigid. That is, it is not a matter of something in common between *a* and *b*, something else common to *b* and *c*. The resemblance is not constituted by a recurrent feature, as winning and losing, amusement, or exercise of skill – sharply distinguishable features of games that threaten us, through their sharpness, with different interpretations of 'game'. Rather, mere resemblance may present us with a lack of definition, a blurring of boundaries, with which same and different meaning are too crude to cope. With this uncertainty it remains unclear whether we have an exemplification of the family resemblance pattern. It is more a matter of finding this way of speaking appealing – no hard and fast divisions need be invoked – so long as we do not command a clear view of the range of uses and the character of the distinctions. And even before we have closely scrutinized the possibilities we can see that there can be differences which bring with them a difference in meaning. It may not be evident how we are to relate 'make of car', 'owner of a house', and 'result of a fire' in respect of their common preposition, but it is clear that we can have two senses with 'dish of fruit' and 'dish of metal'. More generally, it appears again to be a case of 'a family of senses' giving the appropriate characterization.

3.4 Applications of family resemblance

It would seem that a family resemblance account has its best chance of being workable at the point where the concepts of sameness and difference in meaning become blurred. Even then it cannot be ruled out that a fuller investigation of such grey areas will not bring them into line with the clearer cases, and so revive the objection that family resemblance is a recipe for bringing these concepts into conflict. On the other hand, it is perhaps not of paramount interest whether, as formulated, Wittgenstein's account is incoherent, but it is the residual issue – do we have a single meaning, or a whole family? – that looks to be important in the areas where, as with psychological and formal concepts, Wittgenstein applied, rather than merely illustrated, the notion.

The application to psychological concepts is more to the fore in his writings in the early thirties than it is in the *Investigations*, with Wittgenstein constantly stressing the multiplicity of phenomena which answer to 'understanding a word', 'knowing how to go on', 'believing', 'expecting', 'intending', and so on. This lessening dependence on the concept is desirable, given the curious use to which it had been put in seeking to clarify our conception of the mental. Thus, in the *Blue Book* Wittgenstein claims that philosophical investigation has been shackled by the idea that one has to find the common element in all applications of a general term if one is to get clear about its meaning (*BB* 19). He then considers what is involved in an instance of expectation – expecting someone to tea – and concludes that there are endless variations to the process of expecting which we describe by the same expression, the endless variations being a matter of different activities and states of mind. Thus one, but just one, possible development is this:

> At four o'clock I look at my diary and see the name 'B' against today's date; I prepare tea for two; I think for a moment 'does B smoke?' and put out cigarettes; towards 4.30 I begin to feel impatient; I imagine B as he will look when he comes into my room. All this is called 'expecting B from 4 to 4.30'. And there are endless variations to this process which we all describe by the same expression. If one asks what the different processes of expecting someone to tea have in common, the answer is that there is no single feature in common to all of them, though there are many common features overlapping. These cases of expectation form a family; they have family likenesses which are not clearly defined.
>
> (*BB* 20)

The difficulty with this account lies in its implication that an appropriate description of the various activities instanced can be given in terms of *expecting*, as if expecting could, in certain circumstances, be a matter of doing something like looking at one's diary or preparing tea. If someone asks me what I am doing I may say, 'I'm expecting B for tea', but only by way of explaining my actions; I have not offered a direct reply in the form of a description of what I am doing. To give the point a Rylean turn: I may be preparing tea hastily or with deliberation; I do not expect anybody hastily or with deliberation. Here the flight from a single mental process ends in a still more unsatisfactory distribution of *expecting* through a family of behavioural acts.

Similarly with the discussion of understanding in *Philosophical Grammar*: '"Understanding" is not the name of a single process accompanying reading or hearing, but of more or less interrelated processes against a background, or in a context, of facts of a particular kind' (§35). Again we have the identification with a family of processes, and again these processes refuse to accept the descriptions proposed. The later discussion of understanding, at *Investigations* §§151-5, rejects any such identification. A claim to be able to continue an arithmetical series may be preceded by various thoughts, calculations or experiments, but none of these *is* the person's understanding. Not only is there more to the latter than is given by its accompaniments or manifestations, but even if we found something common to the various cases, why should *it* be the understanding?

We can show the reasonableness of this query, but without casting doubt on the possibility of finding uniformity in the concept of understanding, by enlisting a refinement of Ryle's task-achievement framework, itself based on the kind of temporal distinction which Wittgenstein outlines, notably at *PI* 59 and *Z* §472ff. Ryle distinguishes verbs which signify a *task*, an activity or process that takes time, from verbs signifying an *achievement*, something which can be assigned a time of occurrence, but a point rather than a period (1949, 149-52). In the former category we have running a race and looking for one's shoes, in the latter winning a race and finding or seeing one's shoes. Because, Ryle thinks, 'see' always relates to an achievement, there is no question of seeking out a process, state, or experience which the verb might report.

Whether seeing should always be reckoned an achievement is disputable, but to the extent that it should it is better regarded as an achievement which marks the *beginning* of a state of awareness, rather than one which records the successful conclusion of a preceding visual search – a search which, after all, need not have been engaged upon. More generally, there is good reason to extend the achievement category to verbs which signal the initiation of a state, as well as to verbs which mark a terminating occurrence – not just 'stop', but also 'start' – since the distinctive feature, a lack of temporal extension, applies either way.

The use of 'understand' which concerns Wittgenstein at *PI* §151 is one in which an instantaneous mental event is ostensibly reported – 'Now I understand!' – and this fits readily into the re-defined achievement category. Understanding will have duration, but its beginnings may be punctate, and 'Now I understand!' is well suited to recording the moment of its dawning; not, in that event, a matter of recording a mental *process*. Again, to grasp the use of a word in a flash we are not obliged to perform a staggering feat of compression, to survey a multitude of uses in the way a dying man is said to see his whole life pass before him. Whether, in either case, a truth is announced depends on whether the person has from that point on the ability to which he in effect lays claim; whether he can go on to do certain things, as continue the series, use the word correctly, deeds which show understanding in a sense in which this has the logic of a capacity term, such as 'strength'. A man can perform various feats which reveal his strength, but there is more to being strong than doing any of the things he might happen to do. It is now clear why nothing we may find in our minds or elsewhere at the time we make the exclamation will *be* the understanding. On the other hand, the failure of understanding to be exhausted by its manifestations or its accompaniments has no tendency to show that it is not susceptible of a uniform characterization; it shows merely that we have been looking in the wrong direction.

In making clear how understanding avoids fragmentation into a host of behavioural acts, this account is, I believe, faithful to Wittgenstein's later thought as well as to our concept, but it remains true that, at least with certain psychological concepts, Wittgenstein continued to emphasize behavioural manifestations to the point of identity. Those of his defenders who are anxious to rebut charges of behaviourism on his behalf should not overlook the many cases in which their defence would not be welcome. Consider, for instance, the following passage from *Z* §545 (departing slightly from the published translation):

> Being sure that someone is in pain, doubting whether he is, and so on, are so many natural, instinctive, kinds of relationship towards other human beings, and our language is merely an auxiliary to, and further

> extension of, this behaviour. Our language-game is an extension of primitive behaviour. (For our *language-game* is behaviour.) (Instinct).
> (Cf. *Z* §573, *RPP* II, §644)

Family resemblance may no longer be explicitly invoked with such concepts, but perhaps it lingers in the background when the emphasis is on forms of behaviour. We may also note that, although the approach in the thirties is refined by the time of the *Investigations*, there is continuity between the earlier and later analyses in the way the demand for generality is resisted; in both we see a refusal to deal other than piecemeal with instances of understanding, thinking, and other psychological phenomena (which fall outside the category of sensation). Individual cases are not presented as preparatory to giving a unified account, certainly not as materials for a *theory* as to what goes to make up understanding or thinking, but it is precisely an appreciation of their variety that we are to take away from an examination of such cases.

Whatever the importance Wittgenstein came to ascribe to family resemblance in dealing with psychological concepts, when the concepts are formal, as *language, number, rule*, and *sentence (proposition)*, the approach continues to receive prominence in his later work. We shall now focus on the last of these; it is of greatest relevance to topics to come, and in any event the other concepts present largely similar issues. Thus, 'proposition' is said not to signify a sharply bounded concept, but to be analogous in these terms to the concept of a game: 'Asked what a proposition is . . . we shall give examples and these will include what we may call inductively defined series of propositions; it is in *this* way that we have the concept of "proposition"' (PI §135).

There is some doubt, of an innocent and ordinary kind, as to what we might cite in illustration of this concept. Are we happy to call 'You may go' and 'I bet he loses' propositions? Not if 'true' and 'false' are to apply in a natural way, though they may pass if what we have in mind is a more formal, grammatical characterization, along the lines of 'declarative sentence', a characterization which finds its contrasts in equally broad grammatical categories, as imperative and interrogative. It is, of course, just this kind of division that a mere listing fails to declare. I could enumerate a hundred instances of what I was prepared to call a proposition, only to be brought up short by such a possibility, thus revealing that there was a characteristic which I considered determinative of propositional status, and whose divulgence would have short-circuited such an incompletable and misinterpretable listing. And this point holds good despite the fact that *any* definition is open to misunderstanding – the questionable 'levelling' point considered earlier.

In *PG* §69 Wittgenstein implies that we might not reckon as propositions everything that sounds like one, citing 'I am tired', '2 x 2 = 4', 'time passes', and 'there is only one zero'. In *PI* §134 he remarks that '*one* feature of our concept of a proposition is, *sounding like a proposition*', so perhaps there is a change in view, but at all events it is not clear that an appeal to the *differences* between these examples will support the claim that we have to do here with a family resemblance concept. The difficulty still remains that we do not know whether the account of 'proposition' is being supposed to have to answer to our ordinary usage, or to some philosophical variant, but the main point can be made in terms of the more straightforward 'statement'. There are large and important differences between reports of past happenings and statements of intention, but application of the common notion of a *statement* is not thereby put under the slightest threat. Variety in what is stated does not necessarily mean variety in the sense of 'state' – and similarly with 'ask' and 'order'. More generally, there are bound to be crucial differences among sentences having a common superficial form, differences which our grammar obscures, but in so far as 'statement' and 'proposition' are terms of that grammar, they are unlikely to be ruled by the kinds of consideration dear to Wittgenstein, who is anxious to expose just those differences which so often go unmarked and unnoticed. Much more likely is a definition of these forms by way of opposition to such equally broad categories as those of question and injunction. Seen in terms of that contrast, the variegated sentences which Wittgenstein cites present a united front.

Very well, but when, to take another example, I assert 'This is fudge' by way of telling someone what fudge is, what 'fudge' means, and when I use the same words in contradicting a rival description, I am doing something significantly different, with in either case further striking differences *vis-à-vis* words used in issuing a threat or in making a promise. Surely we have here a family resemblance pattern, even if not one that would define 'proposition'? Again, however, I am not out to deny differences, nor to minimize their importance; it is just that to grant these differences is not to grant that there is some term upon which they impose that pattern.

3.5 *An alternative scheme*

The major difficulty with the example of games, as regards both the English and the German term, lies in the consideration that the various features cited by Wittgenstein do not form the basis of a suitable generalization for a univocal concept of game. Similarly with psychological verbs, in his earlier account. A more realistic pattern is, I contend, that of one or more central meanings of a term together with extended or transferred uses or senses. To see this at work, consider the example of 'plate'. The meaning that perhaps comes first to mind is that of 'shallow dish', and there is a closely related derived sense in which the word is used to mean 'plateful', with reference to the contents of a plate or the amount it will hold. Slightly differently, we have a 'cold plate', used of an actual course, rather than of the article on which the course is served. Compare the use of 'dish' in 'a popular local dish'. With neither word is this extended use based on resemblance – the food is not *like* the receptacle – but the principle underlying the extension is closer to that of metonymy or synecdoche – as when a book title stands in for the book: 'The publishers issued several new titles last month.'

The use of 'plate' with reference to the article of crockery is generalized when we speak of a 'collection plate', the idea of a shallow, flat receptacle being preserved, and the condition of flatness remains when we move to 'steel plate' – thin, flat metal of uniform thickness. We move further away when 'plate' is used of a thin coating of metal, and it is again a principle other than resemblance that operates when metal thus coated, or a particular article, is so described, as with 'silver plate'. A further specialization is given by 'plate' in the sense of 'photographic plate', or with respect to other kinds of sheet having a printing surface, and we meet with yet another transferred use when a print taken from such a sheet is spoken of as a plate. General physical form reappears with 'dental plate', and, on a larger scale, with 'plate' used of the rigid layers of the earth's lithosphere, but this may vanish entirely when it is used of a cup or other trophy awarded to the winner of a race. Note too the use in application to the race itself, and, in tennis, for a tournament in which first-round losers participate. Further uses, closer to the more basic ones, are with respect to the anode of a valve, a cut of beef, a horizontal timber joist, and a type of horseshoe.

Suppose we decided to rewrite Wittgenstein's doctrine of family resemblance to tally with this kind of case. It does, after all, present as much variety as one could wish for without simply listing a series of homonyms. Whatever account we give, we shall of course want to make use of the notion of *resemblance*, but the further peculiarities which *family* resemblance imports do not appear to be introduced along with this variety. We note first that it is only if there is some resemblance that there is – obviously – any chance of speaking in terms of a single meaning. And this is possible. There is no unifying some of the uses of 'plate' – e.g., as used with reference to a course at a meal and as used with reference to a rowing event – but in several cases we can discern the general condition of being a thin, flat, sheet – *thin* being of course relative to the other dimensions of the particular item – and in these terms we may group together nameplates, bookplates, photographic plates, the anode of a valve, and even tectonic plates. That is, the likeness in form allows us to speak of different kinds of plate, rather than of different senses of 'plate', so a condition for the applicability of family resemblance is satisfied.

On the other hand, this appears to be about as far as we can go with that account, since quite plainly there is a leading idea to be extracted in all these cases – and a difference in sense once we depart from this idea. It is not enough for a family resemblance analysis that the things which go by the name should be many and various. They indeed are in this instance, but they are *otherwise* various; i.e., otherwise than in respect of the general feature. The Eskimos have many more words for snow than our one. Does that oblige us to acknowledge more than one meaning for 'snow', to allow that this stuff is snow in one sense of the term, not snow in another? Not at all. The shared character of the various forms that qualifies them all as snow is not negated by any unshared features, any more than differences in nationality make for different senses of 'man'.

In arguing that univocity of a term *w* cannot tolerate the kind of diversity of feature in things falling under *w* that family resemblance sanctions, am I perhaps operating with an unrealistically sharp division between same and different meaning? On the one hand, Wittgenstein would presumably not look for a defence of the family resemblance scheme which depended on saying that an ambiguous word could well fill the bill; on the other hand, he might consider it misguided to insist on strict univocity of a term like 'game'. We found reason to doubt that he thought of 'game' and 'number' as having a family of meanings, but it is now beginning to appear that it requires this reading to make his account coherent. If a family resemblance relation between things falling under *w* demands that *w* be taken now one way, now another, then we can avoid something less crude than outright ambiguity only if we can speak of a family of meanings of *w*, as Wittgenstein himself suggests with respect to 'good'. And, as I have indicated, we are not asking of Wittgenstein more than he has shown himself willing to offer elsewhere. Consider this passage from his 1934–5 lectures:

> One could say 'proof' has as many different meanings as there are proofs. All the proofs form a family, and the word 'proof' does not refer to any one characteristic of those processes called proofs.
>
> (*AWL* 116)

If he is prepared to go to this extreme – not, surely, a step to be recommended – it is hard to see why he should not settle for a family of meanings in other cases where there is family resemblance.

With respect to 'plate', there can be no objection to speaking of the different meanings as forming a family, though the principle of membership will not invariably be one of resemblance. I doubt, however, whether such a family is what we should be considering if the example of 'game' is to be our model, the diversity to be found here being nothing like that observed with 'plate'. It may conceivably be held that there is a distinction between games as *sports* and other games, so that golf and tennis are games in a different sense from bridge or backgammon, but in general the differences that make for different kinds of game do not make for differences in the meaning of 'game' – nor indeed do I think that Wittgenstein considered them to do so. On the other hand, if the rationale for applying the term can be as irreducibly diverse as he claims, then we should soon have the kind of marked variation among meanings of the word which would issue in readings as far apart as those of 'plate' as used of a dish, and 'plate' as used of a cut of meat.

Throughout this chapter we have appealed to the observation, seemingly obvious, that sameness in meaning requires a matching sameness in the things to which our words apply. Could it be that Wittgenstein's identification of meaning with use made it easier for him to overlook this truism? (As though, since so much can fall under use, the measure of agreement we might have in the use of *w* with respect to things having nothing relevant in common could override any differences at this level.) However this question is answered, our consideration of family resemblance has not only deflected the attack on traditional definition, but, more important, it has further reinforced the claim of chapter 1 that use must be given this specific focus, must operate at the point where word and world meet, if it is to keep in touch with meaning.

4

Explanations of Meaning

Suppose *The Concise Oxford Dictionary* is right in defining 'game' as '(form of) contest played according to rules and decided by skill, strength, or luck'. None the less, it does not seem that we *operate* with this definition, that it enters into our actual practice in any way. And it is on this score that at least one aspect of the family resemblance account has an apparent advantage. Thus, the idea that we explain by giving examples, with perhaps only a phrase such as 'and similar things' added by way of verbal explanation, serves at least to bring the explanation of meaning into close contact with our usage. From this perspective, it is not so much that a traditionally formulated definition cannot be given; rather, it is not the kind of explanation we customarily do offer, so not one to which our understanding owes anything. So what is the interest of dictionary definitions? Within the more sophisticated areas of the language they may be indispensable, and they may more generally enjoy a normative status, but beyond that it is hard to see any fundamental role for them. Certainly, they would hardly seem capable of supplanting ostensive definitions, which operate in the public domain where common understanding is established, misunderstandings exposed. A person's fumbling efforts at defining a familiar word are of no great concern if his actual usage cannot be faulted, and in like fashion perhaps we need not trouble ourselves with questions about the kind of conceptual breakdown or analysis which a definition would associate with a word. Only perhaps, however. As we shall now see, definitions have more to offer than these considerations would allow.

4.1 *Explanation and definition*

For Wittgenstein, meaning is what is explained in explanations of meaning, in the sense that there is no more to meaning than is conveyed in such an explanation, where the form of explanation is as indicated in the following passage:

> What does it mean to know what a game is? What does it mean, to know it and not to be able to say it? Is this knowledge somehow equivalent to an unformulated definition? So that if it were formulated I should be able to recognize it as the expression of my knowledge? Isn't my knowledge, my concept of a game, completely expressed in the explanations that I could give? That is, in my describing examples of various kinds of game; showing how you can construct other games analogous to these in all sorts of ways; saying that I should scarcely include this or that among games; and so on.
>
> (*PI* §75)

It is true that one can show one's understanding of the word 'game' by describing and constructing various kinds of game, knowledge of the word's meaning being essentially a practical ability, manifested in a correct use of the word in application to actual or imagined games. It is far less clear, however, that giving proof of one's understanding in this way amounts to giving an adequate explanation of the meaning of the word; that depends on how much more can usefully, i.e., non-redundantly, be said or done. Not much with a word like 'beige', say, where 'That is what is called "beige"', uttered while pointing at an appropriate range of samples, is perhaps both as much as one can hope for, and as much as one could desire, but the situation is surely not the same with a word like 'legacy' or 'contraband', or indeed with 'game', where it is in place to speak of the rationale for our treating as games the various activities which we may cite or imagine, and proper to ask what that rationale is. I should scarcely place fox-hunting, canoeing, or hang-gliding in the category, I say, but then you might well be curious to know why, given all they have in common with activities which I am happy to include. Citing instances, and even constructing one game on the analogy of another, do not, as it were, *declare* what is going on, but we should like the exclusion of certain activities to be *explained*. Having been presented with a range of games – e.g., games with balloons, musical games, word games, tagging and chasing games – I can readily enough devise further instances of the type, but always within certain constraints, even if these go unstated. I may not actually say that the activity will, *qua* game, be governed by rules, that there will be something which, acting in accordance with the rules, the players must try to achieve, but this none the less belongs to the framework within which my imaginings take place, and an explanation that makes this explicit is better than one that does not.

Wittgenstein holds that our concept of *game* is completely expressed in the explanations that we could give. This we can accept if the 'could' indicates merely that nothing is wanting on the side of our knowledge. There is nothing hidden here, in the sense of there being something to which we are denied access, and yet our knowledge of meaning need not be something that we have made explicit to ourselves, or should be able to do so at all readily. That at least is so if the more explicit form of explanation, as proposed here for 'game', can be made to relate to our understanding, and it is just this that is our problem.

To take a different example, we naturally think that an accurate account of the definite article in English makes explicit what a native speaker's usage shows him to grasp in more unreflecting fashion. We do not suppose that such an account could be given by many speakers; the principles governing the correct use of 'the' are difficult to lay bare, and it is all too easy to mischaracterize, or simply to overlook, features of the word's use. But how does any such account relate to actual practice, given that none is ever actually invoked? Furthermore, while there are words and phrases for which only the more explicit pattern of explanation seems possible – as 'mortgage', 'bank rate', 'endowment policy' – with a word like 'game' a child does not in general receive anything more than an explanation by way of examples, and with 'the' the pattern of usage to which he is exposed may well not be supplemented in any way by explanatory comment. In neither case, however, does this make for an obstacle to eventual understanding.

There is a natural suspicion that talk of verbal definitions can be brought to bear upon our inarticulate and fluid practice only at the risk of distortion. However, the reasons for thinking that there is something which an account of meaning or usage can be taken to bring to the surface seem still to hold good, and to offer purchase to a notion of definition. Consider the simple example of the difference in meaning between 'bottle' and 'jar'. Although this is a question that may never have engaged us explicitly, it takes very little reflection to conclude that we use 'jar' when the width of the container's opening is close in size to the width of the body of the container, whereas with a bottle we have a neck which tapers to a relatively narrower opening. This plainly recognizable difference is not one that we need have expressed in so many words, but it is clear that it is width of opening (among other things) that guides us in the use of these terms. Not only need we not have formulated definitions of 'bottle' and 'jar'; we may not even have the words which, like 'width', 'opening' and 'taper', such definitions would have to employ – though lacking 'taper', say, we could still make use of contour-defining gestures to the same end. This accords with the claim that a definition does not in general have any reality for us as something we *consult*, but it does not exclude definitions from another role, namely that of specifying the various features of things we look to in making our classifications.

Similarly with a word like 'the'. Rules for the use of 'the' are very much derivative from actual practice; recipes for instructing a newcomer to the language rather than rules which the native speaker invokes. However, they may also be called upon in delineating the factors which dictate occurrence of the article, and in this they are very much relevant to meaning and understanding. Or again, consider the examples of mood and tense. With some languages it may be quite difficult to detail those contexts in which the subjunctive is felt to be required, and to explain why its use is not called for in a number of seemingly comparable cases. There is no expectation that a native speaker will be capable of framing an adequate account of the necessary distinctions. He will presumably be able to give examples of correct usage, but he may be unable to go beyond these in such a way as to throw light on his use of the subjunctive more generally. None the less, there are circumstances which his usage shows him to recognize as calling for this mood, and an account of the subjunctive has a role in making clear just what those circumstances are. And this is a matter of the meaning of a linguistic form. Likewise with tense. The sureness with which a speaker handles quite subtle distinctions relating to tense and aspect may not be matched by a like ability to explain just what factors make a particular form the appropriate one in a given context, but there are patterns here which can with some effort be discerned and which relate to meaning.

The account just sketched has the virtue of showing how definitions and rules may be relevant to meaning in a way that does not involve imposing an unreal, formalistic approach upon the workings of language. My use of 'game' owes nothing to the existence of a definition, to an actual formulation of necessary and sufficient conditions for the use of the word, but there are features that make for character as a game and which we implicitly go by in judging something to be a game, and a definition is not being abused if it is called upon to bring these into the open. When definitions are enlisted for this purpose, it is not sufficient that they actually apply to whatever falls under the concept which they define. If it is a matter of specifying those features which we take into account in pronouncing something to be a game, then of course the definition is restricted to conditions of which we can be apprised, conditions which we are capable of recognizing – as, we note, with Wittgenstein's *criteria* – even if the procedure of making explicit these conditions leaves room for discovery, for possible surprises. We have, of course, no assurance that a satisfactory definition can always be formulated. That depends on the language's having terms for the relevant constancies which we recognize in games, and so forth, and there is no guarantee that we shall have words which, singly or in combination, will allow us to accurately circumscribe the same area of usage.

Recognition of a person, in particular by facial characteristics, offers an apt comparison. I may not be able to put into words what it is that I go by in judging a person to be *N.N.*; indeed, there may not *be* words which I might call upon for this purpose. You would expect me to be able to say *something*, but the generality of what I offer may well not match the specificity of my recognition, in so far as the description I give would fit many people whom I could readily distinguish non-verbally from *N.N.* It may not even be entirely clear to me just what it is that I go by in judging someone to be *N.N.* His appearance, no doubt, but I may be quite unable to pinpoint, let alone describe, the features that weigh with me, that I find distinctive.

Wittgenstein's defence of ostensive definition appeared open to the objection that it was insufficiently discriminating: of course any explanation can be misunderstood, but there is a vast difference between explanations for which success is practically assured, and those for which it is the exception. However, while this objection is relevant, it is relevant only to the extent that ostensive definition is thought of as inviting comparison with other forms of definition. That, clearly, is one of Wittgenstein's concerns, but he also wishes to highlight a *grammatical* point: ostensive definition genuinely *counts* as an explanation of meaning. And this is important for what it tells us about meaning. That is, meaning is something that *can* be conveyed by this everyday form of definition; it is not something hidden, lying beyond what might be revealed by this procedure.

Just as 'definition' is not wholly apt when ostension is meant to do the work, so 'explanation' might here be queried. However, more important is a reminder of the earlier limitations to which ostensive definition was said to be subject, namely the stage-setting, the knowledge needed by the learner before he is in a position to take in any definitions at all, even ostensive ones, and which Wittgenstein sees as induced by *training*. Given that there may be learning without teaching, we shall have to interpret 'training' very liberally, but the point is that Wittgenstein himself allows that what is imparted in ostensive definition bears upon a part only of the usage which the child comes to master. There is an area of meaning that lies outside the reach of ostension. Considerations of this kind appear at this stage to have faded from view, leaving us with an unbalanced picture, yet I am doing no more than stress the importance of that dimension of linguistic knowledge which requires training, or at least which is gradually acquired through exposure to use of words in the appropriate circumstances, and which appears somehow to have lost out to the area of usage in which ostension can successfully operate. Or, rather, I am doing slightly more than that, since I wish to stress the former at the expense of the latter, to bring in under this heading more that pertains to the sense of particular words, rather than just the notions more generally implicated in learning a language. Compared with what has to get across to the learner in the less explicit way, what ostensive definition can in practice provide may be comparatively insignificant.

4.2 *Knowledge and meaning*

At *PI* §82 Wittgenstein writes:

> What do I call 'the rule by which he proceeds'? – The hypothesis that satisfactorily describes his use of words, which we observe; or the rule which he looks up when he uses signs; or the one which he gives us in reply if we ask him what his rule is?

There is a similar variability in talk of features that we 'go by', or which 'weigh with us'. These phrases, along with 'what guides us' and 'what we look to', have a use in which they relate to conscious deliberation and ratiocination, and in some cases just this interpretation is relevant: we satisfy ourselves that the bird has such-and-such markings, shape, and so forth, before pronouncing it a woodpecker. Very often, however, we give no thought to the requisite conditions; that exercise may be a necessity for one who has not mastered the language, but the native speaker is characterized by his more automatic, unreflective – and more assured – responses. For him, a phrase like 'what he goes by' will accordingly have to be parted from any suggestion of articulate knowledge or reasoning in a large number of cases. But since it is less clear what it then involves, is its use really necessary at all?

Once we strip our account of this epistemic dimension, we are left with just the bare association of word and circumstance: we use 'jar' of a container when . . . , and we use 'bottle' when . . . ; or we use the term of a container which . . . . If our aim is simply to specify when the given term is used, no more than the truth of such a statement is needed. However, while these examples look to be satisfactory as pointers to how the two words are understood, that is surely because we are entitled to take for granted that the conditions specified are conditions which are apparent to us in our dealings with bottles and jars. And not only apparent, but key features when it comes to distinguishing the two in these terms. True, these observations are directly relevant to a limited area of use only, occasions when there is no actual application of the word to anything being frequent enough, but the case that is central is surely that where our words make contact with the world, when it is quite apparent that we take this to be a jar, that to be a bottle.

Again, it must be emphasized that this knowledge may be far from the forefront of our mind, not the kind of knowledge that, in general, we can formulate on demand. We may never have stopped to ask ourselves why certain orderings of adjectives may be mandatory – for instance, no rearrangement is possible in the phrase 'numerous highly-qualified Italian technicians' – and even when confronted with examples we may fail to appreciate what it is that governs the ordering. Not merely do we not consult a rule; we do not cite a rule by way of explanation or justification either. Or again, consider the distinction in meaning between 'almost' and 'nearly'. So often are these interchangeable, we can sympathize with dictionaries which define each in terms of the other, though it does not take long to turn up differences: we do not use 'nearly' in such sentences as 'It is almost too good to be true', 'His feats were almost unbelievable', 'Almost nobody came', and 'It is almost as if he wanted to lose.' Why not? With both adverbs we have the idea of 'little short of being', but with 'nearly' what is missing is more of the same, more of what has brought us close to the condition in question. This may also be the case with 'almost', but here what is wanting need not be continuous with what there is already, so that the idea of coming near to the condition may not apply – we say 'very nearly', not 'very almost'. As this invocation of the adjective suggests, it may not be too fanciful to see the original spatial model at work: we are nearly there when only a small part of the distance remains to be traversed, and we maintain this picture when 'more of the same' has application, whereas the model behind 'almost' is more generally quantitative – 'all but'. It may be wondered how there can be such a distinction if its existence comes as news to native speakers, but it is not as if we were introducing factors of which we have no inkling: the division between the spatially analogous and the more generally quantitative relates to factors of which we can be apprised, and which can thus be reflected in our usage. This is simply to approach from another direction the earlier condition of learnability which an adequate specification of meaning can be asked to satisfy.

To take an example of a distinction which is even further removed from any explicit knowledge, consider the claim made by Randolph Quirk (*The Times*, 20.v.85) that a distinction is commonly observed in the use of 'dreamed' against 'dreamt', the former indicating continuity, the latter an episodic occurrence. It may come as a surprise to learn that we differentiate in this way – if indeed we do – to such a point that 'natural' meaning may be thought the most that can be involved. That is, perhaps the stated correlation does hold, but lies outside the scope of linguistic meaning, being akin to a correlation that might obtain between, say, use of a word and some unknown state of the brain. One way of bringing it within the ambit of linguistic meaning would be simply to extend this category to embrace the natural variety, but while the line between the two is in some cases a fine one, I should wish a further condition to be satisfied before allowing that an aspect of word meaning is in the offing, the condition being precisely that we have some connection, however minimal, with knowledge. We should, if there is anything to the suggested distinction, at least feel that something is not quite right when it is not observed. Or, perhaps, the degree to which there is indeed this distinction might be measured by the extent to which there is that response. We are not conscious of using 'dreamt' rather than 'dreamed' in order to communicate episodic character, but what we have essentially, and as is reflected in the sense of something being not quite right, is a correlation with conditions – episodic and non-episodic character – which fall within our cognizance.

'A word has the meaning someone has given to it', wrote Wittgenstein (*BB* 28), apparently requiring that meaning be transparent in a way that I deny to be necessary. But then my denial may well be resisted on the grounds that there is hardly room for surprise or discovery with respect to what one means. My invocation of these recognitional terms is an acknowledgement of what is true in this claim. That is, the relevant facts about our usage may never have occurred to us; we may be unable to come up with a correct analysis without considerable reflection, examining and rejecting various alternatives, and even then nothing better than a very crude account may be forthcoming – and that only with prompting. But we must be able to show our awareness of the distinction by the way we observe it in practice, by showing our sensitivity to the presence or absence of the relevant feature. With conjunctions, for instance, the factors to which we must be attuned reside in relations between things said, as when a statement stands in a certain contrastive relation to what has preceded it in the conversation, a relation that is signalled or acknowledged by use of a term such as 'although'. It may be said that we use 'although' when we think there is a contrast of this kind, but our thinking this may be essentially only a matter of our using that term when, for the most part, there is such a contrast, and being prepared to make a charge of incorrectness, or at least being bewildered, uncomprehending, when the regularity is violated. We give substance to the ascription of the belief in these terms, rather than take use of the word as evidence for a belief which is to be given another form of expression. Indeed, not only may we be fairly inarticulate about what a word imports, but there is clearly something very much secondary about the ability to give a verbal account, especially if that is a matter of stating the meaning in other words. There may be no other formulation, and even if there is, a grasp of the given term may owe nothing to the possibility of this alternative.

Although the preceding view has been developed in opposition to Wittgenstein, it is not clear how far it is at odds with his position. On the one hand, he often appears to regard understanding and the ability to explain as correlative. We should of course be astonished, he remarks, if someone understood the word 'bank' but could give no answer when we asked him 'What is a bank?' (*RPP* I, §679). No doubt, but then this is one example only, with no evident claim to represent the generality of words. Surprise would indeed be natural in this instance, but if the word were 'time' or 'mind' our expectations might be much less. However, Wittgenstein then indicates that understanding – of the word 'sun' – may demand only such things as knowledge of what the sun looks like. If that is the direction we move in, or if explaining requires no more than an ability to give examples of correct usage, then it may well be that, with respect to the problematic terms, nothing of any substance is being demanded by way of a connection between understanding and an ability to explain – though in that case our doubts may well shift to the propriety of speaking of 'explanation' in this regard. Again, alongside Wittgenstein's observations apropos words like 'bank' and 'book' (ibid. §296), where a request for explanation can be met without difficulty, we have his understandable acknowledgement that conceptual relationships are very complex (*RPP* II, §454), that we are unprepared to describe the use of a word like 'think': we learn its use in certain circumstances, but we do not learn how to describe those circumstances (*Z* §§111-14). The analogy he offers looks to be right on the mark with respect to very many areas of the language: a man may be able to find his way about a city perfectly well, yet be incapable of drawing a map of that city (ibid. §121). What is supposedly hard to achieve is not an account which reveals 'think' as having a unified employment; that is simply not to be had at all. We can give examples of use, sufficient to evidence a practical grasp of the concept, but it is one that comprises many manifestations of life, and its employment is difficult to survey (ibid. §§110, 113).

At all events, it does seem abundantly clear that, faced with subtle differences in meaning, e.g., that between 'can' and 'may', or between 'probable' and 'likely', we may well not get a satisfactory account of the nuances from speakers of the language who have given no thought to their usage. There is even a place for expertise, for ensuring that the data considered are comprehensive and representative, and for looking critically at any descriptions of usage based on the data. After all, we do get differing versions – not least from linguists – and any philosophy tutor knows that he might well foist an erroneous analysis on a native speaker – persuading a not unintelligent student that, say, Russell's theory of descriptions furnishes an adequate account of 'the', or that 'unless' means the same as 'if . . . not . . . '. Indeed, given the difficulty in getting clear about the very word 'meaning', we can hardly be expected to give much credence to the suggestion that its character is so much open to view that a distorted account by a native speaker is not a real possibility.

4.3 Sameness and difference in meaning

Our reasons for parting company with Wittgenstein on the topic of family resemblance reflected divergent conclusions on questions of sameness and difference in meaning. That an issue of such moment should peter out in a dispute over something so apparently inconsequential may be felt unsatisfactory. Of what interest is it whether a word has one meaning or a dozen? In many cases it may well not matter one jot; certainly, the concern should not be that meanings are things to be avoided – as though, the very notion being suspect, we should try to make do with as few of them as possible. However, if there is diversity, ignoring it is likely to lead to confusion, and if there is uniformity, ignoring this may mean that significant general patterns go unnoticed. More emphatically, a divergence on what counts here as the same or different is potentially crucial with many philosophical issues; as indicated at the outset, whether there is any future in looking for a uniform account of a key concept such as knowledge – or indeed meaning itself – will depend on just how we deal with this seemingly trivial question of identity. The general issue is, then, worth further consideration.

If we start to run over possible uses to which words may be put, we may find ourselves agreeing with Wittgenstein that there are countless such (*PI* §23); not only as generated by different word classes, but even within a given class or with respect to a given word. On the other hand, we may also wonder what significance there is in this abundance. Might it not be that some uses are more important than others, that when it comes to a grasp of the meaning of a word, there is in fact only a small number of central uses to be considered? Indeed, with many words, if we set out to list the relevant uses we may be hard pressed to get beyond one. Take the word 'tomorrow'. This can occur in any of the various contexts which Wittgenstein lists when trying to get across the multifarious possibilities of use, as speculating about an event, guessing riddles, praying, and so forth, but it would seem that the word enjoys a constant use – to signify the day following that on which the word is uttered or written – unaffected by the differing overall purposes to which the context as a whole is put. For Wittgenstein, however, it is as if each word somehow partakes of the force of the whole utterance in which it occurs, such forces being, moreover, indefinite in number and incapable of being ordered in any sort of hierarchy which would let us fasten on any use or uses as central.

Here we may recall Wittgenstein's remarks in the opening pages of the *Investigations* concerning the ostensive teaching of 'Slab!'. Awareness of what goes by the name does not suffice for full understanding, but there must also be an appreciation of the utterance as something to be acted upon. However, as noted earlier, single words are not generally the bearers of a particular force, so it is dangerous to generalize on the basis of this example. I am thinking here of force as something that belongs with the description of a whole sentence. If, on the other hand, we think more broadly in terms of semantic function, then, as indicated, it would seem that with a word like 'tomorrow' a single such function can be realistically identified. Again, with respect to 'slab', we can allow that naming is preparatory to the use of the word, but the use which the word enjoys as a certain kind of name, or common noun, appears to be fairly uniform. Even if, moreover, we do find ourselves able to speak of different uses, that may simply give further support to my claim that 'different use' does not always keep in step with 'different meaning' – e.g., 'use in a prayer' as against 'use in a riddle'.

It is occasionally thought that unless we have one central use of language of the narrower kind – the assertoric use of sentences being the one customarily selected – a use from which other forms are somehow derivable, there is no explaining the common meaning which words have as we move from sentence type to sentence type. A philosopher has to be firmly in the grip of dogma to imagine that there is any difficulty in appreciating how 'tomorrow', say, does exactly the same job in 'Come tomorrow' as in 'Will you come tomorrow?' However, Wittgenstein's opposing view does not rest on the obvious ground that a single use, or at least straightforward variations on a single use, can be discerned within different sentence types; rather, he simply accepts, and indeed revels in, a plethora of unsystematizable uses. This makes for a curious meeting of extremes, both viewpoints seemingly regarding different contexts as inevitably threatening differing characterizations for all the words within them.

I am again not confident that these observations find a target in Wittgenstein, since the position I am taking exception to seems so plainly wrong, but there is undoubtedly a tendency on his part to emphasize diversity of meaning, and not always on grounds that we should consider adequate. Is it really right to say that, for instance, 'the phrase "beautiful color" . . . can have a hundred meanings, depending on the occasion on which we use it'? (*AWL* 35). He is of course not to be held to a literal interpretation of these words, but does the phrase enjoy even many meanings, where, say, double figures is all we demand for many? Again, Wittgenstein apparently considers the word 'pain' to vary in meaning depending on whether the pain reported is present or past (*LW* I, §899). He allows that the same feeling is spoken of in either case, but claims that there is none the less a difference in meaning because use of the word with reference to past pains brings with it a different *technique*. He gives no explanation of how it is that a difference at that point might provide a ground for speaking of a difference to be located in the sense of 'pain'.

In cases like this, where Wittgenstein's criteria for sameness of meaning are wildly out of line with any established practice, a bad argument – or at least a casual approach to matters of meaning – is sometimes lurking in the background. Take his frequent talk of different meanings for 'is' – as copula, as sign of identity, as sign of equality (*AWL* 98–9, *PI* §558, §561, 175). The difference between, say, 'Williams is the lawyer you met earlier' and 'Williams is Welsh' is a difference in the type of term following 'is'. That, and that alone, is sufficient to account for the differences which lead us to contrast the identity with the predication. We should have reason to find variability in 'is' only if, holding all the other factors constant, we could say that one and the same form of words was ambiguous as between the two readings. Since, however, what complements 'is' has to differ from identity to predication, this is not a real possibility (cf. Rundle 1979, §3). Neglect of this kind of consideration perhaps led Wittgenstein to suppose that no argument was needed to defend his claim that it is specifically 'pain' that differs in meaning in the different temporal contexts.

Again, his discussions of 'can' and 'able' are marred by a failure to keep apart the variety in the verbal phrases with which these may join – 'able to lift', 'able to eat a large dinner' – and the variety, much less, in 'can' and 'able' themselves (*AWL* 81; *BB* 111–17). It is surely only by using the former to inflate the latter that he could come to think of the uses of 'can' as forming 'an enormously large family' (*AWL* 95). At all events, the more critical our approach to the data, the more likely it is that the meanings we find will reduce in number: contextual differences may obscure the common thread of meaning, so it is only to be expected that the initial impression should be one of multiplicity; it is not, though, an impression with which there is any virtue in remaining content.

4.4 The examples of now *and* well

Variety among uses at one level is not inconsistent with constancy of use at another, and indeed it can be the latter that is relevant to the question of the number of a word's meanings. To see how this may be overlooked, consider the *Concise Oxford Dictionary*'s sub-entries for 'now', where the word is said to be, in the relevant use, 'without temporal force, giving sentence various tones: soothing, exclaiming, reproving, explanatory, threatening, etc.' Suggested equivalents are given by *pray, I beg, I insist, I warn you, and yet, you must know, it must be admitted*, and *surely*.

It seems natural enough to speak in terms of the different uses of 'now' – more natural than to speak of its different meanings – and we get a glimpse here of the richness of use which Wittgenstein wishes to emphasize. However, I believe the account to be misleading in this respect. Various sentences are cited in illustration of the different uses, but it is surely the sentence without the 'now' that will ensure that there is a reproving, threatening, explanatory, or other force. Such descriptions as these can be invoked with 'Now why didn't I think of that?', 'Oh, come now!', 'No nonsense, now!', and 'Now Barabbas was a robber', to mention some of the dictionary's examples, but in each case we can recognize the sentence minus the 'now' as having the relevant force. There is nothing specifically explanatory about the 'now' in 'Now Barabbas was a robber'; it is just that what the word precedes can be thus described. Or, if 'now' does in some cases make a more substantial contribution, so that the sentence would not accept the given description if it were omitted, this could be because of the interaction of that sentence with 'now' in its general sense. The word might serve to make clear that what follows is offered in explanation – given certain contextual facts – but to do so as a function of its more general sense and use.

The dictionary may be thought simply to be doing its job in listing these various uses, but only half that job has been done so long as it fails to provide a synthesis of the uses where one is possible; we have been given no more than clues to the general case, not an account of that case from which we might be able to predict further uses, uses which arise when the word is coupled with different types of sentence – though this is somewhat misleading, in so far as it is the further sentences that provide the foundation for speaking of a further use.

How is 'now' to be explained? It is, as here envisaged, a sentence adverb, so not part of the statement, command, question, or whatever, that it would be as a qualification within the sentence. For instance, the question 'Now where was I?' is not to be reported: He wondered where he then was. Compare the use of 'again' in 'Who did you say you were again?', or the philosophically more interesting example of the if-clause in 'If you don't mind me saying, you're putting on weight'. This is not 'if' in a sense different from that which we find in a conditional; it is just that the if-clause here offers no qualification to what is advanced in the main clause, but has again the role of a sentence adverb, relating to the assertion of that clause.

In this use of 'now' the word is said to be 'without temporal force', but that is not altogether correct. The now is the now of *saying*: the word serves to highlight the current utterance, and may bring us back or move us on to some other matter, through the implied contrast with other times, and so with other utterances at those times. So, with 'Now Barabbas was robber', there is a movement to the next stage in the narrative, and since it is felt to be of some significance, it is explicitly signalled by 'now'. A similar focusing on the utterance is possible for questions, commands, and exclamations, as with the other dictionary examples, 'No nonsense, now!', 'Now why didn't I think of that?', and even 'Now, now, behave yourself!', where the repetition serves to convey a sense of greater urgency. It is not implausible to hold that the 'now' which occurs here is in fact the same in meaning as the 'now' which is described as a temporal adverb, since any difference between the two is adequately accounted for by appeal to the syntactic separation, the independence from the accompanying utterance, which the use as a sentence adverb enjoys. So, I see only one word in 'Now, settle down, please' and 'Settle down now, please', the difference coming in with this difference in grammar. The description that suggests itself is: a word with a single meaning, but two distinguishable uses.

It is this pattern of explanation that should be our aim. After all, there is a presumption of a reason in our use of a single word throughout these diverse contexts, a need to be understood balancing any desire we may have to appropriate a word for a new use, and while there is no guarantee that we shall not in the end find ourselves obliged to ascribe a multitude of meanings to a given word, this is a step to be taken only if there proves to be no way of unifying the individual cases, no way of construing them as realizations of a single theme. Subtle variations in overall use – i.e., the use which results from the interaction of the word with other contextual elements – will no doubt be encountered. Think here of the way in which, in saying 'Take care, now', or 'Goodbye, now', one can be talking *down* to a person. Why? This 'now' not infrequently follows an admonition or exhortation, and it could be that, because one might well make use of the 'now' to draw attention to one's words, to set them off from preceding remarks, the speaker sounds as if he is addressing a child, for whom such emphasis may be necessary. We are saying, in effect, 'Don't overlook this'; hence the talking down impression.

There is again a question of interest in the matter of an intentional use where the intention is very much beneath the surface. It seems correct to say that we use 'now' because it serves to highlight the accompanying utterance, but there need be no consciousness of that purpose at any articulate level; on the contrary, there may be considerable difficulty in coming to appreciate just what the role is for which the word is commonly enlisted. To change the example – since we already know the answer with 'now' – consider 'well', as this is used in 'Well, I suppose you may be right', or 'Well, well, what a surprise!', or in 'Well?' uttered expectantly to a silent figure who has just poked his head around the door. The intentionality may manifest itself in a pretty inchoate way. For instance, in formal writing we may feel that the word is out of place, but be conscious of a gap at this point. So, having been posed the question, 'What possibilities are there?', I may wish to respond with 'Well, there is the materialist's answer, and also that of the dualist.' Deny me the 'well' and I feel that something is missing, something that is necessary to ease over the transition, to prevent it sounding too abrupt. But it takes time to arrive at an account of 'well' that explains how precisely it succeeds in doing this, how exactly its meaning is to be explained in this and in other comparable contexts.

We may allow that one who claims to understand 'bank' could not make good that claim if he is unable to dilate upon its meaning, but is it clear that a native speaker must be able to say much of use in pinning down the meaning of 'well'? Here are some of the uses with which he is going to have to cope:

1 Well, who would have thought it?
2 Well, here we are at last
3 Well, perhaps you are right
4 Well, who was it?
5 Well, but what about Jones?
6 Well then?
7 Oh well, it can't be helped
8 Well, well!

It is useful to think in terms of a comparison with 'now'. Both may be sentence adverbs that ease a transition, though each of course relates differently to what has preceded. And, of course, to try to explain either merely by pointing to this role appears unsatisfactory as an explanation of *meaning*. Once more, this is the kind of use that one finds *explained* by an account of what the word means. *Collins Dictionary of the English Language* makes such a questionable move with its description of the occurrence in 'well, I don't think I will come' as simply 'an expression used to preface a remark, gain time, etc.', thus putting 'well' on a par with 'er' and 'um' in not requiring that it mean anything at all.

These sample sentences come from the *Concise Oxford Dictionary*'s entry for 'well', which, as with 'now', offers individual characterizations of the uses. So the word is said to express (1) great astonishment, (2) relief, (3) concession, (4) resumption or continuation of talk, (5) qualified recognition of point, (6) expectation, (7) resignation, and (8) surprise. Once more we should hope to do better than this, and indeed to relate 'well' in these uses to its use as an adverb corresponding to 'good'. Can we? The role of the interjection stands out most clearly when what follows is in answer to a question. With 'Is this a genuine antique?', the question will be aiming at a yes or no response; if all that the person addressed can manage is 'It looks like one', he is likely to add a prefatory 'well' in order to acknowledge the merely partial character of his answer: what he has offered is better than, say,

'I've no idea', but it still falls short of what was sought. Likewise with our initial example of question and answer, where the possibilities which the latter presents go a long way towards meeting the terms of the question, but, since they are not exhaustive, not all the way. And again with an imperative, as when 'Pay him a visit' is greeted with 'Well, I shall try to'; not the assurance of compliance which had been sought, but further in this direction than a refusal to comply. Similarly with 'well' in response to an assertion when we do not fully endorse what has been put to us, but can at least offer qualified support.

The dictionary examples present variations on this theme. On the one hand, a conciliatory note is struck, the speaker signalling a degree of acquiescence in or acceptance of what has been said or implied, has happened or been done; on the other hand, this is coupled with a shift in direction, an expression of surprise, a more challenging observation, a questioning stance. Just as 'but' signals a certain relation between what follows and what preceded, so too the use which is to complement the meaning of 'well' will receive a comparably general formulation – the character of the surrounding context again defining the appropriate association – further uses, as instanced by the dictionary, being uses which exploit this basic association. The relation to 'well' as the adverbial form of 'good' is often remote, but such an expansion as 'that is all very well, but . . . ' may bring out the relation to this use.

There is still much to say about this invaluable word, and I readily admit that the sketch given may be inaccurate. It is – and this is more important than the matter of correctness – no more than a hypothesis that the word allows of explanation along these lines. It may be felt that 'well' is just the kind of word that cries out for an explanation in terms of family resemblance. Perhaps the differences in its uses are sufficiently nuanced to make this scheme inviting, but what is more evident is the utter unhelpfulness of an attempt at explanation which simply lists uses such as the above without interpretive comment, lamely adding 'and others like these'. It is utterly unhelpful, since it is so opaque just how these cases are like one another. To such a point, of course, that *any* talk of sameness of meaning may be in doubt, even the sameness that family resemblance would allow. With such variety in evidence Wittgenstein could be expected to speak in terms of a multiplicity of meanings, rather than of family resemblance. However, while this accords with the paraphrases which, like those of the dictionary, one is initially disposed to offer, the motley of explanations provides a point at which to start rather than to stop, diversity of meaning being something to embrace only after a concerted attempt to discern univocity has failed. In this respect Wittgenstein's general approach seems to be wanting.

5

Varieties of Force

At §21 of *Philosophical Investigations* Wittgenstein observes that, while we do call 'Isn't the weather glorious today?' a question, it is used as a statement, and he notes that one says 'You will do this' not as a prophecy but as a command. In both cases, it would seem, grammatical form is a poor guide to use and meaning. Moreover, not only may the uses associated with different forms overlap, but within sentences of any given category we meet with innumerable uses (ibid. §23). And not merely innumerable uses, but uses whose variety defeats any attempt to subsume them under a uniform characterization (ibid. §24).

Wittgenstein's frequent reminders of linguistic variety are salutary, but variety at one level need not preclude uniformity at another; nor is it clear that there can be no way of aligning grammatical form and linguistic use; that again may be essentially a matter of pitching the characterization of the latter at the right level of generality. Here I am tempted by the following analogy. Our right to ascribe a single shape to an object is sometimes challenged on the grounds that an object manifests a multiplicity of appearances in respect of shape. In fact, of course, such multiplicity is only to be expected on the supposition under attack, the threat coming from precisely the opposite possibility – that, however the conditions are varied, we meet with a constant appearance. Similarly with form and function: rightly understood, apparent dissociations of the two may attest to an underlying uniformity.

The main objective of this chapter is to determine the general shape to be taken by explanations of meaning which bear upon sentential *force*, and in pursuing this aim we shall set forth considerations which for the most part favour unity with respect to the main sentence types. This may or may not have us contradicting Wittgenstein. Certainly, an opposing tendency will be stressed, but it could be that it is for him more a matter of the differences being of greater importance than the likenesses. At all events, the patterns which emerge will not suffice to reinstate one of Wittgenstein's major targets, namely, the attempt to draw together such diverse categories as those of assertion, question, command, and the expression of a wish by identifying their supposedly common content, channelled via the 'sentence radical' (ibid. §22). This representation aims at maximal uniformity, but the uniformity envisaged is not in the language as it exists, and the problems at which it is directed are in any event nugatory. The concept of truth is of course very much bound up with the sentence radical, and the present discussion will be a preliminary to the further investigation of both topics.

5.1 Form and force

The division is not always clearcut, but I shall generally employ the terms 'declarative', 'interrogative', and 'imperative' as labels for grammatical categories, reserving 'assertion', 'question', and 'injunction' for sentences in use, albeit sentences of these types. The difference between a declarative sentence and an associated interrogative form – as 'He is in' and 'Is he in?' – is sometimes spoken of as a difference in *mood*. However, mood is mood of the verbal phrase – indicative, subjunctive, imperative – and in both its occurrences the verb here receives the same description – 'third person present *indicative*' – word order, not mood, being what differentiates the two. It is difficult to make out a case for two distinguishable forms of the verb in these two sentences, and difficult to see why anyone should think it necessary, given the obviously relevant structural difference. Or, if we consider the single form, 'He is in', now with the intonation appropriate to an assertion, now with that of a question, we have again a feature which signals the difference, and if anything a weaker case for speaking of two variants of the verb. Similarly, we might add, with verb forms in conditional sentences. In 'If I laugh I cough', *both* clauses present us with verbs in the indicative mood. I suspect that, despite its frequency, the assimilation of 'indicative' to 'declarative' reflects confusion, rather than just an alternative usage. However that may be, if we fail to locate the variable factor correctly, we may well overlook the possibility of construing a declarative and its corresponding interrogative as functions of a common verbal form in a way that opposes them both to imperatival sentences, where the mood of the verb certainly does differ. That is, while it organizes them differently, an interrogative draws upon the same components as a corresponding declarative sentence – a feature which seemingly gives us a head start in any attempt to unify the two.

When a declarative form is used to generate a question, as with 'The paint is wet?', a kind of diminished assertion results: we utter words whose use could constitute a full-blooded assertion, but by altering the intonation – or adding a question mark – we signify our withdrawal from the full assertoric use, presenting a possible claim in a tentative, probing way, with a view to eliciting confirmation or contradiction from our audience. While we are not to be held responsible for what we say as an unqualified assertion, our invocation of a form of words that is geared to such a use – an unasserted assertion, we might say – gives our hearer or reader something which he may treat as such in the desired respect, viz. as something that can be confirmed or contradicted.

There is a difference between questions thus formed and those where we depart from the declarative word order. The former may be used precisely when we come close to an assertion, offering our words as a possible answer, explanation, or suggestion, as when, in reply to 'Guess what happened today', we venture 'Your cousin rang?' – which might be greeted with 'Right' as well as with 'Yes'. Another frequent use of this form is in incredulous repetitions, as when someone's remark, 'I've passed', is returned to him in tones of disbelief: 'You've passed?' The questioner can hardly believe his ears, and indeed the point of the query may be to establish whether he has heard correctly. In this case what is said may have the force of an exclamation, and be marked as such, as much as a question. Certainly, the different nuances are available to this form in a way they are not with 'Have you passed?', which is geared more to the plain asking of a question, without the further suggestion that something is being queried.

The variety here may be taken to reinforce the rejection of any stable connection between form and function. After all, we have just acknowledged that one and the same sentence may be now assertion, now question, now exclamation. However, while the variety is to be admitted, this supposed consequence is not. First, to look at just the words is to ignore the element which may switch us from one interpretation to another, namely, the differing intonation: that is a matter of a linguistic difference which reflects a difference in use. Second, it is significant that we may invoke the generally assertoric character of the form of words in accounting for its extension to an interrogative or exclamatory use. The use which we should regard as basic to that form is not simply negated, so that we find ourselves faced with a puzzling brute fact – one and the same sentence serving totally different ends – but that use plays a crucial part in the generation of the other cases. So, it is not in the least surprising that the word order of the declarative form should be retained when there is some inclination to go along with an assertoric use of the words, or when, in the other case, we echo what is said, as it were sending it back to the speaker for confirmation. Conversely, it is not at all remarkable that a question formed by inverting the word order should not be enlisted in either of these cases.

Further complications are provided by negation. I say that an interrogative use of a declarative form of words tends to expect an answer which endorses that form, and this remains true when negation is introduced, as with 'Your cousin didn't ring?', though there is then a suggestion that an expectation is being queried, the expectation that the person's cousin did ring. This latter suggestion is one shared by the inverted form, 'Did your cousin not ring?', whereas the version without the 'not' – 'Did your cousin ring?' – carries no such implication. Why? I suggest that we are witnessing here a feature of 'not' which it shares with its uses in assertoric contexts. In general, a negative statement has a higher probability of truth than the corresponding affirmative, so a lesser probability of being invoked for the sake of new information which it presents; rather, a use to *correct* takes over as the more likely: we counter a belief, or expectation, which we take to be mistaken. In putting the question, 'Did your cousin not ring?', we are asking whether a negative form is so, a form that may be supposed to have arisen in opposition to the unnegated version, so it is like asking whether a contradiction of someone's claim is correct. Hence the suggestion that we are querying a presumed – indeed a presumptive – truth, so that the question, 'Did your cousin not ring?', has the force of 'Did your cousin not ring after all?'

The association of 'not' with a use to contradict a belief is seen again with examples like 'Is it not the prettiest baby you've ever seen?' Not a request for information – the answer being thought to be obvious – but a challenge to the person to contradict what the speaker holds true. Given the supposed obviousness of the answer, the utterance is tantamount to an emphatic statement. Similarly with Wittgenstein's example, 'Isn't the weather glorious today?' His characterization of this – a question used to make a statement – can be allowed to pass, but to leave it just at that gives no indication as to how this apparent exchange of roles is achieved. It is not just an inexplicable accident of usage, but the extension of the interrogative form in this direction is *principled*, exploiting general facts about that form – and about negation – rather than imposing a use that is at cross-purposes with its interpretation elsewhere.

Similar observations apply to rhetorical questions in which there is no negation, as with 'Who is to say what is to count as a proof?' Such is the speaker's certainty as to the right answer – including, in this instance, 'No one' – he considers that you have only to entertain the question – and question it assuredly is – to hit upon the right answer. Questions seek answers, even when they are thought obvious to the point that the speaker's endorsement of the corresponding assertion can be assumed. But it is a less direct way of indicating one's commitment to that assertion, not adequately characterized by speaking merely of a question used to make a statement – as if we no longer had the more basic feature of questions as forms of words whereby an answer is *invited*.

Again we may have an exclamatory use of an interrogative form, as with 'Could that man fight!' Exclamations might be thought to constitute a separate species of speech act, but, at least when they are sentential in form, and not just interjections like 'Wow!' or 'Blow!', they are, or are in effect, refinements of the more general assertoric and interrogative categories – the qualification, 'in effect', being needed for such forms as 'What beautiful eyes you've got!' Unlike 'Wow!', this gives us something – an implied assertion – with which we can agree or disagree. No connection between form and function is overturned by an exclamatory use of the sentential forms, which give a relatively full specification of something which occasions a feeling or reaction, as surprise or annoyance, whereas the shorter forms are a focus merely for the latter, and require a knowledge of the context of utterance for an appreciation of what it is that is exercising the speaker.

The observations made with respect to Wittgenstein's example, 'Isn't the weather glorious today?', are also relevant to Donald Davidson's attempt to back his claim that assertion and the indicative mood (*sic*) cannot be closely identified:

> Utterances of 'Did you notice that Joan is wearing her purple hat again?' or 'Notice that Joan is wearing her purple hat again' may on occasion simply be assertions that Joan is wearing her purple hat again.
>
> (1984, 110)

I do not think it would *ever* be right to say that such utterances were simply assertions, but what is true is that certain interrogative or imperatival forms of words may have features which reveal the speaker as committed to some assertion or other, and indeed may have as their main point the communication of the information implied. In the present case it is clearly the particular verb and associated noun clause that generate this involvement. If we had said 'Did you think that Joan was wearing her purple hat again?', there would have been no such commitment, but 'Did you notice . . . ?' is like 'Did you know . . . ?' in what it implies for the supposed truth of the following clause. Again, because you cannot be said to notice something that is not so, we have this same implication with the imperative, an implication that is absent with 'Imagine that Joan is wearing her purple hat again.' Whether there is or is not the implication in question, the interrogative remains an interrogative and the imperative an imperative. Character as such is not imperilled by the consideration that some verbs make a presumption of factuality with respect to the clauses they govern which is not restricted to their occurrence within an assertoric form. More generally, what is relevant to the question of the reliability of a given sign as a sign of force is, of course, the matter of constancy as a sign, the claim that a particular grammatical form, or intonational pattern, is indicative of a certain force being at risk only from the discovery that that force is not standardly present. It is not refuted by showing that we may meet with something *in addition* to the force in question.

Davidson extends considerations of the same kind to other moods:

> we can ask a question with an imperative or indicative ('Tell me who won the third race', 'I'd like to know your telephone number'), or issue a command with an indicative ('In this house we remove our shoes before entering').
>
> (1984, 110)

Once more, I should not wish to deny a one–many mapping of a form onto forces, though I see a difference in the way the force is conveyed which is dependent on the specific grammatical form invoked. It is again a matter of addition rather than cancellation. So while the interrogative, 'What is your telephone number?', is used for making known one's desire for certain information, that desire can be conveyed more explicitly with 'I'd like to know your telephone number.' The character of the two forms is seen in this difference, which is not one that has to be eliminated for the sake of the common end. Similarly with 'In this house we remove our shoes before entering.' A statement it is and a statement it remains, even if the imperatival message is clear. But, because the hearer is required to draw an inference (as to what is expected of him), the message is one that can be missed, despite an understanding of the words.

These and other examples suggest that while the relation between form and force may be one–many, there can be subtle differences in the latter reflected in the exact choice of the former. Consider the sentences, 'Would you like a lift?' and 'Would you mind taking your muddy shoes off the sofa?' It is easy to see how these become offers and requests and not *just* questions aimed at eliciting an answer, but it would again be misleading to say merely that the latter is an interrogative form doing the job of an imperative. The job done is slightly different, and different in a way that reflects the literal meaning of the sentence. So, although we are aiming at a response from our audience, as we should have had we employed an imperative, there is a particular point in making use of the given form, in that it presents the person with the opportunity to express his own wishes. With the blunt imperative, 'Take your muddy shoes off the sofa!', no choice is offered. In saying 'Would you mind . . . ?', we do not expect our words to be treated just as the question they could be taken to be, but while the opportunity for the addressee to make known his own wishes on the matter is, as it were, only formally provided for – an answer, that is, *makes sense* – and not one we are happy to see taken up in a way that runs counter to our own evident wishes, this is enough for the sentence to amount to a polite form, to be preferable in this respect to the peremptory imperative.

5.2 Questions

How is the interrogative form to be characterized? It may be thought improbable that any single formula should fit the variety of possible questions – a view in evidence at *PI* §24 – but of course a single formula does not rule out differences within the genus. True, the definitions currently on offer tend to have the otherworldly character of logicians' characterizations, as when it is said that a question is a function from possible worlds to objects of a certain type (Tichy 1978), or that a direct question denotes a set of propositions, viz. the set of propositions expressed by possible answers to it (Hamblin 1973). Here we see a question not merely assimilated to a name, but to a name with a possibly indefinite and unknowable extension. Or, all questions are 'really' performatives beginning 'I ask . . . ' – as those who have been vouchsafed a glimpse of their deep structure report. Coming closer to reality, the truism that questions seek answers seems a safe enough starting point, so can we simply say that the interrogative form conveys a desire to know the answer? Certainly, the presumption of ignorance can be strong. (To greedy child: 'That's your fourth cake'; reply, feigning innocence: 'Is it really?'; rejoinder: 'As if you didn't know!') However, as is often pointed out, the characterization is too restrictive: the examiner seeks to elicit an answer, even though he knows it already. Still, he does at least *want* an answer, so does this broader condition enjoy the requisite generality? Since the term 'answer' is correlative with 'question', it is perhaps no more wanted in an illuminating account than is the latter itself. However, because the words which are to give an appropriate answer take their shape from the question, we can say that what is sought by the questioner is a form of words complete or specific in a respect which is not merely left open by the question, but which it explicitly marks – as 'Where . . . ?' conveys a desire for a specification in respect of place, 'When . . . ?' in respect of time, and so on, with yes/no questions simply conveying a desire for confirmation or contradiction, qualified or not, of the corresponding proposition.

The main question is whether the desire for an answer is to be introduced into an account of the interrogative form, or whether this desire simply provides the usual motive for asking a question. As an alternative to giving desire a definitional role, it may be suggested that a question need do no more than give expression to, or externalize, our doubt or uncertainty, the question being one which we expect to remain unanswered or indeed consider unanswerable (cf. Lyons 1977, 755). However, is it enough that the words of a question should merely express uncertainty? That by itself fails to do justice to the basic use of a question, a use thanks to which an answer is always at least *invited*, whereas the reference to desire gives a ready explanation of that feature. On the other hand, it is worth pointing out that the word order enlisted in putting a question is not confined to this use, but is also to be found with negative forms. Contrast 'In neither case would they be vindicated' with 'In either case they would be vindicated.' Compare too the use of inversion in presenting a hypothesis: 'Had I known then what I know now, . . . ' Perhaps the most general function of the inverted word order is to detach from assertoric force, the use in asking a question constituting a further specialization.

Even when the question is put to oneself, there is as much sense to the characterization in terms of desire as there is to the idea that one might try to answer one's own question. Again, whether one is addressing another or only oneself, a belief that one's audience will not or cannot provide an answer does not make nonsense of the expression of a desire for such, though in this event the point of putting the question will not be the usual one. We shall not be seeking to *elicit* an answer, but perhaps giving voice to our despair, frustration, or bewilderment: 'Why must these things happen to me?' Even with rhetorical questions we do not lose sight of this desire. The questioner may consider the answer so obvious that there is no need for it to be spelled out, but a failure of his audience to arrive at the obvious means that his purpose too has failed.

Absence of any desire for an answer is in any case something occasionally to be expected, rather than something which refutes the centrality of the association. For some reason I may not want an answer when I ask, 'Who threw that dart?' I have no wish to punish the culprit, but I must at least put the question if I am to preserve my authority. However, I can hardly complain if I do get an answer, precisely because my answerer would have been taking my words at their face value – as giving expression to a desire for an identification of someone. A following 'Don't tell me' would be something my audience could make sense of only as signalling either a change of mind or a desire to light upon the answer myself – a possibility which keeps us within the scheme. Likewise when the questioner wants to show up someone's ignorance. He actually hopes that his question will go unanswered, but is none the less exploiting the fact that an answer is customarily sought with the form of words which he invokes. It is to its character as standard, rather than as invariable, that the association owes its place in an account of the meaning of the interrogative form.

I speak of a desire for an answer as defining this association, not an intention to elicit one. The latter goes further in requiring a belief that an answer can be elicited, and when there is this belief, the association with desire is what the intention exploits: given our fellow speakers' knowledge that such a desire is expressed by the interrogative form, there is a prospect of their responding so as to satisfy our desire once it is made known, and accordingly a place for an intention on our part to elicit an answer by using that form. To distinguish desire and intention in this way may look like an exercise in splitting hairs; on the contrary, nothing less than a proper conception of the relation between meaning and use, and of sentence meaning at its most general, hangs on acceptance of the pattern which the example of questions here illustrates.

On H. P. Grice's analysis, a further role is found for intention in connection with meaning something by an utterance, this being held to be a matter of intending a certain effect in one's audience (cf. Grice 1957 and 1968). Though we shall not find reason to become embroiled in the complexities which develop with this approach, it is not surprising that these should strike some as inescapable when, as with questions, we are dealing with *force*, since force is a meeting point for three species of meaning: linguistic meaning, speaker's meaning, and natural meaning. First there is the matter of the meaning or significance of a particular verbal feature, e.g., of the word order of a question; this might be called 'linguistic' meaning, and it may or may not accord with the second species, what the speaker means by what he says – a notion of some complexity, in that it can relate both to the sense in which the speaker's words are to be taken and to his intention in uttering them. The marks of a question are also signs of a desire for an answer just in the sense that their manifestation gives grounds for an inference to the desire – a matter of 'natural' meaning, our third variety, and one which often occurs without the corresponding linguistic species; e.g., our words may be informed with a distinctive intonation which we impose despite ourselves, as when our delivery betrays impatience, despondency, nervousness, or anger. Just which variety is at stake is not always obvious: the forms 'by x is meant . . . ' and 'x means that . . . ' typically involve speaker's meaning and natural meaning respectively, whereas our first thought may well be that we are dealing with linguistic meaning in both cases.

A question is genuinely asked if in uttering an interrogative form of words the speaker has, or at least represents himself as having, the desire customarily associated with that form. So, if 'Does it hurt?' has merely an illustrative use, the speaker will make no attempt to tie it in with the context, to make clear the reference of 'it'; he will not wait for an answer, prompt further if none is forthcoming, and so forth. The term 'interrogative' will continue to apply to the grammatical form invoked, but 'question' – which tends to be associated with the requisite *use* – is marginally less appropriate; certainly, in such a case we shall not wish to say that a question has been *asked*. The notion of a certain force as associated with certain words is accordingly ambivalent: '"Does it hurt?" has the force of a question' may be a grammatical truth, but it may also be a generalization that can be faulted. On the other hand, if the usual moves are engaged in, the moves appropriate to the customary desire, then even if the speaker lacks that desire, the way he has knowingly fostered a contrary impression may warrant us in saying that a question has been asked.

Is there any significance in the way force is conveyed? That is, an indication of force by means of word order or intonation is suprasegmental; not a matter of just another word, but a feature of sentence or utterance which determines just how the individual words are to be taken, so has a 'metalinguistic' character – bearing upon the interpretation of what is said. It certainly is of some consequence that force can be thus imposed, its detachment from individual words showing how one and the same word may figure in sentences which receive a different interpretation overall – as statement or question, say – and indeed suggesting that we have in such a case variations upon a common theme, particularly when *all* the words are common to the two forms. However, although we have here a category that is in its way distinctive, so long as our concern is with the general characterization of a linguistic form, there is so far no reason to think of signs of force – whether in the shape of word order, intonation, or mood of the verb – as having meaning in a different sense of meaning from that which applies with an individual word, which of course can be the mode whereby force is conveyed, as when 'Would that . . . ' announces the expression of a wish. Or again, we might achieve the same effect by qualifying the main verb with the kind of phrase which, in Fregean terminology, would be said to introduce a refinement of *sense*. We do not normally think in terms of a mood proper to statements of probability, for instance, various parts of speech, as the adverb 'probably', being used to this end, but it could be that a language was richer in moods through being less analytical in this respect – as is indeed true of the Eskimo language – a possibility which goes against defining sense so as to make a sharp divide between it and force.

5.3 Imperatives

The variety we have noted among questions is by way of embellishments of, rather than departures from, a common pattern. Can the same be said with regard to sentences in the imperative mood? One approach to the latter which does scant justice to their variety is that which associates this grammatical form with commands only; and, at the opposite extreme – not one frequented by philosophers – we have the very broad construal of the imperative that equates it with the infinitive. We shall not for the moment ascend to the heights of generality offered by the second alternative, but gradually work our way in this direction from the first position, taking in *en route* such uses of the imperative as those in entreaties, pleas, requests, instructions, orders, invitations, suggestions, recommendations, and exhortations. This richness shows up the narrowness of the starting point, yet the fineness of the distinctions suggests that the extremes of the range which these define are not far removed from one another.

Commands constitute a narrow range of imperatival uses, requiring a fairly formal, structured, set-up, a hierarchy in which some have authority over others, as in the armed forces, a person who is suitably commanded being required to obey in virtue of his subordinate position. Though obviously close to commands, *orders* differ on this score: a person can be appropriately ordered to do something even though he does not have a position in any such hierarchy. If a man orders someone off his property then he may have authority to do so, in legal or moral terms, but while that will make for a difference in his position *vis-a-vis* that of the trespasser, the latter is not someone having the specific relationship to him that he would within the more formal framework required for commands: he would not be under the landowner's command.

Telling someone to do something is a description that applies in either case, though not to all uses of imperatives: *pleas* and *entreaties*, for instance, are not covered. With these we move away from the case where compliance can be enforced, the speaker being at the mercy of the goodwill of the person to whom he makes his plea; or, if that is not quite right – because it is more a matter of something for the benefit of the addressee, as when one pleads with someone to take care of himself – still, it remains a matter where the speaker is unable, or at least unprepared, to impose his will. In fact, when the addressee's interests are predominantly in view, *exhortation* is likely to be the more appropriate category: vocal support for a football team may rise to exhortation, but 'plea' takes us in the direction of *begging* for greater efforts.

With a *request*, the speaker's own interests are generally to be served by compliance, but compliance contingent upon the willingness of his audience; it is like a plea, then, but without the same urgency. A blunt imperative may not convey this conditionality, but additions like 'if you don't mind' or 'would you?' soften the force. With *suggestions*, *advice*, and *recommendations*, it is a matter of a course of action prescribed that is ostensibly for the addressee's good – or again for the good of someone other than the speaker – suggestions often arising when the addressee has already made known the relevant aim, and where there is a greater degree of tentativeness than with advice or a recommendation: if it is intended as just a suggestion, it will not be urged upon the person more forcibly should he show misgivings or hesitation. As less tentative, a recommendation is appropriately made on the basis of knowledge of the efficacy or desirability in some other way of what is recommended. Advising a course of action is even further removed from a mere suggestion – one fails to comply at one's peril, it is implied – and when the advice is against an act with sufficiently serious consequences, we have an instance of a *warning*. Since advice fittingly comes from one more knowledgeable in the relevant respect, *suggestion* or *proposal* is the more appropriate characterization of a first-person imperative, as 'Let's try'. If the imperative is not in response to a statement of a desired end, it may have the character of an *invitation* rather than a suggestion. Consider how 'Bring the children' and 'Take a seat' may be either. With *instructions* and *recipes* we again have a procedure or course of action specified for the sake of the addressee.

So far, the main variable has related to the interests supposedly served by compliance. With our eyes on orders, commands, requests and pleas, we might think that the imperative could be defined as a form whereby we convey a desire for action in accordance with the specification given by the verb. However, this does not always suit advice, instructions, and recipes, where performance of the action may be a matter of indifference to the speaker. Here the rationale for the use of the imperative is the supposed desirability of the action for some other party: we specify a course of action which we believe conducive to the attainment of an end sought by the person addressed. However, whether we speak of action desired or of action considered desirable, we have prima facie a fairly uniform definition of the imperative form. Of course, it is possible to be indifferent to the point that one does not even consider the action desirable, but so long as the speaker at least represents himself as having the appropriate desire or belief he can be said to have engaged in the relevant act.

But surely this characterization does not make a sufficiently immediate connection with action, does not lay due emphasis on the use of the imperative as an instrument, something whereby we can get people to act? Merely representing an action as desired or desirable is not urging it upon anyone. In stating 'I want a hammer', let us say, we do not call upon anyone to do anything, as we do with 'Give me a hammer.' True, but 'I want you to give me a hammer' is a form that better corresponds, reproducing the feature of the imperative whereby it is addressed to someone, and is thereby suited to enjoining action of that person. 'I want you to give me a hammer' can be every bit as demanding as an order. It may not be, but then neither may the imperative, as the example of recipes – 'Take two eggs . . . ' – plainly shows.

While an imperative may often give expression to a desire, this is not to say that it has the same meaning as 'I want . . . '. There is no 'I', no 'want', in the imperative, no scope for the moves which depend upon an *explicit* occurrence of such terms. Although I might have said 'Listen carefully' rather than 'I want you to listen carefully', the latter makes possible various elaborations and contrasts: 'I, and your mother, want you to listen carefully', 'Whatever he may want, *I* want you to listen carefully.' More generally, the different grammatical forms do not all merge into one, the declarative, just because this may be invoked in specifying when they are correctly used. The individual words in a sentence are to be taken seriously. Focus on the sentence as the unit of meaning, and the precise contributions of the component words risk being lost sight of in the preoccupation with a general overall use.

It would appear that the character of what is enjoined, together with other contextual matters – degree of urgency, intention, relation of speaker to hearer – can provide the basis for distinguishing between the various uses instanced, the same grammatical form, with the same general meaning, recurring throughout. But if this much can be left to context, why not also the connection with desire or desirability? After all, the imperative itself says nothing explicit about desire, but only something about action, so should we not in strictness construe that form merely as giving a non-committal specification of a course of action, even if our reasons for invoking the form will no doubt connect it with desire?

In speaking of a 'non-committal' specification, I am alluding to the way in which a verbal phrase occurring in an imperative contrasts with a declarative occurrence of that phrase: no act is reported or predicted, ascribed to or denied of an agent. Stripping the verb of any indices of such function may leave us with the imperative, but it may also leave us with the infinitive. Or is that to be left with the same thing? Here we may recall how other languages make evident use of the infinitive as an imperative: travellers by train on the Continent are requested not to lean out of the window by notices reading *'Ne pas se pencher en dehors'* and *'Nicht hinauslehnen!'* Context, clearly, serves to convey an imperatival use, but the form itself has a generality that transcends this particular application.

I say that either an imperative or an infinitive may emerge when we have a bare specification of an action, when any indications of declarative character are removed, but we might also arrive at a subjunctive, and here again we have a possibility that languages may adopt. Thus Spanish with subjunctive *'Venga!'* for 'Come!' And, while we have only a vestigial subjunctive in English, what does persist enjoys a relevant use in such contexts as 'God defend New Zealand', 'Perish the thought!', and 'Woe betide anyone who crosses me!' The description, 'expression of a wish', arises naturally here, *wish* going with the third-person case where events are not so much in the speaker's power to influence as when there is a person addressed to whom one makes known one's will with a view to eliciting action. It is also worth noting that even if we have to do with an imperative form, *wish* may, because realization of the happening specified is known or thought to be out of the hands of the person addressed, give the preferable characterization. Consider 'Get well soon' and 'Have a good time' – and perhaps also 'Know that we shall be thinking of you' and 'Understand that this is conditional upon your good behaviour.' However, it may be felt that 'Get well soon' does not altogether shake off the injunctive role which the form more usually has, any insistent repetition giving the impression of a futile order as much as of a heartfelt wish. A better example is perhaps 'Die!', uttered while seeking to despatch one's victim. Here the resemblance to the subjunctive, as in 'Perish the thought!', is very close, the character of the imperative as a form of words addressed to someone being all that would appear to distinguish it from the subjunctive form – though again that is enough to introduce a hint of *telling* someone to do something.

The use of imperatives in giving voice to a wish takes us still further away from a narrow command-oriented conception of imperatives, but not from the account in terms of an action desired or considered desirable. In terms of this condition we may speak of a constant meaning of an imperative – say, 'Go to sleep!' – whether it be advanced as an order or merely constitute the expression of a wish. The example of wishes shows again that an injunctive use is to be reckoned *further* to the basic imperatival use, appropriate when the action is thought possible for the addressee. We found that a question could have a role even when the speaker thought that an answer was not to be had; that is no obstacle to expressing one's desire for such. Similarly with imperatives. We may for the most part seek to elicit action when we make use of an imperative, but when this is precluded there is still the underlying expression of a desire or wish to give point to our utterance. Indeed, it is through this connection with desire that we explain how the words can be used in this way in those cases where action is thought possible. The use to enjoin or prescribe does not constitute the meaning of the form. Once more the shape of this analysis is important in the larger scheme.

Where a question mark perhaps remains is on the matter of the propriety of treating in a uniform way the imperative as used in giving expression to a desire of the speaker, and the imperative as used in giving advice or instructions, or in making a suggestion. The difference between these cases, between telling someone *to* do something, and telling someone *what* to do, is such that we may feel we have misunderstood what was said if, for instance, we mistake an instruction for an order. Against this, it is not implausible to make the notion of desirability carry the weight in *all* cases: whoever's the interest affected, and whether it be merely an expression of a wish or a cry to action, an action is ostensibly being advanced as desirable. At all events, whichever way we go, the increase in meanings contemplated is minimal: from a paltry one to a mere two. If we can speak of innumerable uses, that just shows that uses are not counted on the same basis as meanings, but in any case we have only a small number of central uses, further subdivisions being adequately defined by reference to the multitude of factors that context can provide.

6

Meaning, Intending, and Asserting

Approaches to sentence meaning commonly divide over the relative importance, and even relevance, of truth conditions and communicative intentions. Prima facie, 'mean' is congenial to an analysis in terms of the latter, and we shall now explore this possible involvement with regard to the declarative sentence, the major sentence type remaining to be examined. First, however, the principal uses of 'mean' must be disentangled.

6.1 Mean *and its subjects*

'Mean' is often thought to be a word of many meanings, the record for locating ostensible multiplicity probably being held by Ogden and Richards, who found that 'no less than sixteen groups of definitions may be profitably distinguished' (1923, 248; cf. 186–7). I also see some variety in the word's behaviour, but I shall be less ambitious, putting forward just two major divisions, with two further subdivisions in each. With the example of German in mind – in part to keep us close to Wittgenstein – let us make an initial division between uses of 'mean' in which its subject is a word, or some other non-personal object, and uses in which its subject is a (designation of a) person. (I use 'subject' both for the linguistic item and for whatever it may single out.) The further subdivisions within each of these may be illustrated as follows:

(N)	Non-personal subjects:	1	What does 'id' mean?
		2	Dark clouds mean rain.
(P)	Personal subjects:	3	What did Freud mean by 'id'?
		4	I meant to tell you.

Here (1), word meaning, is grouped along with (2), where to mean something is to be a sign of it – so-called 'natural' meaning. (3) also involves meaning with respect to a word, but now with a person as subject of the verb, and (4) gives us 'mean' as a virtual synonym of 'intend' – not quite identical in sense, since we favour 'mean' when there is an action to be explicated; so, either 'I did not mean to hurt you' or 'I did not intend to hurt you', when the injury occurred, but 'I do not intend to alter my plans' rather than 'I do not mean to alter my plans'. This near equivalence does indicate that 'mean' has at least two senses, but it is in general not clear whether we have to do with different senses, or simply with overall differences which derive from other features of the contexts in which the word is met. For our purposes it is the bare fact of the differences that matters, rather than the possibility of construing them as differences in the meaning of 'mean'.

It will be noted that the two uses of greatest concern to us, viz. (1) and (3), are not placed together. The grouping given may not seem the most natural, but I wish to lay emphasis on the differences which come with the change in subject, despite the common concern with linguistic meaning. In English we treat as one the uses under (1) and (3), whereas in German two distinct cases are recognized – *bedeuten* for (1), *meinen* for (3) – and indeed it is reasonable to say that a word or other inanimate object can hardly mean something in the way that a person can. Such is the difference, we can readily understand why the use of 'mean' with a word should be felt closer to its use with other inanimate subjects, closer even than is (1) to (3), a single word, *bedeuten*, being used in German for both. (1) and (3) also move apart if, as is plausible, we bring under the latter category such examples as 'He meant the one in the middle' and 'She means what she says'. (3) and (4) can be drawn together, as their common range of subjects would indicate, though a difference is suggested by the more straightforward substitutability of 'intends' in the latter. With 'I meant that you should draw that conclusion', we may be able to replace 'meant' by 'intended', but if the sentence is offered in elucidation of something said, this variation is not possible. Similarly, if we ask what was intended by a remark, this is likely to be a query as to why the remark was made, rather than a request for an interpretation of the words used. For intention we want something that might have come about as a result of something done, so not 'I intended that he may have caught a cold'; on the other hand, as clarifying one's words, 'I meant that he may have caught a cold' is standard.

Wittgenstein's interpretation of meaning as use is made chiefly with respect to *Bedeutung*, word meaning. However, just as the meaning of a word is not a mental image with which the word is associated, so meaning something by a word is not a matter of engaging in an accompanying mental act or experience; it is accordingly not surprising to find him connecting use with meaning in the sense of *Meinung* (*LFM* 40–1). Clearly, the two notions of meaning are very much intertwined, and, especially for an English speaker, easily confused. I suspect that running them together is one of the chief sources of mentalism about meaning. It seems at least a possibility that meanings are 'in our minds' if it is a matter of what *we* mean, and this is naturally carried over to meaning as an attribute of linguistic items. Add to this the possibility, again very real for an English speaker, of confusing meaning something by a word with intending something thereby, i.e., (3) and (4), and the diversity of philosophical thought on meaning is seen to be in no way remarkable.

Other confusions in which misconceptions concerning 'mean' (3) are implicated arise in connection with rule-following, a central topic of *Philosophical Investigations*, and one that has been the source of much current interest in meaning. The problem may be approached through the challenge presented by Saul Kripke's benighted sceptic, who thinks it possible that a person could have meant '+' in its usual interpretation with respect to the sums which he has actually calculated, yet have meant a quite different function in the case of the larger numbers with which he has as yet not operated. Perhaps he meant the 'sum' of any numbers greater than 56 to be all equal to 5, for instance (cf. Kripke 1982, chapter 2, and for an acute analysis of the issues, Baker and Hacker 1984b).

I speak here of a problem, but in fact it is not at all easy to get anything going by way of a real difficulty when the meaning of words or symbols is at issue, since it soon becomes clear that the person's usage will already have taken care of the application in the disputed area, the area where he had never explicitly invoked the operation in question, the appearance of novelty being quite misleading; either that, or there proves to be no question of an entitlement to say that 'plus', say, was meant. To find anything more than a passing difficulty we have to turn to instances of speaker's meaning for which the appeal to usage is not available.

First, the simple case. The notion of meaning something may arise in connection with following a rule when we clarify an instruction to an errant pupil with some such observation as 'I meant you to write 1002 after 1000, not 1004', the pupil having been charged with generating the series of even numbers. To say one meant such-and-such might seem to require that one let one's mind dwell on the relevant possibility, but the endlessness of the possibilities in the present instance, coupled with our inattention to any of them in advance of our statement of what we meant, is thought to leave the status of the latter perplexing. What of the negative part of the claim, viz. 'I did not mean you to write 1004'? This may appear correspondingly easy to satisfy: if I gave no thought to it then of course I did not mean you to proceed in this way, just as I did not mean you to start writing down the letters of the alphabet or the words of a song. That way of going wrong simply did not enter my head. However, if failure to give explicit thought to the possibility in question does not make it right to reject 'I meant you to . . . ', it is likewise wrong to accept 'I did not mean you to . . . ' on the same basis.

Consider then 'I meant . . . ' when no thought has been given to the instance in question. Matters are straightforward so long as we are dealing with a direct application of an unambiguous phrase, as with the expansion of the series, 'add 2'. If someone proceeds: ' . . . 998, 1000, 1004', we can say both 'I didn't mean (like) that', and 'I meant 1000, 1002'. Perhaps the affirmative response is more in need of justification, supposing we gave no prior thought to the particular number, but it can hardly be held to be problematic. After all, our instruction was to add 2, and what has been done simply does not count as doing so. That consideration is enough to take care of it without our having to address questions as to what went through our head when we issued the instruction. Take the extreme case, where the series is simply 2,2,2,2, . . . , and where at some point the person introduces a 3. Here we are simply describing a development which we should not count as continuing a succession of just 2s, and then asking why that would not accord with the instruction given. Granted, 'what we should count as . . . ' presupposes a certain uniformity in human practice, a uniformity that might not have existed and might one day cease to exist, but such possibilities do not put current truth at risk.

So far, then, nothing non-trivial, but now suppose that the person is asked to develop a more complex series, as that given by

'$y = 17x + 29$'. If the pupil proceeds, '46, 63, 80, 98', going astray with x equal to 4, can we really say that we meant 97 at the last place, not 98? There is a contrast with the correction given in 'I meant 1000, *1002*', in that this is a direct or immediate application of the rule 'add 2', whereas to reach 97 in the present instance requires us to *work out* the relevant value. Of course, there can be uncertainty as to when we may speak of 'working out', or 'calculating', but we are dispensed from having thought ahead when we say 'I meant . . . ' only if what completes this can be represented as a trivial application of the instruction, a matter of 'what we call . . . ' or 'what we count as . . . ' where these are associated with a direct or immediate application, a matter of how, as a matter of brute fact, we proceed. Wittgenstein is perhaps too ready to allow that one can say one meant . . . , his concern being to dispel false conceptions as to what this involves, notably having moved in thought to the possibility at the time (*PI* §187). He seems to be happy to have the whole issue reduce to the example of the series 2,2,2,2, . . . (cf. *RFM* I–3).

While it is questionable to say that one meant 97 in the above example, 'I meant you to *write* 97' is perhaps easier to justify, but only as a simple adaptation of the original statement of intention: I meant you to expand the series correctly, and that requires giving 97 at this point. At all events, the qualification which a more complex series demands does not alter the basic pattern: either 'I meant . . . ' is not warranted, or it rests on a triviality. Recourse to established usage, to 'what we understand by . . . ', might be thought simply to bypass the problem, which is concerned precisely with cases which usage to date has not yet encountered. However, the point is that no genuine novelty is presented by the future cases, no gap that might require a thought on our part to fill it; or, rather, it is only when there is no novelty that we can be justified in saying 'That is what I meant' when we have given the case no thought.

Consider now the possibility of an eccentric understanding of '+'. As with the more complex series, we should surely balk at saying that 5, 125, or any other number was meant as the sum of 68 and 57 by one who had never performed the addition – an eccentric use of 'meant' indeed. However, I take it that what is primarily intended is along the lines of the question, might not the person have so understood '+' that he was committed to giving 5 as the answer to 68 + 57? To this the answer is a clear 'No' so long as doubt is not being cast upon the person's grasp of addition with respect to lesser sums. That is, while he is envisaged as having never carried out a sum with a number as large as 57, he will have carried out the individual steps involved in, say, adding 57 and 68: 8 + 7, 6 + 5, and 11 + 1 will none of them be new to him, nor any of the other steps that enter into such a calculation. But then, to get an answer other than the right one, he would have had to do something at variance with what he has done to date, since one at least of the component steps must be the locus of his error. There is a straightforward reduction here of the 'novel' case to a repetition of familiar moves. But might not the person have proceeded differently when faced with 68 + 57, despite his proven ability to handle the smaller numbers? That is not the issue, the question being whether an answer other than 125 would show him to have deviated from the technique of adding which he had already mastered. However, it is true that he might have proceeded differently. Something quite extraordinary could have overtaken him – it is just that, until special considerations are advanced, all the evidence is on the side of supposing that he would have proceeded in the expected way.

I say that this is not the issue, but suppose that these component moves are also made the sceptic's target: we envisage an orthodox reading of 'carry', say, but only as confined to the contexts of actual use. Clearly, there is then no question of how the term was meant outside these contexts, and if the claim is that, despite the pattern established, the person's usage would have taken the unexpected turn imagined, then it is again quite unfounded.

It is thought that to answer the sceptic it must be shown that the person so understood '+' that he was *committed* to giving the answer 125. The question now is: what exactly does this mean? and the answer is simply: if he had come up with any other answer he would not have been adding (correctly). He was implicitly committed to giving 125 as the answer, not through having already performed and accepted the sum, but merely on the strength of his (supposedly standard) usage, and that is just to say such things as that if he had ceased to use '+' so that 8 + 7 came to 15, if, for instance, he had maintained that this was so unless numbers larger than 56 were involved, then we simply should not allow that he was using '+' as we do. But however we were to judge, might not what he did still be addition by his lights? No. Not in a sense which would allow consistency with his earlier practice. But suppose that, in the situation depicted, there is a quite general adoption of this deviant usage, yet an emphatic insistence: we are going on as before. Then this describes a situation in which people mean something different by 'we are going on as before'. Note that while in saying that what is contemplated is not what we should call adding, or adding correctly, I may be right or wrong, there is no right or wrong about the general practice – of accepting as addition what we do accept; there need be no harm in saying in such cases that 'This is *F*' amounts to 'This is what is called *F*', but that is not '. . . what is *correctly* called *F*'.

This way of construing the notion of being committed to a certain way of proceeding – viz. any other course will not count as continuing in the established way – is of crucial importance elsewhere, trivial though it may seem. Consider the problem which Michael Dummett poses for a (modified) conventionalist view of logical necessity (1978, 169–70). We may regard the axioms and rules of inference in a branch of mathematics as secured by stipulation, as registering certain conventions, but this gives no account of the necessity that attaches to the theorems which we may then derive; here we meet with a necessity that is imposed upon us, that we have no means of escaping. Once more, however, the same pattern of explanation applies: to accept the axioms and rules of inference just *is* to accept whatever we allow as an instance or application of them; to say that we are committed to these consequences, that we *must* accept them, can mean only that we cannot be described as abiding by our original commitment if we do not, or at least that we are then failing to carry through an application of these rules. There is accordingly no call to endorse – nor to ascribe to Wittgenstein – a more thoroughgoing conventionalism, to regard the mathematician as dispensed from proceeding in a way that is responsible to his usage to date. Wittgenstein is not suggesting that the mathematician's inferences are without foundation, but is tracing their source to our practices, to what *we* count as correct rather than to what is dictated by a reality which is independent of our practices and to which our inferences must answer (cf. *RFM* I–116).

In these simple examples we let what is meant rest on what the word or symbol means, the apparent infinity of cases being no more than what we should count as repetition of the same. But what of those occasions when the words cover more than one possibility, when, for instance, there is an incompleteness about what we say? So, when I said 'Read!' I meant 'Read out loud, not to yourself!', yet nothing equivalent to these words need have passed through my head. Or again, we may have to resolve a lexical ambiguity: 'I meant light in colour, not in weight.' There appears to be greater scope for a problem here, since we cannot let the established usage of the word carry the interpretation.

Suppose first we are dealing with a present utterance, so talking of what we mean as much as of what we meant. Here it is a matter of how we are, or wish, to be understood, and we determine that by offering an explanation aimed at giving clearer expression to our present state of mind, our sincere avowal being definitive in that respect. A past case need not differ from this: the circumstances are such that we might still repeat what we said in the same state of mind; or, at least we consider our beliefs, attitudes, and purposes to be sufficiently constant and enduring in the relevant respect that the lapse of time does not introduce a factor of any significance. On the other hand, it may be that we have to conjecture how we should have clarified what we said, in which case there will be no question of a sincere categorical declaration, 'I meant . . . '. Compare the case where, interrupted in mid-sentence, we later confidently state, 'I was going on to say . . . ', even though we had not formulated the thought to ourselves at the earlier time. Such confidence is well placed so long as we can now pick up where we left off, in the sense of continuing to give expression to the state of mind we were in when interrupted, the wrong model again being that of having to cast our mind back to a thought which we had articulated at the time of speaking. With the passage of time there may come a change in what we are disposed to say, but, this aside, there is nothing more puzzling than when we give uninterrupted expression to our thought.

6.2 Mean *and complementary acts*

As ascribed to a person, meaning might be taken to be a mental act *par excellence*, and indeed an act that is infallible: we can go wrong with what we say or point to, but not with respect to what we mean. But is it right to think of meaning as in any sense an act? That one does not *do* anything in meaning something by a word or action appears to be evidenced by the absence of qualifications which might express the *manner* in which one means something. Such an approach is developed by Dennis Stampe: if *A* obviously (clearly, certainly) means *x* then what is obvious is not the manner of *A*'s meaning *x* – *A* does not mean *x* obviously, in obvious fashion – but what is obvious is simply that *A* means *x*. The adverbs reveal themselves to be sentence adverbs rather than adverbs of manner (Stampe 1968, II–III).

This consideration might be offered by way of defining a sense in which meaning is not doing something, as much as by way of establishing that claim, though what that sense is is not altogether clear, as there remain some adverbs of manner which may be invoked, as when we say that a remark was meant unkindly or disrespectfully. These qualifications tell us *how* the remark was meant, even if they do not convey how something was *done*. True, this is 'mean' as it equates with 'intend' – more or less – but then the verb in that use is, I should imagine, no more supposed to report an action than when it is a matter of meaning that such-and-such is the case. We might, then, look for a relevant distinction within the class of adverbs, or we might try to specify more directly in what way meaning is to be considered non-active. Relevant to both points is the question whether such verbs as 'blush', 'faint', 'age' and 'die' should be said to signify something we do. Adverbs of manner can apply – we may age suddenly and die slowly – but ageing and dying might well not be reckoned *actions*. However, what appears to exclude these is the consideration that we cannot be said to age or die *intentionally*, these being things that happen to us, rather than things that we accomplish. Consideration of possible adverbial qualifications will be relevant in so far as this makes plain the intentionality of a verb – the adverb 'intentionally' obviously being of special importance – but that character does not make for a general prohibition on adverbs of manner.

On this test, 'mean' is excluded from those verbs which signify things we do. It has, we note, no use for an imperative form; meaning is not a matter of bringing something off, is not to be considered a successful achievement, as when, in singing or swimming, one succeeds in singing or swimming – *contra* what is suggested by the book title, *Learning How to Mean* (by M. A. K. Halliday, Edward Arnold, 1975). In this it compares with other psychological verbs, as 'expect', 'fear', 'suspect' and, of course, 'intend'. We do not intentionally expect trouble, fear snakes, or suspect others' motives, though that is not to say that 'unintentionally' will happily qualify these verbs, since its use may suggest that one's fearing, say, was what came about when something else was aimed at, when of course there will have been no question of aiming at anything.

It is worth pointing out that 'mean' differs from 'refer to' on this score, despite Stampe's claim that the latter gives one of its meanings, e.g., in such a sentence as 'He means the one in the middle' (Stampe 1968, VIII). We can speak of referring to someone audibly, in public, repeatedly, by means of a name, or in order to show our acquaintance with that person, but we cannot be said to mean someone audibly, in public, and the rest. Since Stampe thinks that 'mean' does not describe something we do, it is curious to find him equating it in one of its uses with 'refer to', when this bears all the marks of a phrase which does signify a doing.

The different behaviour which 'mean' displays *vis-à-vis* verbs like 'refer' does not favour any equation of meaning with use, we may note, since the relevant verbs are precisely those which do signify a use. However, it is plausible to suppose that, at least when we have a personal subject for 'mean', there will always be a complementary use. We must reject a supposed sense of the verb in which it would equate with 'refer to', but we may see the relation between the two as intimate none the less. So, consider the contrast between what is said and what is meant. Our words may have us speaking of *x* when it is *y* that we mean; or again, it may be that they fail to specify the relevant object or region of space sufficiently narrowly. In both cases what we mean is what our words are directed or aimed at, where this is as decided by our intentions. I use the letters 'PVC' intending to single out a certain substance. This is an act which may or may not succeed – I could be under a misapprehension as to what goes by the label – but if it does then the two notions, the stuff *singled out* (by the letters), and the stuff *meant* (by me), satisfactorily converge. 'Mean' here contrasts with 'have in mind', at least in one use of the latter. I may have someone in mind as I use a name, but merely having someone in mind need not engage with any act of saying, as meaning the person in question when I use the name determines what the phrase is aimed at, the intended reference.

Reference is, of course, too narrow to do justice to linguistic use generally, but could it be that a specification of what is meant is a specification of a condition which defines the success of *some* associated act, or whose successful uptake defines success in this respect? Application of the pattern is particularly inviting with whole sentences, as, e.g., imperatives. Here the relevant act is one of conveying a desire for action in accordance with the given terms. Meaning is, again, not communicating, expressing, or the like, but what is meant will be what is aimed at with the imperative, what defines its success.

To seek an elucidation of meaning by bringing to light the act or acts which it complements looks to be a move in the right direction – very much the right direction if the aim is to pass from the broad perspective of meaning as use to a more specific account in terms of communicative intentions. How does this approach work out when we turn to our main topic, that of meaning something by a word or words? First, it does not seem that we should be looking for an *act* in this instance. There is of course the act of uttering, but while I may mean 'carping' by 'captious', I do not mean the latter by *uttering* 'captious'. Likewise with writing. By 'it' I may mean the weather, and by 'It is fair' I may mean that the weather is mild, but I do not mean the weather by *writing* 'it', nor do I mean that the weather is mild by writing these words. The construction simply does not expand into a form in which a reference to uttering or writing is made explicit; nor does any other act come readily to mind as filling the bill, but there appears to be a confusion here of 'mean' followed by an *explanans* with 'mean' followed by an infinitival construction, as 'mean to describe' or 'mean to convey', contexts in which it bears the sense of 'intend'. In this respect the example of the imperative is misleading, since it is a matter of what is meant by the words only in the sense of what is meant (or intended) by uttering them, any success being success of the historic *act*, whereas it looked as if something were true here of the words in a way not to be found with 'captious'.

Suppose we take the relevant constructions at their face value, i.e., accepting that it is a matter of something meant by a word or words, and not by an act. Might not the pattern still hold, in the sense that the notion of an associated aim has a place? We may say that by 'refute' journalists commonly mean 'contradict'. This is not simply: that is how they understand the word, since journalists cannot be said to mean anything by the word unless they themselves use it, and this is not implied by the paraphrase. But is it not a matter of: that is how they wish to be understood?

If this is the correct pattern, we bring in a communicative element, use of 'how *A* wishes to be understood' supposing an attempt to get something across to an audience. A plausible construal in many instances, but is it appropriate to the general case? A less demanding formula would identify the potential opposition as between what is said and how the speaker's words are to be taken if we are to understand him aright, but without the implication that he actually seeks to be understood; perhaps it is of no interest to the person whether or not anyone takes any note of his words. However fundamental communication is to language, it would be a mistake to interpret meaning *v* by *w* in such a way that its application to someone who is making no attempt to communicate is excluded. Mothers may speak to their babies with no expectation of being understood, yet meaning this rather than that – i.e., using the words in this sense rather than that – and there is nothing amiss with the suggestion that certain uses of language may be solely for the benefit of the speaker, as with some instances of counting, or when we list intended purchases. Again, we might issue instructions to ourselves in soliloquy, provide a commentary on what we are doing, give voice to a question that is exercising us, attempt to set our thoughts in order, to clarify rather than communicate them.

The difficulty with this style of argument is, of course, its vulnerability to the objection that the uses of language cited are in all cases secondary. Better, perhaps, simply to confront the communication theorist directly with the alternative indicated: meaning this rather than that is a matter of using the words in this sense rather than that; not a triviality, even with 'meaning' in place of 'sense', since it is a matter of *Bedeutung*, whereas what was to be explained was *meinen*. And the analysis has a consequence that is far from trivial, in so far as it implies a reliance of speaker's meaning on word meaning which stands in the way of one of the communication theorist's main aims, viz. to explain the meaning of words and sentences in terms of speaker's meaning.

There is confirmation for this analysis in the paraphrase of 'mean' as 'wish to say', a common rendering in many languages. To speak in this way requires us to allow that a person may wish to say *w* even though *w* is not a word with which he is familiar, which may be thought odd, but it is no odder than saying that the speaker means *w*, where *w* is unfamiliar to him; in either case, what determines suitability of *w* is nothing other than its having the meaning it has. No communicative act is introduced, but the wish is simply that the word used should have the meaning specified; a matter of a wish or desire, not that one's act of speaking or writing should have a certain effect, but that what one says should have a certain character.

As well as meaning *v* by *w*, we have also meaning what one says to consider. Given that the latter reports nothing episodic, that we may mean what we say without giving close thought to our words, it may seem that the notion is best characterized in negative terms, a matter of what we say prompting no misgivings from us, no desire to retract or qualify. However, to pinpoint the relevant grounds for retraction we have to introduce the notion of the word or words as being warranted for the speaker. Suppose a person says, 'I have never given the matter any thought', and we ask him whether he really means 'never'. Our question is whether choice of that word is justified in the light of what he knows or believes, whether it gives correct expression to his state of mind.

While we may invite the speaker to have second thoughts about the accuracy of 'never' without having to suggest an aim to deceive, the question whether the person means what he says will often be a question as to his sincerity; not only does what he says not represent what he thinks, considers warranted, but he is well aware that this is so as he says it. Suppose that a person says that he is worried. Then for him to mean what he says it is sufficient that he be giving truthful expression to his thought; it is the satisfactoriness of his words in that respect that is at issue, not any intention he may have in giving voice to these words. Or again, one who cries 'Stop!' may have a number of ends in view with his utterance – to draw attention to himself, to alarm someone, to get someone to stop. With the latter it may seem that we have given the specification required for an account of meaning what one says, but again it is the faithfulness of what is said to the speaker's state of mind that is at issue – did he really want the person to stop? – and not the effect intended. What is meant looks back, to an agreement with the speaker's state of mind; what is intended looks forward, to a result to be achieved. Of course, if, as is usual, the question of intending to communicate something arises with an assertion, then what is meant may well be what the speaker intends to communicate, but the words used can be satisfactory in the former respect even though the utterance is unsuccessful in the latter. In sum, the idea that speech has a purpose or purposes may be thought to make for a presumption that intending should enter into meaning, but to expand on any such purpose is to expand on meaning to *F*, not on meaning what one says, or meaning such-and-such by what one says.

6.3 Assertion and intention

We turn now to the analysis of the declarative sentence. The role customarily associated with this form is that of assertion, but we have already seen that the association is far from invariable, such a sentence also being familiar in an interrogative capacity. A closely related use which again falls short of the assertoric is that in which the words uttered constitute a guess. A contestant in a quiz who ventures 'He was an Elizabethan playwright' in hope rather than in knowledge of the answer to 'Who was John Donne?' is not making the kind of *claim* that 'assertion' would imply, and in contexts where the speaker is doing no more than report another's words, character as a claim is even more remote. Again, consider the possible enlistment in presenting a merely hypothetical situation: 'You're walking along when you see someone trying to break into a car. What do you do?' Or: 'A piece of iron with a cavity inside it is heated. Does the hole become larger or smaller?' It seems appropriate to align this suppositional use with that of the same words occurring as antecedent of a conditional – 'If a piece of iron . . . ' – the traditional term 'propositional' being apt in either case, and raising the question whether what is common to this cluster of uses is a recurrent proposition. As a link between the two we have the intermediate 'You try to be helpful and he simply ignores you.'

What are we given with these examples? Half a dozen different uses showing that grammatical form is a poor guide to semantic function? Or a central use that is variously exploited? I allow that at one level the description, 'a single form with multiple functions', is correct, but variety within a given general use need not contradict the unity which the variations exhibit *vis-à-vis* some other broad category. However, form does not fail as a guide so long as it is allowed to take in the various factors whereby one interpretation rather than another is *marked*, as intonation or punctuation may indicate a question, or 'if' herald a suspension of assertoric force in the clause which follows. The cases which remain genuinely ambiguous on subtraction of those that are marked are hardly numerous, but order rather than anarchy is to the fore, the interesting challenge again being to identify a common use or uses which are embellished rather than obliterated in the variations.

One aspect of this general challenge, and one that will be our main concern, is to identify what remains constant when we abstract from the diversity within occurrences of assertion itself.

Though not, as I say, the only role which the declarative form enjoys, this is the one commonly taken to have the strongest claim to priority; it is also, correspondingly, the most likely target of objections to attempts at singling out a use of language that can be regarded as central.

Before proceeding, we might mention a number of uncertainties concerning the nature of our quarry. There is, first, a question as to the range of grammatical forms to be associated with assertion. Does this extend to, for instance, the construction in 'What beautiful eyes!'? Such an exclamatory sentence lacks the explicitness of 'She has beautiful eyes', and is without a natural negation, but, as the possible response, 'True', indicates, its behaviour none the less comes close to that of the explicit assertion.

Second, we note that there is a degree of uncertainty with respect to non-serious uses of the assertoric form and the question whether the speaker is actually making an assertion. Do we assert anything when we start a joke with 'A chimpanzee walked into a bar and ordered a pint of beer'? The usual verdict is 'No', and while I am going along with it, usage is not so clear cut as to make this mandatory. What of ironical uses, as with 'You really do know how to make someone feel wanted'? Grammatically, we might say, this counts as assertoric, but if we wish to exclude it we have reason to do so in the way that belief is counter-suggested.

Third, there are clearly differences from member to member in the family which includes asserting, stating, affirming, declaring, and claiming. To state, for instance, is to set forth openly and explicitly; we can state, but not assert, our age and address, and the contrast to the fore is with what is merely implicit, whereas assertion finds its contrast in denial. 'Assert' may also suggest that, while the speaker's degree of assurance is high, there is little by way of backing for what he says. We shall be speaking largely in terms of assertion, but with the broader family in view rather than the nuances particular to this member.

If *A* means what he says when he asserts *p*, then he is speaking truthfully, an implication which falls far short of what is required for a communicative intention. This does not of itself show that a characterization of assertion in terms of an intention which this speech act serves is excluded, since the relevant intention might find its way in via another route; many, for instance, would think it evident that assertions have truth as their aim. However, if we consider how an association with intention might be understood, we find reason to suppose that a relevant definitional role for the notion is not to be had.

In the most basic respect, there can be a failure of intention in that we might actually fail to assert anything. A fundamental breakdown, since it involves something as drastic as one's assertion not even taking shape. Clearly, the minimal requirements for success in doing something describable as asserting fall well short of the achievement of truth – or of having any impact on an audience. Another possibility is that, while succeeding in making an assertion, we fail to achieve what we aim at thereby, where this is an end that lies outside the mere production of the assertion. We may grant that the general character of 'assert' is such as to invite specification of such an intention: the verb signifies something we *do*, something which is within our control, which we may engage in for a reason; it is not like 'slip', 'age', or 'forget'. However, while an aim or purpose will almost always be present – beyond that of merely accomplishing the act – none such is to be read into 'assert', any more than it is with 'say'.

As a contrast, take the verb 'fish'. I may succeed in fishing just in the sense that I do something which counts as fishing, and my fishing may then be successful in that I manage to catch something. With 'assert' we match the first, minimal, sense, but whereas knowing what 'fish' means we can specify what constitutes this further success, there is nothing corresponding to this second step with 'assert'. Of course, most of the aims we have in asserting *require* truth, but then most aims require that we be heard, understood, and not ignored. Truth is not *the* aim – as if we could rest content with what we said so long as we had advanced a truth, whatever it might be – and as a feature required, it, or at least the closely related notion of being *right*, belongs as much with *guessing* as with asserting. The speaker will, of course, want to be recognized as asserting something, and not putting a question, say. Use of the declarative format goes some way to ensuring such recognition, though the desire for this cannot without circularity enter into a characterization of the act. This is not in any way to detract from the importance of the richer intentions into which assertion enters, but what matters is that we should leave room for these, not that we should reveal them as definitive of assertion. If we seek an intention in this capacity, we shall arrive only at the rudimentary intention indicated, but that is not a matter of an intention which one may have *in* asserting, which is surely what is wanted.

Even if intention does not enjoy a significant definitional role, we may be reluctant to see truth's claim to centrality end at this point. Granted, performative utterances would seem to require that both be dismissed, an assessment as true or false being out of place with 'I declare the meeting open' or 'I propose that we adjourn'. However, such departures from a truth-stating use are very much the exception – and not even allowed by all to be departures – to such a point that we might reasonably hold out for a connection with truth, even if this can be sustained for a subclass of assertions only. With this subclass in view, a useful, if slightly awkward, formula to enlist is the following: in asserting, the act in which we engage is one of representing things as being a certain way; equivalently, what we are doing is making things out to be thus and so. This characterization does not serve to pinpoint asserting, as opposed to stating, etc., but it is usefully geared to the character of the declarative form and the role which this enjoys when the associated linguistic act is described by any members of the broader family to which 'assert' belongs.

The relation between assertion and truth is clearly revealed by the respective paraphrases, 'making things out to be a certain way' and 'things being as they are made out to be'. I am supposing a sense of the former which requires that one who is described in these terms understands what he is saying, and this is a matter of knowing what it is for things to be as represented, i.e., knowing what it is for what one says to be true. So, on this reading, in saying 'You are pawky' I can be said to make you out to be pawky only if I understand what 'pawky' means, which is a matter of knowing what it is for you to be as I say. However, while an intention to make things out to be as they are has as good a claim as any to an association with the act of making things out to be a certain way, it is clear that it takes no more than success at the latter for an assertion to have been made. On the other hand, it is clear that a person could not have the concept of assertion without that of truth, and this consideration, coupled with the basic character of the truth-stating intention, should be enough to satisfy anyone who wishes to see truth accorded a central position.

There is a parallel between this account and the accounts given for injunctions and questions. It is tempting to think of the primary role of injunctions in terms of trying to get someone to act, but we saw that an imperative could be used in a standard way even when it was known that action was impossible. This did not make its use without point, since it could still serve to express a desire or wish. Likewise with assertion and the various intentions which might be held to be implicit in it. There will often be little point in giving voice to an assertion if, say, it is thought to convey nothing new, but it can be that we are acknowledging or drawing attention to something we take to be already known, perhaps to remind, perhaps to show that we are not ignorant. Consider the surprised observation, 'You weren't at the meeting', where an explanation may be sought, or 'You are not being quite candid', where there is no intention to tell the person something he does not already know. As with both injunctions and questions, we want a very general characterization of assertion, one that can accommodate the various uses. In these terms the suggested account is suitably austere, allowing assertion to merge happily with the customary range of intentions – to inform our audience that *p*, to remind them that *p*, to show that we are aware that *p*, to show, or have them believe, that we think that *p*, and so forth.

The phrase 'make things out to be' aims at a high level of generality. Is it so high as to be intolerable? For Wittgenstein it may well be, yet it is difficult to see how any point that he might reasonably wish to make should be at odds with this analysis, which, after all, aims merely to identify a common denominator in our cluster of terms, 'state', 'affirm', and the rest, which already apply with even greater generality. To repeat, a highly general account is compatible with variety within the category defined, provided that the variety reflects an elaboration of, rather than a departure from, the standard use. For instance, it may be that the assertion is incorporated in an exclamation, or that the words constitute a challenge – '(You) can't catch me!' In neither case need assertoric status come under threat. On the contrary, maintenance of that status may be required for the particular application.

However, there is a case for saying that the idea of making things out to be a certain way is in one respect broader than that of assertoric use, in that it applies when the words are advanced with a greater degree of tentativeness than when assertion, as here construed, is involved. Not when the words actually constitute a question, but with pretty well anything less than this – as with a guess or suggestion. It is accordingly worth reiterating how, in contrast to guessing, asserting involves a *claim* as to how things are, a preparedness to stand by, to offer support for, what one says, to maintain it in the face of doubt and denial. Along with the idea of something we are prepared to defend goes that of something we purport to believe, and it is this that the liar exploits. Lying requires the speaker to make a particular use of the declarative form, viz. an assertoric use, and it is because of the way this involves standing by what one says that the liar may persuade someone that he takes what he says to be true. Whether or not our formula is to apply with respect to guessing, we have a spectrum of uses of the declarative form, differing in the degree of commitment, of tentativeness, involved. In certain cases, notably with interrogative and suppositional uses, we undoubtedly leave behind the straightforward assertoric use, but even here the continuity with the latter is readily perceived. We shall return to this question.

In offering 'represent things to be a certain way' as illuminating 'assert', the intention is not that the more complex phrase should necessarily mirror the structure of a declarative sentence by featuring 'things' as a variable for a noun phrase. That is, in saying 'The stars are bright' we could be said to be representing certain things, viz. the stars, as being a certain way, viz. bright. Such an application of the formula has its place, but it tends to presume a subject-predicate sentence when we should like the formula to apply whether or not this pattern can be extracted. We represent things as being a certain way when we say 'A drink would be welcome' or 'There must be some misunderstanding', despite the absence of a logical subject. But we can also be said to represent things a certain way if we say 'What beautiful eyes!', and while this may be tolerable, we seem to move a little too far from what is normally thought of under the heading of assertion with such a form as 'You silly old fool!', which the formula likewise fits.

If our aim is a more restricted account of assertoric use, the verbal component is the natural unit to fasten upon, since other constituents, e.g., noun phrases, are likely to behave in this context just as they do in, say, a question or an injunction: the role of the demonstrative is constant throughout 'This is taken', 'Is this taken?', and 'Take this', any variability being located in the verbal phrase. With the question, for instance, there is no way in which 'this' can come within the scope of the query, as if its applicability, like that of the verbal phrase, were a matter on which information was sought. This observation leads naturally to a characterization of assertoric character which centres upon the *variable* part of the sentence: when the declarative form is enlisted for an assertion, the verbal phrase is being advanced as a correct description, a description applicable to something or someone which context, along with the remainder of the sentence, serves to identify. For the most part this will be a matter of affirming a predicate of something named by the subject, though in some cases just the area within which the relevant item is ostensibly to be found will be specified, as with 'Here is a match', and in other cases the affirmation will be with respect to a time and place, but with no explicit indication of a subject, as with 'It is late' or 'There will be trouble.'

The importance of relating our characterization to the verbal component is twofold. First, in drawing attention to the way assertoric force is centred on the variable part of a sentence, rather than distributed equally throughout, this approach helps correct the monolithic conception of sentence meaning that continues to mislead so many; second, and more specifically, there is the consideration that we have with the verbal phrase a unit that is qualifiable by adverbs, and in particular by negation. The more general characterization in terms of 'a phrase advanced as an applicable description' would apply to the adjective in 'The empty glass was filled' and 'Fill the empty glass', the commitments of these forms as regards the adjective being similar to those of 'The glass is empty.' However, it is this latter mode of occurrence, when 'empty' is incorporated within a verbal phrase, that can with some reason be taken as central, since it is only then that it becomes the explicit focus of affirmation and denial. With this further refinement we can exclude 'What a silly old fool!' from the category of assertions, while not exaggerating its distance from that category.

6.4 Belief and convention

One who uses the declarative form will normally take things to be as he represents them; to such a point that, unless it is cancelled by speaker or context, there will be a presumption of belief so overwhelming that the speaker who does not take things to be as he says will be guilty of insincerity. More generally, in the eyes of many the communication of belief vies with the specification of truth conditions for the honour of throwing the greatest light on the concept of assertion. And it does indeed seem a safe enough claim to affirm that belief is in some sense bound up with assertion; not, however, to the point of making it out to be essential to the latter. A person who lies when he says 'We have never met before' is asserting something, despite his lack of belief; nor does belief find a place with certain avowals, as 'I despair of ever getting him to see sense' – though there is, of course, a related condition of sincerity. Close to this latter species is a performative utterance, as with 'I apologize', which offers no foothold whatsoever as to belief.

No one would dream of claiming that belief is essential to assertion in a sense that would mean its refutation by the example of lying, but it may well be held that it remains central in the standard case, notwithstanding these various counter-examples. A more serious difficulty is that of relating belief to assertion in such a way that it is not presupposed by the latter, thereby excluding an appeal to assertion in explaining belief. So, consider a use of the declarative form, perhaps in a primitive version, as this might come from a small child: 'Allgone milk', or 'That mummy's nose', let us say. If the child were a Gricean adult, it could be expected to be uttering these words with the aim of instilling a belief in its audience. A possibility here as well, but when belief makes an entry at this level in our account, it need not be as something presupposed by the use made of the declarative form; rather, the child's utterance could be the occasion for talk of belief in its regard to be introduced for the first time, with respect to the matter at hand. The child says 'Allgone milk'. With what intention, if any, we may not know; perhaps it is just openly registering the milk's absence. However, in so far as this description at least is warranted, we can appeal to the utterance to *give sense* to the idea that the child thinks that the milk is all gone.

In many instances it is difficult to conceive of a belief as being entertained if the subject has as yet no means of expressing that belief, and examples of the present primitive kind are fittingly considered precursors of those occasions when the belief has been inwardly formulated prior to its disclosure, occasions when the speaker may have given some thought to better ways of stating what he wishes to get across. In the simpler case it is not that we hypothesize a belief on the part of the child, but that we appeal to what it says – and to what it does – in giving substance to an ascription of belief. We are not explaining the utterance, as we should if we considered the belief necessary to account for it, nor, more generally, are we to regard that utterance as (independent) evidence for the belief; we might wish to say, with appropriate provisos, that to affirm p is to express a belief that p, but that is not to elucidate what is going on with the utterance; it is by way of offering a *redescription* of what is taking place. Compare the relation between action and desire. The favoured philosophical pattern is one in which voluntary action follows on an experienced desire, but the case which should have priority is that in which the character of the subject's movements is such as to warrant a redescription in terms of desire, without our having to hypothesize an antecedent mental event.

As just intimated, there is no necessity that we should be able to discern any intention behind the child's utterance, which may simply be a spontaneous response to the person or thing to which it is attending – an expression of recognition or surprise. Certainly, no communicative intention is necessary if we are to speak of a genuine use of language. Early speech is often asocial, psychologists inform us, the child commenting in some detail on its own actions but with no concern to be understood, or even heard, by others (cf. Hickman 1986, 26-7). Conversely, the child's understanding of an assertion does not require any hypotheses on its part as to intentions. If, in saying 'The kitten is under the table', our intention is that the child should believe something, perhaps (quite exceptionally) that it should think that we have a certain belief, then this is an intention which could well escape the child, despite its understanding of what is said. It is a trivial truth that the child must be able to discern an intention if it is to know that the speaker is seeking to communicate, but it is only the expression of belief, not an intention to get it across – or to get across how things are – that it need appreciate in order to latch onto the assertoric character of what is said. Likewise, it is not the child's asocial use of language that poses a problem, but the relevant difficulty is one of determining whether the child has displayed the appropriate reactions and the appropriate adaptation of word to circumstance that make possible a redescription in terms of belief.

We can now give a more accurate description of what I spoke of above as the rudimentary intention involved in assertion, this being, at least in the most common case, an intention to express a belief. When assertion is characterized in terms of the particular use made of the verbal phrase – advancing it as a correct description – it is also clear that belief is implicit, since it is a matter of the speaker offering – in a format which conveys just this – a description which he (ostensibly) believes to be correct or applicable, these latter terms being preferred to 'true', which is better suited to the assertion as a whole. Likewise when we invoke 'making out to be'. This requires buttressing with a psychological ascription, to the extent that there must at least be the semblance of belief if its use is to be warranted.

Finally, a word about convention. There is a sense in which this notion applies to language at large: it is not the happiest description, but we may speak of the link between linguistic sign and thing signified as 'conventional' by way of contrast with natural signs. However, it is sometimes supposed that convention has a more substantial role to play in the characterization of such speech acts as asking, enjoining and asserting. In Dummett's view, for instance, to understand assertion we must appreciate the general convention which governs the utterance of declarative sentences; specifically, 'there is a general convention whereby the utterance of a sentence, except in special contexts, is understood as being carried out with the intention of uttering a true sentence' (Dummett 1981, 298).

We may prefer to speak of a convention whereby something is *deemed*, rather than *understood*, to be so-and-so. At all events, there could be a convention whereby we were deemed to believe what we say, or treated as believing what we say, in certain circumstances – to take the preferable alternative to 'intend to say something true'. However, whichever we opt for, there are objections: a person thus treated, and accordingly held responsible for various consequences of his utterance, might protest that he did not make out that he actually believed what he was saying, that it should have been apparent that, for instance, he was only joking; i.e., that it is not a convention that justifies saying that he really made an assertion, but something which he deliberately conveys – as Dummett himself suggests (ibid. 300). The notion of a convention has appeal in view of the apparent indifference of such terms as 'assertion', 'question', and 'order' to the matter of the speaker's mental state. Clearly, however, it is important that the mental state should be accurately characterized. If, with regard to questions, a desire to know the truth is taken as the leading candidate, it is natural to appeal to considerations of convention to defend the claim that one who lacks this desire – as a knowledgeable examiner – may none the less have asked a question (cf. Dummett ibid. 331, 356). However, the more plausible candidate is that of simply wanting an answer. With this broader characterization we lessen proportionately the scope for an appeal to convention, and once we add the derivative condition, that of deliberately giving the impression of wanting an answer, we do away with it entirely. Similarly, to say that an order has been given it is enough that the speaker should have represented himself as having the relevant desire through his use of the imperative form. The supposition that the speaker has the expected desire is simply false, not a conventionally secured truth, while the supposition that he has issued an order is true, but not a truth that requires the invocation of a convention.

7

The Sentence Radical

In discussing both sentence types and the concept of meaning we have given prominence to questions of uniformity. It is not that this feature is in itself one of outstanding virtue; it is just that, given the possible loss in understanding if what is common is overlooked, the right methodology is surely to seek to accommodate diversity *within* any apparent sameness. As it happens, we have found reason to stress certain differences in use which 'mean' presents, but our attitude should none the less continue to be one of caution towards claims that, e.g., meaning as it applies to words is not as it applies to sentences, that it changes yet again as we move from one sentence type to another. The present chapter takes its start from a clear example of continuity, viz. that evident in the vocabulary common to declarative, interrogative, and imperatival forms. Whether we are considering words or sentences, we must do justice to the constancies as well as to the differences that we meet with from one such context to another. The question is how we are to do so while remaining true to the language as it is.

Perhaps the most favoured approach in this spirit is the following. Such related sentences as 'She is singing', 'Does she sing?', and 'Sing!' are held to present us with a common thought, proposition, or supposition, the speaker now asserting it to be true, now asking whether it is true, now commanding that it be made true. To bring out this continuity we may rewrite sentences of the three types in accordance with the schemata, 'It is the case that *p*', 'Is it the case that *p*?', and 'Make it the case that *p*', with 'that *p*' – the 'sentence radical' – expressing the common thought. The recurrence of *truth* in characterizing the uses of these sentence types reflects the likely rationale behind such transformations: by revealing how the words contribute to truth conditions, the same in each case, we show how a uniform account of their meaning is possible, despite the overall differences in force.

If assertions, questions, and the rest present us with nothing more than an unsystematizable range of uses, there is little prospect of identifying the recurrent factor which the sentence radical purports to isolate. That is one threat that has been warded off, the variety so far sampled not being such as to weaken the links between form and function to any significant degree; on the other hand, the invocation of the radical goes far beyond what has been defended in this respect, seeking unity right across sentence types and not merely within them. In this chapter we shall touch upon some of the ways in which uniformity is suggested, at the same time indicating why the sentence radical does not furnish the means for doing it justice. First, however, we shall look further at sentence meaning and the considerations which pave the way for the introduction of the radical.

7.1 Sentence meaning

Consider the question: what is the meaning of 'I'm not sure, but I think I've seen him somewhere before'? Is this a legitimate query? And what of more extended stretches of discourse? Once we reach paragraph length, surely, the rationale for speaking of *the* meaning may no longer be apparent in the face of the many words with their many meanings.

Perhaps we are more comfortable speaking of *the* meaning so long as the words can be regarded as constituting a single verbal unit, or at least as relating to a single theme. However, I do not think that we are too bothered with any such requirement, that we consider use of the definite article unjustified so long as we have not integrated the totality of meaningful elements in some such way. The meaning of the whole just is what we get by running through these, and their interrelations, whatever the shifts in theme. For some, however, the unitary character can be provided only by a suitable non-linguistic correlate – a single thought, perhaps, which our diverse verbal forms may embody. For those so inclined, sentence meanings become shrouded in mystery, problematic entities the nature of which it is for a theory of meaning to discover, entities which – to continue with the inapt terminology – such a theory is to describe or characterize. This project tends to be associated with a conception of the sentence as the primary unit of meaning, the meaning of an individual word being taken to be the 'contribution' which the word makes to the meanings of sentences in which it occurs. However, the two standpoints are distinguishable. The sentence can in some sense and for some purposes be regarded as primary without our having to lumber it with any mystifying concomitants.

It is clearly wrong to say that a word has a meaning only in a sentence. I have not written down a meaningless mark if I write 'tiger' and nothing else. 'In a sentence' is here the kind of misplaced locational qualification that we see with the temporal clause in 'You can know something only when awake.' Or again, saying that a word has meaning only in a sentence is like saying that an object has a weight only when it is on the scales; it is not like speaking of a substance as having an existence only in a compound.

But in the absence of sentential contexts, there could surely be no such thing as linguistic meaning? It is true that while an individual word may have a use by itself – 'waiter' as a summons, 'cheers' as a toast – in general the assistance of other words is required. What is important is whether a linguistic form, simple or complex, has a use as it stands; we shall speak of a sentence if it does, otherwise not. The thesis that the sentence is fundamental is acceptable if it simply recasts the claim that occurrences of words in which they are put to use are basic. Indeed, while it does not suit meaning, the context principle is readily transformable into a correct observation about use. Adverbs and adjectives, clearly, have no use in isolation, but only when united, explicitly or implicitly, with other parts of speech; we use pronouns to single out persons and things, but a complementary act, as of saying something about the referent, is required before the use of a pronoun can be described in this way. Without such a complement, we note, we are no more entitled to ascribe to a proper name a use to refer than a use to summon. Because word meaning presupposes a use, and because the latter requires a sentence (by definition), there is accordingly an interpretation of 'Word meaning presupposes a sentential context' in which it is true; but it remains a needless distortion to say that a word has a meaning only in such a context.

Wittgenstein's identification of meaning with use might be expected to lead him to a questionable application of the principle. It receives favourable mention at *PI* §49 in reference to the claim that naming is not a move in the language game, and elsewhere he makes the more sweeping declaration, 'To understand a sentence means to understand a language' (*PI* §199, *BB* 5), which might be thought to support the extreme holism sometimes encountered, as in Davidson's rendering of the principle:

> If sentences depend for their meaning on their structure, and we understand the meaning of each item in the structure only as an abstraction from the totality of sentences in which it features, then we can give the meaning of any sentence (or word) only by giving the meaning of every sentence (and word) in the language.
>
> (1984, 22)

As I understand Wittgenstein, he is not committed to the absurd thesis that we can understand nothing until we understand everything; rather, despite the unqualified form of expression, what is being advanced is along the lines of the more modest claim that, given any sentence, we could not understand just that sentence and nothing else. On the one hand, an ascription of understanding is unwarranted unless the speaker has shown or can show himself to be master of the language more generally (*PI* §199); on the other hand, the significance of the sentence itself cannot be taken in unless its links with other parts of the language are appreciated (*BB* 5).

As indicated, the view of the sentence as primary tends to lead on to a monolithic conception of sentence meaning: the move from word meaning to that of the sentence is conceived of as a move to a new kind of unit, something more than the sum of its parts in combination; it is a whole in which the meanings of the individual words have become submerged, their identities blurred, something with which we might be presented – in the guise perhaps of a thought – prior to having apportioned parts of it to individual words. Or, starting from the other end, we might come to a realization that this meaning is somehow engineered by combining the constituent atoms, the individual words, in a certain fashion, so that it might make sense to observe: how ingenious to produce that meaning in that way! At all events, there is supposedly a significant question as to how parts and whole are related: how, on the one hand, we might *derive* – or '*compute*' – the meaning of the whole from the meanings of its parts; and how, on the other hand, we might *work back* from the meaning of the whole to the meanings of its component words. And this is all surely nonsense. There is no such animal as the meaning of the whole in the intended sense, something over and above what can be specified by detailing the meanings of the words and their interrelations, including signs of force, but the idea that an important task awaits linguists and philosophers, namely, to show how the meanings of sentences depend on the meanings of words in the given language, is a task or programme of equal significance to that of showing how the letters *c-a-t*, arranged in just this way, spell the word 'cat'. We do not have an independent grasp of the meaning of a sentence in such a way that, with this meaning before our minds, we might set ourselves the task of working out just how the given words combine to yield it; our explanations do not, fortunately, require us to start by trying to get across the meaning of the whole, let alone presume that this is grasped, before proceeding to explain what part is contributed by what word. To assign the sentence priority in a way that would have these consequences is clearly wrong-headed. To say that the meaning of an individual word is a theoretical entity postulated for its explanatory value *vis-à-vis* sentence meanings is, if anything, even more fatuous. In giving an account of the sentence we clearly rely on the individual words meaning what they do. Given this reliance, it would be absurd to turn around and say that meaning was somehow less assured for words than for sentences, and of course absurd to entertain talk of 'theoretical entities' in either connection.

The target of these criticisms has been a misconception of the relation between the individual words of a sentence and the meaning of that particular sentence. Prima facie, it looks to be a different question if we ask how the former relate to a *general conception* of sentence meaning (cf. Dummett 1978, 448). Given that such a conception can be had in advance of constructing the particular sentence, we can make sense of the idea that the words of the latter should have in some way to accord with the former: sentence meaning requires this, this, and this; word *w* supplies the first, *v* the second, and so on.

Consider this possibility in relation to the dictum that the meaning of a word is or consists in the contribution it makes to the meanings of sentences in which it occurs. Our first thought may be that this crude identification is not even a starter: to say that the meaning of a word *is* its contribution to something is to couple terms having irreconcilably different grammars; we can say that the meaning of a word contributes to the meaning of a given sentence, but only in the uninteresting sense that the word is one of the words that go to make up the sentence. However, perhaps both points can be met by saying that the meaning of a word is to be *explained* in terms of its contribution to sentence meaning, where it is the general conception of sentence meaning that is now in play. After all, something like this would seem to follow from our claim that a person cannot have an understanding of individual words until he has an appreciation of their use in sentences – not, we may note, a claim which requires that either word or sentence have primacy over the other.

The suggestion that this form is *de rigueur* for explanations of meaning is at first sight less than compelling. Such explanations, whether verbal or ostensive, do not usually make reference to the larger contexts in which the word being explained may occur, but they can be satisfactory none the less. Still, it could be that there is an incompleteness about our ordinary explanations – much as an explanation of one noun in terms of another relies upon an understanding of, rather than explains, nominal character. But what is there to be said about a word, bearing in mind its diverse sentential contexts, which goes beyond what is possible if we consider the word in isolation? The word 'ladder' will occur in a range of sentence types – 'This is not much of a ladder', 'Get down from that ladder!', 'Might I borrow your ladder?', and so forth. Clearly, 'ladder' does not change in meaning as we pass from one sentence to another, but it is true of the word in all its occurrences that it is the word for a certain kind of object. This is what we might say when considering the word without regard to its larger contexts; what is to be added if we allow ourselves to draw upon the latter? Until we have before us an account of sentence meaning of the desired generality, it is difficult to know how this question might be answered.

An approach to the sentence which supposedly offers a framework in which the meanings of individual words may be explained is provided by the sentence radical, soon to be examined, and a more satisfactory alternative will be proposed in §10.3. However, whatever the formula invoked, it should in no way be allowed to detract from the importance of the individual words which go to make up the sentence. Consider questions. There can be levels of description at which we do not distinguish between 'Does it work?' and 'Doesn't it work?', yet a difference in meaning is apparent: the negation in the latter is not idle, its presence indicating, as we saw, that a presumed truth is being queried. Similarly with the pair 'Do you understand Dutch?' and 'Do you understand Dutch or don't you?', the former being being readily answered by 'Only a little', the disjunctive version discouraging answers which do not endorse either disjunct. These variant forms present us with differences which lend themselves to straightforward elucidation if we attend to as much as is obvious – the words which set the one apart from the others. Ignore this, treat the whole sentence as the unit, perhaps as indecomposable, and what is obvious is likely to escape altogether our scheme of explanation.

7.2 *Conjunctions and force*

One approach to drawing together seemingly unlike linguistic forms, and so perhaps identifying the unity which the radical demands, is to argue for the applicability of such evaluations as 'true' and 'correct' to sentences of whatever type. Thus, Elizabeth Anscombe queries whether there is any reason other than a dispensable usage for not calling commands true and false accordingly as they are obeyed or disobeyed (1957, 3), while Michael Dummett holds that 'correct' and 'incorrect' might be enlisted for this purpose, and also that 'true' and 'false' might be extended to (certain) interrogatives, such a question as 'Is it time we set off?' being deemed true if the correct answer is 'Yes' (1981, 305–6; 1978, 117–18).

It would be difficult to maintain that the case for a common character is actually advanced by such proposals. As things stand, we attach no meaning to speaking of 'Keep still!' or 'Must you whistle?' as true, and while the proposals in question could be said to tell us what we might mean if we made this extension, it would of course be an extension which required a new understanding of these terms. We can allow that there is an analogy between, say, commands that are obeyed and statements that are true, but the decision to extend truth to the former can add nothing to the considerations which make for the analogy. The whole substance of the suggestion resides in these considerations, nothing being implied by the use of 'true' that could not have been inferred without its assistance.

When appeal is made to a 'theoretical' concept of truth – one that is not required to answer to our everyday concept at all points – we may suspect an attempt at glossing over unwanted departures from what can meaningfully be said with the word in its usual acceptation. Not a charge I am levelling in this instance, but there is still the risk that the true significance of the word may be lost, but this loss covered up when the word itself is retained. Certainly, so long as we do not command a clear view of the complexities of actual usage, it is difficult to be sure that we have not introduced a distortion with our abrogation of the usual conceptual links.

In this connection it is worth indicating just how close the ties are between truth and assertion. If a declarative sentence is advanced merely as a guess, then while the guess may be on target, in so far as the speaker does not actually *assert* anything, 'correct' or 'right' are the preferred terms of appraisal, not 'true'. Indeed, though 'sentence' is a current favourite for identifying truth-bearers, its indifference to any assertoric act makes it a poor choice. Again, whilst thoughts have been taken by others to be the primary bearers of truth, it is in fact awkward to say that, e.g., one's first thoughts on the matter were true. Likewise, not 'I suspected he had called, but it wasn't true'; rather, 'but it wasn't so'. And not 'He hoped they would go ahead, but it wasn't to be true', but simply 'it wasn't to be'. Again, even though it may be the declarative form that is used in putting a question, as 'You are ready?', we cannot respond to this with 'True', and it is a needless distortion to represent this question as equivalent to 'Is it true that you are ready?', given the way the latter envisages an assertion to the effect that the person is ready.

It is of interest to note that, while truth's ties with assertion prevent the response 'True' to either 'Are you ready?' or 'You are ready?', the form of the latter provides us with enough for 'Right' or 'Correct' to get a grip. Without resorting to stipulation we can secure a point of contact between declarative and interrogative in these terms, even if wh-questions remain outside the scheme. Can anything be done to draw either form nearer to the imperative? Here is a curious possibility. It may appear beyond dispute that an imperative has no place within the antecedent of a conditional. However, consider the sentence, 'If you be good I'll take you.' That the action is envisaged as coming about in response to an imperative is not an invariable implication of this form, but the possibility of such a reading is enough to give sense to the notion of an imperatival occurrence at this point, and hence to show that imperative and declarative are not as far apart as might be supposed. Indeed, it would seem that 'are' is favoured over 'be' when an imperative would not be used. So, not 'If you be first to die . . . ' or 'If you be so much stronger . . . ', which, if they occurred, would present us with archaic subjunctives rather than imperatives, but in either case 'If you are . . . '.

The closeness of compliance to truth, as just indicated, discloses an unexpected affinity between imperative and declarative, and continuity is also revealed in the way adding 'or *p*' to an imperative may give us an alternative to the state of affairs that follows upon compliance, as with 'Hurry up, or you'll be late.' Only in this sense do we have what could be described as an alternative to the imperative itself, and while not in general interchangeable with 'If you don't hurry up you'll be late', this conditional defines a substantial overlap between the two. Likewise, 'and *p*' as a declarative addition to an imperative generally envisages compliance with the latter, *p* presenting us with something further to, and often consequential upon, the situation as thus brought about. This is so whether action is enjoined, as with 'Give me a screwdriver and I'll fix it', or whether the 'imperative' simply gives a variant conditional form: 'Give me a place to stand and I will move the earth'. Somewhat similarly, with 'Did you speak, or am I only imagining things?', the alternative which the second disjunct presents is an alternative to the possibility raised by the first; it is not an alternative to raising that question. There is no denying the intimate links between the different sentence forms. The problem is to give an account that does not obliterate or distort them.

Oddly enough, an advantage claimed for an account of sentences in terms of the radical is that it explains the impossibility of getting an imperative into an antecedent. We might have supposed that two sentences, each with its own force, could be linked by sentential connectives. Why not? However, on one view of the matter, this would be a mistake: force applies to the whole complex, what the connectives link being merely sentences considered as having a sense, as yet neutral between the assertoric, the imperatival, and so forth. As Dummett expounds the argument, if we do not 'notice' this fact,

> we can easily think that the disjunctive command is formed by joining two commands, and the conditional command by joining a statement and a command; and we may then rack our brains to discover why we cannot join two commands by means of 'if' – why we cannot get an imperative into the antecedent.
>
> (1981, 305-6)

Even supposing we disallow the occurrence in this position of an imperative in the way just explained, the argument still appears to be defective. Its unqualified form suggests that it is aimed at sentences or clauses linked by *any* connective, but with 'and', 'but', and conjunctions generally we need an independent demonstration that what we conjoin are neutral expressions of a thought, the indication of force then attaching to the whole, not to the individual parts. It is surely two commands that are joined in 'Open the door but don't let the cat out', or 'Be quiet and pay attention.' Furthermore, the corollary, that the whole context be endowed with a uniform force, does not work for, say, 'I know it is late, but could you take a quick look at this letter?', where there can be no disputing the description, 'a statement conjoined with a question'.

Dummett is, of course, aware of the existence of such combinations, and does not wish to press unreservedly the thesis that a sign of force 'cannot significantly occur within a clause which is a constituent of a complex question, but can attach only to a complete sentence as a whole' (ibid. 327). However, given this 'cannot', his claim that the exceptions do not affect the essential soundness of the thesis is hard to take. As not expressing 'thoughts', wh-questions are held to lie outside the scope of the thesis, but if we can happily allow the shift in force evident in 'I've found the coffee, but where is the sugar?', how can there be a general prohibition against such heterogeneity?

Leaving aside the dubious consideration that the sentence radical is at least thereby given something to do – or so it is supposed – it would seem that the example of 'or' provides the spur to this singular thesis. Thus, there is some awkwardness in speaking of 'Either sing in tune or don't sing at all' as a disjunction of two commands, in that the speaker does not issue the command 'Sing in tune' if the words occur in this way. Rather, the imperatival force governs the sentence as a whole, and not the disjuncts taken separately (ibid. 303). However, we could hardly rest content with this as an argument, since it is a peculiarity of the term 'command' – which we have seen to be far from correlative with 'imperative' – that has been fastened upon, rather than an essential feature of 'or'. If the disjuncts embody suggestions, advice, instructions or invitations, as in 'Heat in a moderate oven or brown under the grill', or 'Call in or just drop us a line', then we can more readily describe the disjuncts individually in such terms.

Even with commands, where it does seem correct to hold that

force attaches to the whole complex, it has still to be shown that a description in terms of the radical is apposite. That description is given sense in terms of a particular grammatical form, as in 'Bring it about either that you sing in tune or that you do not sing at all', and nothing of that character is discernible in 'Either sing in tune or do not sing at all.' To convey the idea that the words 'sing in tune' occur here without the force which they may carry in isolation, we might describe them as constituting a 'potential' command, but that still does not reveal what we get in this way as identical with what is similarly yielded by 'you are singing in tune' when this is dissociated from its assertoric force – as the general approach requires. Finally, even if we can make sense of the thesis in application to this example, we have been given no licence to generalize it to other conjunctions. To repeat, there is no reason whatsoever not to take at their face value such complex sentences as 'Whereas Brian is on the silent side, his brother is extremely loquacious' – two assertions linked – and the account does not even begin to make sense when there is a change in force, as with 'Although he thinks the world of you, take care!'

The attempt to impose the radical upon us in this way is more than likely to go hand in hand with a general misconception of the part played by truth in the explanation of conjunctions. The picture which comes across in Dummett's discussion is very much one of natural language as a system of communication designed by and for logicians, questions of the significance of linguistic features, as those of 'and', being decided solely in terms of the contribution made to inferences. A truth-functional role for 'and' requires, of course, that it link units capable of truth values, so any attempt at making that role essential to the conjunction falls down with such familiar combinations as 'When does the debate begin and what form will it take?' However upsetting it may be for those for whom the logician has the last word on its interpretation, it has to be accepted that this conjunction, like many others, can unite two questions, commands, and the rest, and that a satisfactory account of its meaning must gear it to the generality that this requires. When a connection with truth emerges it emerges only through the character of the sentences conjoined, not through 'and' itself, which makes no demands for any such association. There is no call to assign priority to the declarative case, but the logical powers of the conjunction here in evidence are derivable from a consideration of the constant sense which it bears in application to requests, orders, questions, greetings, and exclamations, as well as to statements. (Cf. Rundle 1983 for details.) Those who seek to defend a truth-functional account of the conjunctions of interest to logic have thought it sufficient to meet objections directed to their occurrence within declarative contexts. Such objections – e.g., that 'and' has a temporal connotation – are often misguided, but in many cases the easy victories gained do little to vindicate that account if the usage of the conjunction is to be explained more generally. To bring into line the recalcitrant contexts – as imperatives linked by 'and' – the uniform rewriting offered by the radical seems to be the only resort possible. Hence, in large part, its appeal, despite its desperately implausible character. And, of course, with or without the sentence radical, a truth-functional account is a total irrelevance with the general run of conjunctions, as a brief survey of temporal and consequential connectives soon reveals.

The thesis to which Dummett gives qualified support is the thesis that 'a sign which conveys force must always relate to the whole complete sentence in which it occurs; it cannot form part of a subordinate clause' (ibid. 316). Let us then suppose that examples such as 'Since you have to go, is there any point arguing?' are thought to constitute *two* sentences, so can consistently be assigned two forces. We can, perhaps, tolerate this idiosyncratic way of counting sentences, but such an example as 'Take the medicine he gave you' would still refute the hypothesis: overall imperatival character does not debar the sentence from incorporating a declarative condition in the subordinate clause, 'he gave you'. Nor should we go along with the consequent differentiation of the clauses common to such pairs as 'Ask the man who is sitting opposite' and 'Will you ask the man who is sitting opposite?' Far from being absorbed into the imperative and interrogative forces of the main clauses, the assertoric character of 'who is sitting opposite' stands out against the clauses to which it is subordinated. Or, to say that the force of the whole is the force of the principal clause is not to deny that clauses with a different force may occur within the whole.

7.3 The radical and interrogatives

We turn now to a more direct consideration of the sentence radical, beginning with its application to interrogative sentences. Given that the radical may present us with a form of words that does *not* figure in the sentences under consideration, the approach which calls upon this contrivance to reveal continuity amongst sentence types is unpromising. Indeed, it is worse than that. Not only is the radical inapplicable to wh-questions, as 'Why bother?' or 'Who cares?', but even when it does apply it merely presents us with a systematic way of avoiding, rather than resolving, the supposed difficulties. Forsaking 'Will he agree?' for 'Is it the case that he will agree?' may lead to featuring 'will' in the preferred way – as part of the radical – but of course this does nothing to show how the use of the phrase now charged with signalling a question, viz. 'Is it . . . ', relates to its use in assertoric contexts. Compare the suggestion that the language might have had no specific interrogative form, that we might instead have made do with such assertoric variants as 'I should like to know . . . ' or 'I ask . . . ' – as Wittgenstein suggests at *RFM* Appendix III–1. Since these are completed by questions, albeit indirect questions, it is difficult to argue that a genuine alternative has been advanced.

So also with imperatives. Replacement of 'Sing!' by 'Make it the case that you sing!' simply relocates the imperatival element in the new phrase, 'Make it the case . . . ', and so presents the same problem as supposedly arises with 'sing', or with any other choice of verb, viz. how are we to explain the unambiguity of the occurrences of 'make it the case' in 'He will make it the case that . . . ', 'Make it the case that . . . ', and so on? All that the scheme has to offer is the futile expansion of the latter as 'Make it the case that you make it the case that . . . '. Likewise, of course, with the even more inapposite 'Bring it about that . . . '.

When considering how the declarative sentence was to be elucidated, we found it appropriate to focus upon the variable element – the verbal phrase – passing over those terms which, like pronouns, are constant in behaviour whatever the sentence type. If that approach is correct, there is simply no call to characterize all the words of an assertion in such a way that the continuity of use when we move to another context is problematic. Given, trivially, that it is only the variable elements that pose the problem which the radical is called upon to resolve, we can accordingly ignore the radical and attend just to the smaller phrases.

Suppose, then, we consider the verb common to the contexts 'Does she sing?' and 'She sings'. Here we are being asked to compare a finite form with the infinitive, and it is not clear that the comparison will tell us anything specifically about occurrences of the latter within questions, since the comparison would be the same if, instead of 'Does she sing?', we were to call upon 'She can sing' or 'No one will sing' to illustrate the use of the infinitive. If, on the other hand, we take a form that does vary in a relevant way, as 'can' in 'She can sing' and 'Can she sing?', it is difficult to see where a problem lies. The auxiliary does not mean anything different in either – it is, after all, the same form of the verb in both – it is just that its applicability is being enquired after, rather than affirmed. If asked to explain the verbs 'push' and 'pull' we should try to get across the distinctive actions with which each is associated. The grammar of this word type allows for the possibility of affirmation or interrogation with respect to these verbs, but explanations of their meaning need not tie them to either possibility in such a way that the other is excluded, or becomes in the least problematic. Likewise with 'can'. We noted earlier a danger attending Wittgenstein's example of the language game with 'Slab!', the way word and sentence are here one being unrepresentative. For the most part it is possible to characterize signs of force in such a way that the identifiability of individual words, the recurrent units in the various sentence frames, is *presupposed* – not something that the overall force of the sentence somehow makes uncertain.

As befits the common mood of their verb, assertion and corresponding question are very much variations on a single relation, and while it does not need reduction to a common form to show this, a common form is what we have with 'She sings' and 'She sings?' – and have without being obliged to pretend that the language is other than it is. With 'She sings?' we have a suspension of assertoric force, but what the person is being asked to consider is essentially the same whether it occurs asserted or unasserted. In this respect it need make no difference whether the words are taken one way or the other, though when interrogative status is recognized the person addressed will appreciate that he is being *invited* to endorse or contradict what is being put forward. There is no difficulty in seeing how or why the same words can be retained with a switch from assertoric to interrogative use, but it is also true that this account makes it plausible to join the proponent of the radical in assigning priority to the assertoric case. If, in treating 'She sings?' as appropriately confirmed or contradicted, we are not treating it as having the essential character of an assertion, at least we could seemingly not have any understanding of this role if we were not conversant with an assertoric use of the form.

Whatever the shape a question takes, it is surely intelligible only to one who has a grasp of the general form of an answer, and, if we are talking about questions generally, such a grasp means an understanding of the assertoric form, an understanding that is clearly presupposed by such answers as 'probably', 'with difficulty', and 'sadly not'. The question may have been 'Can he swim?', but answers in these terms require recourse to the corresponding assertion for their interpretation. Indeed, there is some temptation to construe many questions as actually embodying assertions. With 'Why did you refuse?' do we not imply a belief that the person we are addressing refused, the query relating to the reason for the supposed refusal? There is undoubtedly a presumption of such a belief in many cases, but we note that the reason behind a question can be the eventual exposure of the falsity of the proposition supposedly endorsed, so we do not appear to have here a condition for the correct use of this form. However, that there are close links between assertions and questions is plain enough; they are there on the surface of the language, not a matter for conjecture – as if we were dealing with relations between a declarative sentence and one, perhaps in the realm of deep structure, that gave the *real* form of the question, and whose existence could be known of only by argument.

To find a problem with questions formed by inversion, we may call upon the widely used 'does', since it is not apparent that this has the same meaning in questions as in assertions. Has it indeed any meaning at all in the former? Is it not perhaps just a formal device used to generate a question? Following Diver 1964, we might propose that 'do' be grouped along with the modal verbs, 'can', 'may', 'should' and 'must'. These verbs relate, in the given order, to an increasing scale of likelihood, at the top of which 'do' is naturally placed. So, 'He did try' is of course close to the plain indicative, 'He tried', but whereas the latter indicates an unquestioned certainty, 'did' is appropriate to a questioned certainty: we say 'He did try' if there has been some doubt on this score, if, though an unreserved affirmation is now in order, the matter has been thought open, hypothetical.

This is an attractive approach, in that it finds a niche for what would otherwise seem an anomalous verb, but there are uses of 'do' where the connection with certainty is hard to detect, as when it serves to avoid repetition of a more specific verb, e.g., 'Charles lives abroad' – 'So does Emily' – though it may be that 'do' as a lexical proform is to be considered a different use. The auxiliary can plainly bear the suggested interpretation when we shift from the declarative to the interrogative, but while it is possible to read 'Did he try?' as asking whether it is *really sure* that he tried, in a way that is not open to us with 'He tried?', it would seem that in general this contrast is to the fore only if 'did' is stressed, and if the contrast is what we want, we do better to retain the declarative ordering: 'He did try?'. At all events, because we generally make nothing of the contrast in the inverted form, there is nothing here to counter the impression that 'does' is a somewhat empty term, serving only to signal a question, with no implications beyond those present when subject and main verb are inverted. If we have to accept that a difference in meaning may go with different occurrences of the word, that simply refutes an assumption made by those who invoke the radical: not all words do mean the same in both assertoric and interrogative contexts.

Indeed, why should the words which occur in the one context invariably occur in the other at all? Could we not imagine a language in which terms like 'why' and 'when' made an appearance in interrogatives, but in interrogatives only? All this would require is that indirect questions not be a feature of the language, and that is not hard to accept. Nor is it difficult to see how we might come to an understanding of such words. Suppose that the interrogative adjectives 'which' and 'what' were never encountered outside direct questions. We could still learn that 'which' was appropriately used when it was a question of selecting from a determinate, given range – 'Which colour do you prefer?' - 'what' likewise being in place when something was to be specified, but where the range from which the selection was to be made was more open – 'What colour do you prefer?' – the demonstrative element in 'which' being absent. As other linguistic categories, such as exclamations, make abundantly clear, such constancies between word and circumstances of use are not confined to terms within a declarative sentence.

The help which the radical offers has looked dubious in part because it requires us to make certain sentences out to be something they are not. Not only that, but the virtual absence of the radical from actual language threatens it with a location in a purely conjectural realm where it is debarred from any engagement with the forms of words which present the initial problem. Suppose, then, we disallow appeals to the radical which apply only to the language as reconstructed, and try to redescribe the target sentences as far as possible in terms which would fit the reformed versions. There are two ways in which this might be possible. First, we have seen that different uses of the declarative form are intelligibly cast as variations on a common theme to the extent that the variation lies in the degree of tentativeness with which something is advanced. In these terms, given a suitably broad reading of 'represent things to be a certain way', or some kindred formula, we may bring together asserting, guessing, indulging in make-believe, and presenting a supposition or a hypothesis. Second, even if there is no general use under which all these particular acts can usefully be subsumed, a single underlying *relation* may provide a common thread. The notion of predication is sometimes held to apply to all indicative clauses, whether asserted or not. The distance between these two extremes may disallow an explanation of predication in terms of a common use, but there is still the possibility of turning to the domain of structure rather than of acts, of fastening on a common *form*. So, for instance, such a relation as that which a verb has to its subject or object will be maintained throughout variations in force.

Either of these approaches provides a corrective to the superficial view that it is only words that are common to the sentence in its different uses, offering some support to those who wish to speak of words as having a common sense but with different forces imposed upon them. It is most unfortunate if the idea that there can be a distinction between sense and force gets tied to the acceptability of the radical. The differences between asserting, supposing, asking, and the rest, do not have to be represented as differences in the meaning of the single indicative form that may figure in all, but this form can be uniformly characterized as having the status of a (grammatically) possible truth, and it does no harm to think of a common sense as being defined in these terms – or, more accurately, in terms of *correctness*, since this is the notion which we saw to apply to each of, e.g., 'You are ready' and 'You are ready?'

Given that we are dealing with a single verbal form, it is not at all remarkable if, one way or another, we can find a common denominator to its diverse applications. However, not only do wh-questions continue to remain outside the scheme; so, too, does the imperative, if in a different direction, to such a point that talk of a different mood looks to be appropriate. Furthermore, if we try to bring indicative and imperative into line by saying that one who utters an imperative is expressing a desire that the person addressed act so as to make a certain proposition true, we require an understanding of the assertoric form that cannot be taken for granted in the general case. What is needed is an approach which takes the language as it is rather than as a preconceived scheme would have it be. We have taken the first steps in this direction; the next few are equally straightforward.

7.4 The radical and imperatives

We turn now to consider the imperative in greater detail. With 'She sings' and 'She sings?' there is little to argue as regards continuity of meaning, though the relation of the former to 'Does she sing?' has emerged as more complex. Making out a case for continuity over the assertoric/imperatival division looks likewise to be more challenging, in that we have now moved to a different mood. An interrogative draws upon the same components as the corresponding declarative sentence, even if it does organize them differently, whereas the shift to the imperative is a shift to a less directly related use of the verb. A language with just questions is problematic, a language with just imperatives seems not, but we appear to have a genuinely independent form. Of course, a common thread is apparent in the idea of an action specified, whether it be a matter of compliance with that specification or mere conformity with it. That is, an account of what has to be done to comply with an imperative agrees with an account of what has to be done if the corresponding declarative form is to apply, thus giving sense to the idea of a common condition associated with the verb. This parallels the indicative case, where an explanation of the meaning of a verb goes the same way whether an assertion or a question is envisaged.

To pursue further the matter of continuity we shall take up our unanswered question concerning the relation of the imperative to the infinitive. The major division between imperatival uses appeared to be one which followed the division of interests, the desires of the speaker being to the fore with orders and pleas, those of another party with advisory and instructional uses. Asked for advice we may dutifully respond, no doubt showing a desire to be helpful, but whether or not our advice is heeded may be a matter of no concern to us. Here I am thinking of an imperative uttered in response to 'What should I do?', 'What is the best thing to do?', and the like, but there is a question whether the words which give our answer, as 'Call a plumber', really do qualify as imperatives. They exhibit the right form, but since what completes 'You should . . . ', say, is an infinitive, that perhaps is what we have. Or is there in fact any difference between the two?

The suggestion that the imperative might be nothing more than the infinitive (without 'to') looks at first sight implausible, but use of the latter in reports of the former is evidence of at least a close relationship, as when the warning, 'Stand clear!', is reported as 'He told us to stand clear', or when the plea 'Let me go!' is reported as 'She begged him to let her go.' The most striking indication of an actual identity of infinitive and imperative is seen from responses or additions to the latter which seemingly require that it have the character of the former, as with the combination in 'Pay attention, won't you?' or when we respond to the invitation, 'Have another cake', with 'Oh, may I?'. On the one hand, the imperative is clearly present; on the other hand, the intended completions of 'won't you?' and 'may I?' equally clearly call for an infinitive: 'Won't you pay attention?', 'May I have another cake?' We may also note how an imperative may be repeated without the speaker's being committed to an injunctive use. So we are told, 'Take out another mortgage', to which we reply, 'Take out another mortgage? Why not?', or 'Take out another mortgage? What a suggestion!' (Cf. Bolinger 1977, chapters 8 and 9, where the claim for a single form is based very much on such considerations.)

It is also worth mentioning a use which, from a grammatical point of view, appears to qualify as imperatival, but which has no connection with desires or wishes. I am thinking here of such sentences as 'Move and I shoot' or 'Give me a place to stand and I will move the earth'. An imperative having the force of an order, request, invitation, or any of the other categories considered, is not extractable from such a combination when it is intended as a conditional – 'If you move I shall shoot' – yet it is to all appearances the imperative mood that is invoked in the presentation of the condition.

The case for regarding imperative and infinitive as essentially one is stronger than might at first be supposed. There is, after all, no explicit mention of desire or desirability in such a form as 'Give it to me', but the more negative features which it shares with the infinitive - an absence of the further determinations to which the declarative form is liable – seem all that can be safely ascribed to it, even though in many contexts – notably those in which the description 'infinitive' is not customarily sanctioned – the only point that we shall be able to see in giving a specification of an action will be to have someone act in accordance with that specification.

However, notwithstanding the common form of imperative and infinitive, any thoroughgoing identity is questionable for the obvious reason: there is a distinctive use of that form which warrants us speaking of a specialized meaning that goes with the imperative, much as questions involve a specialized meaning associated with the inverted declarative word order, itself a more general phenomenon (cf. §5.2 above). Conceived of as a bare infinitive, a phrase like 'stay away' does not enjoy an independent use, but is in need of further words to complete it into a full sentence – e.g., 'I shall stay away' – whereas with the imperatival use the same words can by themselves constitute a 'move in the language game'. One who knows about 'stay away' only what is true of its occurrence in both contexts, its non-committal specification of an action, and has no idea of the use to put forward the action as desired or desirable, has simply not yet grasped one meaning of the form. The reference to desire is of course not at all explicit, but that is no reason for denying the connection: we should surely allow that a sentence like 'May he regret every word!', or even 'If only she would ring!' – the nearest modern English has to an optative – gave expression to a wish.

It is true that we can greet the order 'Bring in the coal' with 'Why can't you?', without having the sense of making a pun, and this does mean that in some sense we have identity of meaning. However, what weighs with us here is just the availability of *some* form of the verb for 'can't' to pick up. After all, we can equally allow 'Gerald works late. Why can't you?', and the third-person form 'works' is not felt as an embarrassment even though what 'can't' requires is an infinitive. Furthermore, with some linkages any imperatival force may have to be discarded. Most notably with the entry of negation, as when 'Move your queen' is offered in response to 'Is there anything you'd say I shouldn't do?', but not only here. 'Try to make a fool of me, would you?' reads differently depending on whether we have an imperative or an infinitive, and 'Can't you arrange for a replacement?' does not necessarily equate with 'Arrange for a replacement, can't you?' It should also be said that while the infinitive can do duty as an imperative in French, German, and other languages, this is so in more formal contexts rather than in face-to-face encounters. Finally, we might note how the pronoun 'you' can accompany an imperative, but not an infinitive; e.g., 'You stay out of this', 'You be quiet'. Sometimes 'you' may enjoy a vocative use which separates it from the verb – 'You (there): pay attention' – but there does not have to be this separation. It is no doubt because the imperative without 'you' comes first to mind that a conditional with an imperatival antecedent is thought an impossibility – 'If be good, . . . ' is just not English. The pronominal form 'If you be good, . . . ' puts the matter in another light, and serves even more convincingly to disqualify the infinitival thesis. That thesis is best stated by saying that the infinitive retains its identity as such even when incorporated into an imperatival use, but when 'you' is kept this appears impossible to sustain.

The occurrence of sentences like 'Give me a place to stand and I will move the earth' serves only to make clear, through the contrast offered, the standard interpretation of the imperative form. A purely conditional reading may be favoured when, as in this instance, the first clause presents an impossible condition, but the construction lends itself to the more familiar use, as far as that clause is concerned, and with this we are surely required to read the verb differently. With 'Give me a screwdriver and I'll fix it', the speaker could intend 'Give me a screwdriver' as a request – or not. It seems right to locate the options at this point, to make this form of the verb the source of the different readings overall, and if that is so – and if it is right to regard the mood as imperative either way – we have to recognize a more specialized reading of that form, a reading which associates prescriptive force with it as a matter of meaning rather than as a matter of a contextually determined addition to a univocal expression. Similarly with ambivalent sentences without 'and', as 'Give him all the help you can, he won't thank you for it.'

While we go too far in the direction of generality if we allow the infinitive to absorb the imperative, it is true that some apparent uses of the latter can as well be regarded as uses of the former, as when 'Call a plumber' is uttered in response to 'What should I do?' – though it is far from obvious that all such uses of the form are to be thought of as presented in response to a real or supposed question. However, the data which gave some support to an identity can at least be invoked to show the close affinity between imperatival and non-imperatival uses of a verbal phrase. We have seen how imperative and infinitive agree in presenting a course of action in a hypothetical, non-reportive fashion. We have seen too how the infinitive gives the standard way of reporting an imperative, and we note how, while the notion of action in response to an injunction is absent from the ostensibly imperatival use in such sentences as 'Laugh and the world laughs with you', what we are left with is the notion of a condition, which might equally be formulated in an indicative clause.

Also worth salvaging from the hypothesis of an identity is a recognition that imperative and interrogative are not necessarily exclusive categories, that they can be so understood that a form like 'Take out another mortgage?' can be held to belong in both. Given the way such a query may be elaborated by 'Is that what you want me to do?', or 'Is that really what I should do?', this unexpected overlap serves only to reinforce the connection of the imperative with desire or desirability, but it does show that the assertoric and interrogative uses open to a verb in the indicative are matched for the imperative by a use in actually advancing an action as desired or desirable, and one in which we *query* whether an action is thus envisaged – cf. also 'Tell him what?' as a response to 'Tell him!' Indeed, if our concern is to see where unity lies, we should do well to question the usual division into declarative, interrogative, imperative – in part simply a reflection of the confusion of 'indicative' with 'declarative' mentioned earlier – and fasten instead upon the divisions marked by the different *moods* – indicative, imperative, subjunctive. (Though these are themselves in much need of further scrutiny.) Here it is of interest to recall that Frege came to regard assertion and corresponding question as expressing a common thought, having initially refused to take this step, but still did not consider that these were to be joined by the imperative (cf. Frege 1892, 1918). It is a pity that his good sense in drawing the distinction along these lines has not always been emulated by his followers.

Just as a verb in a question can be taken up in a declarative sentence without the slightest feeling of discontinuity, as when we follow up 'Can you come?' with 'If you can, . . . ', so, as we have observed, imperatival and non-imperatival occurrences fit naturally together: 'Eat up! If you don't, . . . '. Recall, too, the way an imperative might make sense in a conditional: 'If you be good I'll take you'. What is perhaps most important is the way the case for continuity can thus be made out at the level of the individual word, the unit that is uncontroversially common to the diverse sentence forms. We are not obliged to ascend to the more complex that-clause, and therewith to *pretend* that the various sentences are not what they patently are. Sameness at the acceptable level is a matter of the same action qualifying both as what fulfils an imperative – whose performance counts as compliance with it – and as what may be reported by a corresponding declarative form, an agreement which provides the core of common meaning, to such a point that we have no sense of incongruity in shifting between imperatival and infinitival uses of the same verb. It remains true, however, that the indicative and the imperatival uses are independent, in the sense that neither presupposes the presence in the language of the other. One of the main questions to put to any account of meaning is whether it makes clear how the meaning of the given form could be grasped, and it does not require a connection with truth for this to be apparent.

The question of continuity in meaning of the words which occur in different sentence types is, then, more restricted than is customarily supposed. That is, what is presented as a major problem about such types reduces to a relatively minor problem concerning different uses of verbal phrases. Focusing on the larger units distorts the issue from the outset, making it seem as though the differences to be accounted for are deeper than they are – another instance of the damage for which an unswerving adherence to the idea of the sentence as *the* unit is responsible. A revised approach on this front is necessary, and it would also appear desirable to redraw the usual divisions among sentence types in a way that does justice to distinctions in mood.

8

Meaning and Truth

Given the extent to which intention was played down in our account of assertion, it might seem that our sympathy must go instead to the notion of truth conditions; what else remains with which to define meaning? On the other hand, the inadequacies of a truth-functional account of conjunctions, along with the futility of the sentence radical, present an obvious setback to the usual attempts at making truth central; in addition, we have the objections from those who consider 'true' to be essentially redundant, with nothing whatsoever to offer in elucidating meaning. Granted, a possible bearing upon meaning is not exhausted by the particular misapplications so far contemplated, and there is unquestionably more to be said on truth's behalf than is allowed by supporters of the redundancy theory, at least in its cruder forms. However, while truth does not suffer emasculation at the hands of that account, we shall find that the obvious restrictions on its applicability remain, leaving it with no advantages not shared by a more generally relevant notion of correctness.

8.1 Truth and redundancy

Over a wide range of cases, truth furnishes us with a surprisingly effective instrument for forcing apart words which come close in meaning. The members of such pairs as 'intention' and 'motive', 'monologue' and 'soliloquy', 'referee' and 'umpire', may appear indistinguishable, but by seeing how replacement of one by the other can make for a shift from truth to falsity, we may come to an appreciation of the distinctive meaning of each. Conversely, if ringing the changes on, say, 'beseech', 'implore', and 'entreat' fails to generate possible differences in truth value, we may conclude that we are without anything on which to found a difference in meaning. In the *Blue Book*, Wittgenstein points to the various decisions possible on the question whether a hammer is used in different ways in hitting a nail and driving a peg, the suggestion being that sameness of use with respect to words likewise presents us with a matter for decision (*BB* 58). However, if we want use to keep in step with meaning, uses which result in different truth values *cannot* be reckoned the same. It is dangerous to think in terms of sameness and difference in use as always relative to a purpose or interest if this is taken to allow the individual's interest to be decisive. There is in the background the general concern with truth which has to be respected whatever the individual's aim.

Though intimate, the relation here implied between truth and meaning appears innocent enough. How might its propriety be queried? Objections to calling upon the services of truth frequently exploit difficulties in finding a suitable worldly correlate for a sentence or statement. If the objections come from supporters of the redundancy theory, they are likely to be particularly hostile towards any attempt to have truth achieve anything of substance, let alone provide the key concept in elucidating meaning. On this account, 'true' is simply swallowed up by the associated proposition in accordance with the equation, '"*p*" is true = *p*', and it is vain to look to truth to find a relation of words to world which might be of value in defining their meaning, or for anything else. Since the knowledge that, say, 'Television encourages violence' is true if and only if television encourages violence simply reduces to the 'knowledge' that television encourages violence if and only if television encourages violence, we can give short shrift to the claim that understanding a sentence consists in the apprehension of its truth conditions. There is nothing here to apprehend beyond a triviality.

This is the argument as presented by Dummett, under the supposition that the whole explanation of the sense of 'true' is as given by the redundancy formula (1981, 458). However, one of the main problems posed by the redundancy theory is to find any developed form of it that lives up to the name, and the issue of interest is to see whether more sophisticated versions have anything to offer on the relation between truth and meaning. The simple equation just given represents Wittgenstein's summary treatment of the topic at *PI* §136, but more has to be said to accommodate contexts in which 'true' is predicated of propositions which the speaker cannot specify, as with 'What he said was no doubt true.' It may be argued that since truth will always be truth of some proposition, and since this circumstance is one we can handle, there can be nothing of substance that eludes the analysis proposed. However, on that analysis it also appears impossible to say what it is that true propositions have in common. Perhaps this can be shown, but eliminate 'true' and it cannot be said. More generally, we can make difficulties for attempts at dispensing with 'true' by having it occur as part of a phrase which requires that the statement to which it relates be maintained in its quoted form, as with '"There cannot be both an irresistible force and an immovable object" is true in virtue of the meanings of the words.' It is really for this rather elementary reason – that we have simply lost what we were speaking about, typically a statement – that we can dismiss the reduction of 'knowing that "Television encourages violence" is true if . . . ' to 'knowing that television encourages violence if . . . '.

Use of 'true' is often held to import an allusion to a statement in another sense, in that we say such things as 'It is true that inflation has fallen' when someone has made, or is envisaged as making, the statement in question. Such an allusion accounts for the ineptness of 'I wonder if it is true that they have forgotten', say, as a paraphrase of 'I wonder if they have forgotten', and we have already remarked on the similar character of 'Is it true that you are ready?' as a rendering of 'Are you ready?' This presupposition of a statement is not a general feature of the construction which 'true' exemplifies; it is not shared by, for instance, 'It is evident that inflation has fallen', but it appears to be more specific to 'true'. Since a question of truth arises only once a statement has been made, or is envisaged as made, it is not surprising that an ascription of truth, even if hypothetical only, should imply just such a circumstance, so this may be all that is required by way of explanation for the infelicitous occurrences. Whether or not that suffices, it is significant that the status of 'true' as a predicate of a statement goes hand in hand with its use to exclude the kind of failing to which this mode of speech is liable. Someone says, 'The economy is booming', and we ask, 'Is that true?' – i.e., is it not perhaps something of an exaggeration, without foundation, a lie even? To address our query more directly to the subject matter of what was said we should say simply 'Is it?' Note also 'That is so', which is a stronger contender for the role assigned to 'That is true' by those who consider 'true' redundant. The words 'That is so' serve to endorse or reaffirm, but as a unit which behaves as a whole more like a statement variable than a predication with respect to the statement as subject. Hence, I suggest, the inclination to think of truth as harbouring a more substantive relation than is offered by these other forms. We shall see how this inclination may lead to distortion when we consider the notion of what makes a proposition true.

To meet the problem posed by unspecifiable bearers of truth, it is natural to take advantage of the fact that, if there is something to which 'true' can be applied, then, whether or not it can be specified, it will be assertoric in form, it will purport to state how things are. Being true will be a matter of being as stated, so 'What he said was no doubt true' becomes 'Things were no doubt as he stated', and two propositions are both true if in each case things are as stated. Thus, as well as '"*p*" is true = *p*' and '"*p*" is false = –*p*', Wittgenstein explicitly presents 'What he says is true = Things are as he says' as part of his account at *PG* §79, this latter being a close relation of 'This is how things are', the formula offered in the *Tractatus* as giving the general form of propositions (*TLP* 4.5; cf. also Strawson 1967, 13–14). In the *Investigations* it is suggested that it is because of its status as a proposition in its own right – as against the unstructured '*p*' – that the formula recommends itself for this further role as a variable, and as such it presupposes an understanding of what goes to make for propositional character (*PI* §134). That, however, does not debar it from throwing light on such character – more, I should say, than the family resemblance alternative then advanced.

As well as querying the value of 'This is how things are' in shedding light on propositional character, Wittgenstein finds fault with the invocation of truth to that end. Given that we do not have a grasp of truth and falsity independently of having a conception of the nature of their possible bearers, it is not satisfactory to define a proposition as whatever can be true or false (cf. *PI* §136). Whether these considerations are thought to cast doubt on the earlier appeal to the equation of 'What he says is true' with 'Things are as he says' is uncertain. One would hope not, since without the help of some such equivalence it is difficult to see what remains for dealing with the problematic occurrences. Granted, whenever there is truth there is a proposition that is true, and the redundancy formula specifies what that comes to. However, there is still something missing, and something which the further equation supplies, viz. a means of providing a general specification of the condition which true statements severally satisfy. Compare the similar failing of the semantic conception of truth, which specifies recursively how truth is realized for certain symbolic forms, but not in such a way that we learn what, as truths, the different forms have in common. Again, if the effect of coupling 'it is true' with 'that *p*' is to convert the latter into an assertion, there is still the question of what 'true' must mean to secure that outcome; and, equally pressing, the question as to the sense dictated for 'false' by the consideration that 'It is false that *p*' takes us to 'not-*p*'. The formula is silent on these matters.

On the other hand, while necessary, any further elaboration in terms of things being as stated serves to generate *paraphrases* of 'true', rather than to provide a recipe for its elimination. A redundancy theory does not maintain simply that the word 'true' can be dispensed with. That is of no interest if it simply means introducing a variant phrase in its place, but for a theory worthy of the name we should wish to see a demonstration of the eliminability of any and every expression having the sense of 'true'. In saying, e.g., 'What *A* says is true if and only if things are as *A* states', we are not illustrating such a theory, but simply giving a contextual paraphrase that is to be assessed as correct or incorrect just like any other.

We might put it like this. The analysis dictates a reading for '"*p*" is true', or the more natural 'It is true that *p*', as 'Things are as "*p*" states', or 'Things are as one who states "*p*" states them to be', and this could well have been our starting point, our basic definition; having set out to define 'true', we could have advanced this possibility directly, rather than via an attempt to cope with the particular case of propositions that have not been specified. We should not have dreamt of calling this a redundancy theory, for it would be so plain that it qualified as a non-eliminative paraphrase.

We have, then, reason to reverse the approach of those who consider 'true' superfluous: the term merits a definition applicable in all its occurrences, albeit one which may reveal it as eliminable in certain of these. 'True' is not, as it were, just an assertion variable, but, as remarked above, it is because of its sense that its union with a proposition can issue in the corresponding assertion. Likewise with 'false'.

So long as we have to rely on an equivalence between being true and being as stated, we are not in a position to regard 'true' as dispensable. However, our account of truth can still be in the spirit of the redundancy theory. Thus, however exactly it is to be formulated, that account arises in opposition to the traditional correspondence theory, and it could be that the chief aim of its exponents is negative: to deny that truth involves anything like the kind of *relation* that the correspondence theorist sees at its heart. If we can be rid of 'true' altogether, we have a graphic demonstration that its role is not to convey such a relation, but this extreme is not demanded by that denial. An advocate of redundancy might be content, then, with the following observation: 'true' does not signal a relation, in the sense that it does not signal a relation *beyond* any that may be affirmed in affirming *p* itself.

Granted that a relation having *p* as one of its terms is not in question, the suggestion is that 'true' may none the less draw upon a relation *within p*. That surely makes sense, and makes sense without our having to entertain worldly items any more exotic than the referents of the names and other patently referential terms which occur so abundantly within our statements. In the simplest case, the relation thus allowed will be one in which a non-performative predicate is (advanced as) true of its subject, a very different relation from one in which the whole assertion is mapped onto its supposed worldly correlate, a *fact*. A statement can make ample contact with the world without our having to fabricate a bogus correlate for it as a whole, and when the demand for extra-linguistic links is met in the way proposed, it is difficult to see why the redundancy theorist should resist the relations invoked. What is important from his perspective is surely the idea that 'true' adds nothing to what is implicit in the associated proposition. Just this is the attraction of the formula, 'things are as stated'. Its necessity shows the necessity for defining rather than eliminating 'true', but it maintains the neutral role of the latter, its capacity to be absorbed into the proposition through doing no more than duplicate what is already implicit therein – unlike 'assertible', say, which clearly goes beyond what is actually stated. If the notion of assertibility can find its way into truth, it will be only in so far as it is implicit in the proposition on which 'true' is parasitic.

For one who supports the modified redundancy theory outlined above, it is not merely difficult to refuse the relation given with 'things are as stated', it is clearly impossible. We note, however, that once we move away from subject–predicate forms, little by way of articulate structure is replicated by this formula. With 'Here is a key', for instance, we are not saying of something named 'here' that it is a key, but the adverb simply demarcates the locality where the description ostensibly applies. Similarly with 'There is a key', and not merely when this features 'there' as an adverb of place. In the 'existential' reading, what we have is a variation on this pattern, even though 'there' has weakened considerably, losing its deictic force and approaching more to 'somewhere'. None the less, even when any correlative notion of reference has given up on us, the idea of the verbal phrase as having application would appear to remain of relevance, and to allow us to speak of a word–world relation. That some such duality is required is suggested by noting what happens when it fails, assertion having then to give way to some other use of language. Consider the use of a name in an identification, as 'That is Henry'. Because there will be someone or something to which the name is fitted, rightly or wrongly, someone singled out by 'that', we have a use for correctness as it applies to assertions, viz. as truth. With no such purported identification-cum-fit, we should have the name in some other role, as when 'Henry!' constitutes a summons, and where correctness will be judged in a quite different way.

However, as far as the modified redundancy theory is concerned, the merit of 'things are as stated' is likely to be essentially negative: we can speak in these terms without any fear of endorsing a relation of correspondence. That at least is the hope; it is not entirely clear that the formula distances us from a reading of 'true' that is in tune with the correspondence theory. We shall shortly give reasons for thinking that this hope is indeed fulfilled, but first it is worth indicating why that theory is one to avoid.

8.2 Truth and correspondence

It is suggested by Dummett that the correspondence theory expresses one important feature of the concept of truth that is not expressed by the formula, 'It is true that *p* if and only if *p*', viz. that a statement is true only if there is something in the world *in virtue of which* it is true (1978, 14). It is not difficult to show that some such claim must be at the heart of a theory which presents us with the following two conditions for the truth of a proposition *p*, so understood that there is a matter for debate: (1) it is a fact that *p*; (2) the proposition corresponds to that fact. Here, plainly, the second condition is redundant: *p* is true if and only if it is a fact that *p*, so there is no need for any more of a correspondence than is already required by this equivalence. All that is implied in this respect is a correlation; not some form of structural mirroring, but simply that for any true proposition there will be an associated fact. However, while that deprives correspondence of any substantial role or content, the theory remains of significance in so far as it is supposed to present us with a correlation between a linguistic item, the proposition, and something in the world, the fact. And that is what Dummett's formulation makes explicit.

This purified version has the merit of diverting attention from correspondence, which has an innocuous enough interpretation, and directing it to the more basic underlying shift in level from words to world. Some such shift likewise seems desirable if there is to be any significance to an invocation of truth conditions in explaining meaning, there being, one would suppose, more to such an appeal if these are thought of as worldly conditions which we represent verbally by means of a paraphrase, than if the paraphrase can be said to constitute such conditions.

There is no denying that if *p* is true then there is something in virtue of which it is true, something that makes it true. That just means that there is something in which its truth consists. Any halfway plausible characterization of what it is for *p* to be true will satisfy this condition. To take a close analogy, if Smith is tall then there is something in virtue of which he is tall, in which his tallness consists: he is tall in virtue of being above average height. The redundancy theory must, if it is to have any plausibility, find room for this notion, and in its extended form it can. What makes (or would make) 'Spring is here' true is spring's being here; that is what the truth of the proposition consists in, and that in terms of the theory's more general formula is a matter of things being as 'Spring is here' states.

It is not difficult to make sense of 'what makes *p* true', but we leave the platitudinous for the problematic if we hold that this phrase can have a worldly reference. It is important to note that this is where the difficulty lies. The objection is not that we are given no more than a triviality with such forms as '"Spring is here" is true in virtue of spring's being here.' If 'spring's being here' picked out something in the world, then it would do just what those who seek a word–world relation ask of it, and it would do this every bit as well as a form of words that might be reckoned less trivial. After all, since the latter will be acceptable only in so far as it has the same reference, it reveals a considerable misconception to think that the apparent triviality of the form of expression used disqualifies it from its intended role.

In 'Spring is here' we can make sense of a referential function in respect both of 'spring' and of 'here', but neither denominates something that makes the proposition true; on the other hand, the move to 'spring's being here' is not a move to a phrase which identifies something in the world, as both season and locality may be said to be. If *making true* were in any sense a causal notion, such an identification could be expected. Perhaps the Almighty could make 'Spring is here' true as a result of His actions, but He would not then make it true in virtue of being, as is surely required, the answering state of affairs. For the proposition to be true it suffices that things should simply be a certain way; the *making true* does not in addition require action upon something. Likewise, what makes Smith tall – his being above average height – does not do so causally. Perhaps his genes and his diet did that, but they are not what his tallness consists in.

But what makes *p* true is the fact that *p*, and that surely is something in the world? Not if a 'linguistic' reading of 'fact' is the right one. On this common view, 'fact' means something like 'true statement', or perhaps 'true thought', so in talking of facts we make no exit from language. However, it is easy to see that these paraphrases will not do: 'He came despite the fact that he was tired' is not to be rendered 'He came despite the true statement that he was tired'; more generally, true statements are statements, facts are not. On the other hand, it is not necessary to regard facts as a subclass of statements or thoughts to challenge the supposed worldly reference. First, while there is no simple equivalence between 'fact' and 'true statement', this does not show that the latter does not offer, in a more roundabout way, a means of re-expressing everything couched in terms of 'fact'. Second, a more accurate formulation of the initial thought is: what makes (or would make) *p* true is its being a fact that *p*, and whether or not facts belong in the world, its being a fact that *p* does not appear to have such a status.

Whether we attack *fact* directly, or the particular gerundials, as 'Smith's being tall', to which it may occur in apposition – or 'its being a fact that *p*' – we do not confirm the belief that something in the world may await identification with such phrases. What has to be justified is the locational implication given with '*in* the world'. With terms in the category of 'fact' the task looks hopeless. It is a fact that herpes is caused by a virus, but we attach no clear sense to the question, where is that fact to be found, when does it exist or occur? Nor can a fact be seen, heard, touched, or otherwise detected, by sense or by science; nor do facts make their presence felt by acting on anything. It is possible to give an account of the grammar of 'fact' in which it is not simply not thought of as being true of a worldly item; it is not true of anything at all (cf. Rundle 1979, chapters 7 and 8). I shall not press this construal, since conditions for being true of something are so generous that some sense can be found for this notion, but whatever is decided here it would seem there could hardly be less to be said for worldly status. It is a triviality to say that facts can be facts about things in the world, but that does not put facts in the world along with such things.

Similar observations apply with the more specific gerundial phrases with which the key moves may be made. *Some* notion of reference may be sustainable in their regard, but in the use relevant to our concern nothing with a worldly location is singled out. Corresponding to the sentence, 'Jean danced', we have the sentence nominalization, 'Jean's dancing'. This has a reading in which it can designate something in the world, a certain activity further describable as elegant and energetic, and which can enter into various worldly relations: it can be observed, imitated, and interrupted, delight the onlookers and disturb the neighbours. In this reading 'Jean's dancing' is patently nominal in its behaviour, as further elaborations – 'Jean's elegant dancing' – reveal. However, other expansions of the phrase are also possible, as 'Jean's dancing gracefully' and 'Jean's not dancing', expansions which are appropriate to contexts in which the phrase has a predominantly *verbal* character. Take 'Jean's dancing gracefully surprised us.' The actual activity can surprise us when we are there to witness it, and 'Jean's graceful dancing surprised us' incorporates an appropriate designation of that activity. But her dancing gracefully can surprise us when we simply learn of its occurrence, where what surprises us is that she danced gracefully, and here there is no singling out of a worldly item; no more than with the suggestion that her dancing gracefully *would* surprise us. Similarly, Jean's dancing gracefully can be said to make it true that Jean is dancing gracefully, but in saying this we are uniting two comparable expressions in a somewhat empty way, not operating at the different levels required to relate word to world. 'Jean's dancing gracefully' is here no more than a grammatical variant on the clause 'that Jean is dancing gracefully'. It does not substitute for 'Jean's graceful dancing', which indeed may designate something in the world, something capable of entering into causal relations, which can be given a time and place of occurrence warranting the locational idiom. And this is one of the more favourable examples. What would make 'No survivor has been sighted' true is no survivor's having been sighted, but it is difficult to find *any* use for 'no survivor's having been sighted' in which it might be thought to identify something in the world. Again, production of the gerundial corresponding to a sentence with dummy 'it' – '"It is nearly Easter" is true in virtue of its being nearly Easter' – is a purely mechanical affair, not a move that waits upon our devising a locational interpretation of 'its being nearly Easter'. Of course, an implication of factuality may be carried by the gerundial, but again that can be accepted without our having to make sense of the question, 'Where is its being nearly Easter?'

How do we lose out, what goes unexplained, if such phrases as 'what makes *p* true' are denied a worldly reference? Certain psychological verbs, notably 'mean' and 'think', provide one of the strongest incentives to put this notion to serious work. Suppose, for instance, that having said 'Help yourself', we clarify our invitation with 'I meant: have one or two chocolates, not the whole lot.' In offering such a clarification we need not be disclosing to our audience something that we had made explicit to ourselves when first we spoke. Hence the question: how can it be true that we meant just this if there is not something about us in virtue of which it is true that we did? (Cf. Kripke 1982, chapter 2).

In *Zettel* Wittgenstein remarks: 'The mistake is to say that there is anything that meaning something consists in' (§16). This is acceptable if taken as a denial that any act or process, whether antecedent to or accompanying the utterance, is to be identified with one's meaning something, but to say this is not to say that there is then nothing that makes 'I meant *x*' true: it is true in virtue of my meaning *x*, where 'my meaning *x*' is now the gerundial, which lays no claim to identify anything with spatio-temporal co-ordinates, whether in my mind or without. But that is not a peculiarity of 'mean'; it holds for any verb in this use. Application of 'what makes *p* true' leaves things as they are, engaging us in no commitments of a substantial kind; it in no way prejudges the precise logic of 'mean', but will be consistent with whatever proves to be an appropriate account of the verb. That is where the real work lies, work which was carried through to some degree in §6.1 but which is not assisted by intoning the empty maxim: when *A* means *x* there is something which makes '*A* means *x*' true.

An attempt to extract something of substance from the notion of 'something in virtue of which *p* is true' may also be directed at conditionals, as 'You would be happier if you changed your job.' According to Dummett, if such a proposition is true, there must be a non-trivial answer to the question, 'What makes it true?' (Dummett 1976, 89). This can be agreed, but because of the meaning of the given words, with 'would' in particular playing a crucial role. It is not that we have a sentence with a certain interpretation, together with an independent principle which, applied to the sentence, yields the conclusion as advanced. An analogy is provided by the claim that a child cannot *just* be disobedient, that there has to be a form that its disobedience takes, a particular disobedient act. This is forced upon us by the character of 'disobedient', not by some independent principle.

The debate between realist and anti-realist provides the setting for a discussion of conditionals in these terms, and the same area is home to confusions generated by 'what makes *p* true' in its application to past-tense propositions. If, as is supposed, what makes *p* true is something having a datable reality, then it risks being lost with the passage of time, and we are left wondering what there can be to make such a proposition true. So, let *p* be 'On Midsummer's Day in 1447 the temperature in York fell below freezing.' There may be no supporting records, but our normal understanding of *p* would be as a proposition about conditions which could have been ascertained at the time rather than about what can be ascertained now. We should happily agree that *p* is either true or false, again thinking of the possibilities as envisaged from the past rather than from the present perspective. Matters alter dramatically, however, if it is argued that if *p is* true, then there must be something *now* that makes it true. 'There is something that makes *p* true' is then not just an innocent if empty gloss on '*p* is true', but a seemingly formidable obstacle to applying the laws of classical logic.

This suspect transformation depends on attaching a particular significance to '*p* is true'. To see what the rationale is that in fact underlies choice of tense, consider the alternative given by 'If *p was* true, . . . '. In general, the point of introducing 'true' is to align the supposition with someone's statement, actual or imagined. Thus, 'Suppose it is true that the temperature fell below freezing' is geared to a present statement, 'The temperature fell below freezing', whereas 'Suppose it was true that the temperature fell below freezing' can also accommodate a statement in the same terms but made in the past. In terms of the suggested paraphrase of 'true', it is a matter of supposing that, as *is* stated, *p*, and supposing that, as *was* stated, *p*. That is where the significance of the tense lies; it has nothing to do with the implication that there still is, rather than just was, something making the proposition true. This account needs refining for the case where 'was' is replaceable by 'were', but again without sustaining this implication.

To see the significance of 'It is true that *p*' over the bare *p* in terms of this allusion to a stating has every appearance of trivializing truth. There has to be more to the concept than can be provided by this secondary feature. And of course there is more to the form with 'true': whatever significance there was to the simple *p* – which is just what the formula in terms of things being as stated extracts. However unremarkable it may seem, this formula is the one to invoke to get the measure of truth, a formula which makes plain how the allusion to a statement arises along with an appraisal in the most significant respect possible for a statement. It is important to note that in giving this as our account we are not joining with those who consider it sufficient to observe that utterance of 'It is true that *p*' serves to confirm or re-assert *p*. The formula is grammatically equipped, in a way this observation plainly is not, to clarifying what it is for *p* to be true, so can cope with such contexts as 'If *p* is true, . . . ', as well as revealing what true statements have in common. As already noted, it is also important that we stop with this formula, resisting the temptation to read into 'true' any condition which, like assertibility, might prevent it from being assimilated into its associated proposition. We shall return to these topics, along with the wider debate between realist and anti-realist in which they figure.

8.3 Truth conditions and meaning

It may seem that, while the notion of correspondence has no work to do in an account of truth, we cannot ignore the fundamental insight of the theory in which it is enshrined: if *p* is true there will be something in the world that makes it true. If the preceding argument is correct, even this minimal version founders; it is not the correspondence theory purged of a questionable relation of correspondence and retaining only that element whose acceptability all must acknowledge, but it preserves the basic error of that theory. The duality required for truth is no more than is implied by talk of things being as stated. The redundancy theory was criticized for making use of this notion, but because of the damage thus done to the claim that 'true' is superfluous, not because there is anything amiss with the formula – understood as providing a logical equivalent; it would be going too far to claim synonymy. Nor is there a commitment to correspondence in its use. If 'things' did duty for a designation of a fact, and if the latter were 'in the world', then the formula could be exploited by the correspondence theory, but since facts lack the required status, there is no such threat. True, the idea of a duality, of something to which our words are fitted, looks very close to the idea of something which makes our statement true, but it is clear that the persons and things which may have the former role do not enjoy the latter.

What now are the prospects for explaining meaning in terms of truth conditions? Not at all good, if knowledge of the meaning of *p* is made out to be knowledge of a paraphrase of *p*; on the other hand, to speak of what makes *p* true is not to speak of what, in the event of its truth, would constitute a worldly correlate of *p*; nor, as we shall see, is a suitable extralinguistic item introduced by the noun clause in such forms as '"Television encourages violence" means that television encourages violence'.

However, these futile manoeuvres do not exhaust the possibilities. We saw that the redundancy theory in its primitive form was not congenial to a truth-conditional explanation of meaning, but we also saw that while such an account breaks down with its assimilation of 'knowing (etc.) that "*p*" is true' to 'knowing (etc.) that *p*', the successor to that account is not open to the same objection. Knowing that 'Television encourages violence' is true is on that view a matter of knowing that things are as stated by one who utters these words, and knowing what the statement means can correspondingly be taken as a matter of knowing how things have to be for it to be true.

Can this approach be faulted? It is clear that an explanation which does no more than specify truth conditions is going to be insufficiently discriminating, given that sentences which differ in meaning can sometimes plausibly be said to be true in the same conditions. As has often been observed, making synonymy hinge on such agreement leads to a conflation of all mathematical truths – being always true, they are true in the same range of circumstances, so, on this account, 'say the same thing'. Even with pairs which come as close as 'It's not something I should want myself' and 'I shouldn't want it', the presence in the one of meaningful terms absent from the other gives sufficient reason to speak of a difference in meaning overall, though of course the two cannot be prised apart by relating either to circumstances which are differently relevant as regards truth. Similarly with the subtle difference between 'It is fair . . . ' and 'It is not unfair . . . ', or between 'He suffered' and 'He did suffer', differences which a preoccupation with truth is likely to render incomprehensible.

It is held that true mathematical propositions are true in the same circumstances, but is this so on every way of reckoning sameness? Surely, by taking into account the particular content and structure of propositions, it must be possible to define a notion of truth conditions with a specificity which matches the possible diversity of subject matter, so that, e.g., propositions about ellipses will not be true in the same conditions as propositions about complex numbers. And such an approach need not be confined to pure mathematics. Consider the pair of sentences, 'Three-quarters of the children were present' and 'One in four of the children was absent.' In so far as we might wish to speak here of a difference in meaning, it will be for the reason indicated, each sentence having terms with no equivalent in the other, but we can still make truth the key notion if the identity of the unshared terms is determined by what they are true and false of. On that test there is a clear divergence in meaning between 'present' and 'absent', and one that is passed on to the larger contexts. This attention to the individual word is particularly desirable with mathematical propositions, given the unclarity of 'the conditions in which *p* is true' in their regard.

However, not only do we have to deal with terms whose grammar takes them right outside the scope of considerations of truth, but familiar difficulties also remain with terms which are co-extensive yet non-synonymous. Take the pair 'log *e*' and '1'. Granted that substitution of the one for the other has no repercussions on the truth of their larger contexts, the difference in the concepts exploited by the complex expression is still an overriding difference as far as synonymy is concerned: we can have an understanding of unity without having the slightest familiarity with either logarithms or the exponential function. Nor is it satisfactory to leave it to ascriptions of belief and the like to show up the difference, to make use of the circumstance that '*A* thinks that log *e* is even' could be true, yet '*A* thinks that 1 is even' false. How might this (clearly logical) 'could' be justified other than by appeal to a possibility which the difference in meaning is seen to leave open? Certainly, it would be absurd to suppose that the possibility is first established and a disagreement at the level of these expressions only then inferred.

Although substitutivity *salva veritate* is inadequate as a sufficient condition for synonymy, its shortcomings can to some extent be remedied. Sameness in application may not ensure sameness in meaning, but it is clear that a *difference* in the latter is assured by a difference in application. We can extract from this a condition that comes close to being necessary and sufficient for synonymy if we require that, with respect to the two phrases under comparison, each meaningful term (or part of a term) in the one be matched by a term in the other which agrees merely in its application. Starting at the other end, the suggestion would be that for terms which agree in not subdividing into further meaningful parts, agreement in application then counts as *sufficient* for synonymy. When that point is reached – as, e.g., with the pair 'wager' and 'bet' – have we not eliminated every possible divergence which might give content to a difference in meaning?

This approach to synonymy is a considerable advance over one that fails to give full weight to the individual terms which go to make up the larger unit – the kind of Platonism which sees the important questions as decided by contemplation of what is expressed rather than of what expresses. However, can we be confident that we have synonymy so long as truth and truth alone is allowed to be decisive? There is an obstacle in that 'what *w* is true of' operates at a less discriminating level than does the simple *w*, demarcating a range of subjects rather than the more specific *character* of the subjects with which *w* is associated. The possibility is thus not excluded that, despite the non-synonymy of *w* with *v*, 'what *w* is true of' and 'what *v* is true of' identify exactly the same individuals. Everything that has weight has volume, and vice versa, but weight and volume remain distinguishable properties. The problem is not avoided by requiring that we rule out differences in application in the way proposed.

Perhaps this is not an insuperable obstacle, but finding a way around it does not help when truth simply has no application to the given terms. Furthermore, even without going to this extreme, there are other difficulties to be reckoned with. Consider again 'almost' and 'nearly'. Not identical in meaning, but substitution may proceed less than smoothly without truth value being affected, a degree of stiltedness or unidiomatic character being all that results. We say

'Almost nobody agreed', not 'Nearly nobody agreed', yet the inappropriateness of the latter does not amount to falsity. Similarly with the pairs 'probable' and 'likely', and 'spoke' and 'has spoken'.

How serious are these divergences? The problem would appear to lie with 'false'. There is a difference between 'He spoke' and 'He has spoken', but while the wrong choice may incur a charge of incorrectness, to speak of falsity is to go too far, with its suggestion that we might actually affirm the negation of the statement substituted. The difficulty is particularly acute when the statement does not even have a negation, in the sense of a contradictory. A good illustration of the possibilities is presented by if-clauses. In some instances a conditional has a natural contradictory, but much of the disorderly behaviour of this form stems from the more usual absence of an appropriate negation. Consider 'You will be ill if you eat this soup', where the role of the if-clause compares with that of a temporal term such as 'tonight' in its relation to negation. If someone rejects 'You will be ill tonight' with 'You will not be ill tonight', his dispute may be with the temporal condition; not that the person will not be ill *tout court*, but that he will not be ill at the time specified. Similarly, the 'not' bears upon the if-clause in 'You will not be ill if you eat this soup' if the claim is that the person will not be ill as a result of eating the soup; not that eating the soup is a means for avoiding illness, though this latter is the likely reading if we reverse the order of the clauses, taking the if-clause outside the scope of the negation: 'If you eat this soup you will not be ill.'

Simply choosing the more favourable order is, however, no guarantee that the if-clause will be sufficiently integrated within the main clause to behave as an adverbial subject to negation – e.g., 'He will buy the property if it is large enough' – and with other conjunctions, as 'although', a suitable contradictory is more generally unavailable. I reveal a misconception in saying 'The drum was heavy, although it contained only water', heaviness not running counter to what can be expected in such a case. However, while an explicit affirmation that heaviness is thus counter could be rejected with 'false', 'although' does not present that condition in an explicit form. Because '*p* although *q*' does not have a contradictory, the notion of falsity in its regard may be obscure, even though its truth remains relatively unproblematic.

Can we then settle for 'true' and 'not true' as making the appropriate division, the latter being broader than 'false'? Not as far as 'although' is concerned, since rejecting '*p* although *q*' as not true surely requires us to reject one of the clauses; it does not negate the relation given by the conjunction in the way possible for 'if' or 'because'. Again, 'but' signals a shift in theme, while 'and' signals continuity, but lack of contrast or continuity is not a suitable basis for the appraisal 'not true'. Finally, 'not true' may be an improvement on 'false' with other types of term, but the condemnation which it gives is still excessive with respect to the erroneous use of 'nearly' for 'almost', as also, in all likelihood, with such pairs as 'hit' and 'strike', 'shut' and 'close', and 'end' and 'finish'.

The example of 'although' takes us to the major problem for the supposed centrality of truth, namely, the presupposition of a certain grammar. Our characterization of the assertoric form fastened on verbal phrases. As indicated when the relevance of truth was initially canvassed, this extends to a large slice of the lexicon. Subordinate clauses, for instance, can often be thought of as presenting complex predicates in a way that brings them into the scheme, since they may become the focus of affirmation and denial in much the same way as a simpler adverb. But while we can handle a multitude of phrases within this framework, we are throughout working at the predicate end of the sentence, dealing with variations and complications of the central theme - being truly or falsely affirmed – and where a particular meaning is reflected in just what such a phrase is, or can fail to be, true of. However, this is not the right pattern for, e.g., pronouns. French *vous* and *tu* are differently used, but misuse need not issue in falsity, a failure to be true, or meaninglessness. More generally, the terms that occur at the subject end of the sentence do not receive a characterization that ties them to occurrences within just such sentences, but, as already observed, a word such as 'this' can be explained in a way that is indifferent to its surrounding verbal context. Indeed, what holds for 'this' holds generally for the kinds of phrase which may occur at the same point, phrases like 'every dog', 'several candles', 'some flowers', and the rest. Truth is a dominant concern with the declarative form, but that does not require a uniform account of the role of any and every term that can have a place within that form. Nor do we have to force 'this' and its ilk into the ill-fitting role of being true of something.

What is the basic reason for regarding truth as central to meaning? The standard reply would appeal to a correlation of the sentence with its truth conditions, whereas for reasons indicated the advantages would seem to lie with an approach aimed at the individual word, and laying emphasis on the non-contingent tie between 'what *w* means' and 'what (kind of thing) *w* is true of'. However, not only has it still to be shown how the gap between these is to be narrowed, but the leading idea which the latter embodies and which makes for its appeal is surely more general – that of a term's being *applicable*, of its being correctly used in certain circumstances, whether or not we have the particular grammatical form that makes talk of truth possible. A conjunction is correctly used if the sentences it links have the requisite character, but it does not have the role of affirming that character of anything. Again, in the broader class of adverbials to which conjunctions belong we have terms such as 'however', 'besides', and 'all the same'. These occur in association with declarative sentences, but no alteration to possible truth value is effected by prefacing 'I should like to try' with 'all the same', or adding 'besides' to 'You never know what might happen.' However, this disconnection from truth value does not threaten learnability, or rule out any notion of correct application. Likewise with the distinction between the perfect and the simple past, as 'He has whistled' and 'He whistled'.

Then, of course, we have the large area of linguistic meaning which pertains to force, and for which truth has largely no relevance. We do not *assert* a desire for action when we issue an imperative, nor a desire for an answer when we ask a question. Even if the words of a question, an exclamation, or the expression of a wish have a use that is somehow parasitic on a declarative use, there will be a facet of meaning not taken in by the latter. Such cases may be avoided simply by declaring that we are not currently concerned with meaning in this sense, but merely to say this is not to ensure that there is the supposed difference in sense. Indeed, the danger in not reckoning force to the normal category of meaning is that truth in consequence takes up a greater proportion of the remaining semantic space, so that we attach excessive significance to it.

Let us return to the example of 'The drum was heavy, although it contained only water.' If our quarrel is with 'although', we cannot correct the speaker by contradicting what he has stated; not even with 'It is not true that . . . ' do we achieve the desired focus. On the other hand, the necessity of a more roundabout form of repudiation – 'What do you mean? Heaviness is just what you'd expect, given that it contained water' – merely reflects a difference in the way the conjunction presents its relation, rather than a radical difference in the kind of relation presented. Thus, suppose our concern is to give a fruitful categorization of sentence connectives generally. We shall be interested in such divisions as those between the temporal, the consequential, and the contrastive, but in explaining these categories we shall not be inhibited by the failure of the truth-conditional approach. Because of the recognizable character of sentences which find their way into such frames as '*p*, although *q*' or '*p*. However, *q*', it is clear enough how a person can come to an appreciation of the kind of relation in which the sentences stand. For instance, we use 'however' when what follows presents a countervailing consideration to what preceded. The fact that we do not *assert* that the relation holds does not leave us uncomprehending; it is just that an assertion would incorporate an expression for the relation within a particular grammatical form, a form which has advantages in the way it enables us to endorse or reject instances of the relation, but which is not a *sine qua non* of intelligibility. Given that no significant obstacles are put in the way of our understanding when truth ceases to be of relevance, the pressure is off us to tolerate the distortions which inevitably follow so long as we insist on finding a place for this concept at every point.

Finally, even when truth's claim to explain meaning meets with no opposition from grammar, it has still to face the apparent priority of meaning itself. The definition of truth in terms of things being as stated might have been expected to draw a charge of narrowness: could it not as well be a matter of things being as hypothesized, feared, or imagined? The close tie between truth and the specifically assertoric use provides the basis for a reply to this objection, but not a reply that meets the related point about meaning. Learning the meaning of 'allotropic' is as much learning how things are hypothesized to be by one who hypothesizes that *x* is allotropic as it is learning how things are stated to be by one who states that this is how *x* is. Uses of language in which we lay claim to truth presuppose a meaning for the words enlisted, much as, in Wittgenstein's analogy, measuring presupposes a system of measurement (*RFM* I–156), the relevance of truth remaining simply as was noted at the outset: because of the two poles of affirmation and denial offered by the declarative sentence we are able, with certain words, to bring matters of meaning into focus; attending to no more than what affects truth enables us to set aside, in Fregean fashion, the extraneous considerations that threaten to find their way into an account of meaning when a concept as all-embracing as that of use is invoked. Important though this may be, it is the extent of truth's relevance, not the beginnings of an account which takes in all types of word, clause, and complex sentence.

9

Meaning and Grammar

While he may not have said 'Don't ask for the meaning; ask for the use', words which we can more safely attribute to Wittgenstein are 'Don't ask for a definition; get clear about the grammar' (*AWL* 164). A definition of number is not what is needed to remove the puzzlement of the question, 'What *is* a number?', but for that we must get clear about the grammar of the word 'number' and of the numerals. Likewise with 'mean' and 'meaning'. In Wittgenstein's broad sense of the term, the grammar of these words is our abiding concern, given our aim of commanding a clearer view of their behaviour – though, for reasons already indicated, that is not to say that a definition would come amiss. There is also a place for grammatical investigation of a more conventional variety; in particular, some of the lingering problems posed by the larger linguistic units require attention to grammatical detail. The results of our inquiry will be largely negative; some confusions may be removed, but beyond that it is what we do *not* say that is important, especially on the topic of clauses, a fertile source of misconceived theories of content if the grammar is misconstrued.

9.1 Meaning and reference

In attempting to explain how the meaning of a word can be something external to language, we naturally invoke what Wittgenstein speaks of as a 'transitive' use of 'mean' (*BB* 161). However, we must take care here, since the more plausible cases are likely not to involve word meaning as in '*si* means "if"'. As already remarked, a word can hardly mean something in the way that a person can, and this consideration makes itself felt in a number of ways. The sentences, 'By "estragon" he means "tarragon"' and '"estragon" means "tarragon"', are equally acceptable, but once 'mean' takes a referential complement, a personal subject is favoured: 'By "estragon" he means tarragon' or 'By "estragon" he means a certain aromatic plant', rather than '"estragon" means tarragon' or '"estragon" means a certain aromatic plant', where 'means' gets drawn, quite inappropriately, into the reading in which a personal subject is specified.

We note that a passive form for 'mean' is often awkward, e.g., with '"lie" is meant by "prevaricate"' and 'Fire is meant by smoke'. Here 'mean' comes from (N), but since we can say 'It was meant as a surprise' and 'That is the one that was meant' – 'mean' now in a (P) use – it would seem that we are simply witnessing a further aspect of the distinction between (N) and (P) uses, resistance to the passive revealing itself as a mark of the former. So, the form '"lie" is meant by "prevaricate"' forces "prevaricate" into an inappropriate 'agentive' role, as if it were a matter of something meant by the word in the way it might be meant by a person. Similarly, if someone observes, apropos of one's car, 'There's a funny noise when you reverse', we may ask, 'What does that mean?', but not so readily, 'What is meant by that?', the latter being geared more to the case where some person means something by the noise.

However, if this approach is correct, how is it that we cannot say 'Smoke is what is meant by fire', but can say 'Smoke is what is meant by *fumée*'? It has been suggested by Stampe that there is a derivational rule which accounts for the acceptability of the latter – which is a cleft passive rather than a passive *tout court*. This rule prescribes that if, say, 'Smoke is what *fumée* means' derives from the string, 'By *fumée* Agent means smoke', then the further form, 'Smoke is what is meant by *fumée*' is allowable. Since 'Fire is what smoke means' will not have such a source, the parallel form is not allowed (Stampe 1968, XI).

For anyone sceptical of the value of appeals to supposed derivational histories, the explanation in this form will not count for much. Moreover, it would seem that the proper order has been reversed: if a certain form is (un)acceptable, then we can have a rule which prohibits or permits it, but the rule follows on rather than determines (un)acceptability. Nor, furthermore, is a passive allowable only with the cleft construction, as 'By *fumée* is meant smoke' demonstrates. However, it is possible to extract a less questionable point from this explanation, a point which supports the claim that only 'mean' in (P) will go into the passive. We might suggest that, despite appearances, the form 'Smoke is what is meant by *fumée*' does not draw on 'mean' from (N), does not arrogate an agentive role to *fumée* in a way that makes it impossible to suppose a suppressed reference to a human subject, someone meaning something by the word. Thus, the corresponding direct question, 'What is meant by *fumée*?' is rendered in German as *Was ist mit 'fumée' gemeint*? Again, while we can say 'By "the tricolour" is meant the French flag', it is not incomprehensible that '"the tricolour" means the French flag' should be less acceptable. These uses of 'mean' are to be distinguished, in so far as a personal subject is implied with the former: the 'by' here is instrumental, not agentive, its real attachment being shown by replacing 'is meant' by 'people mean', to give 'By "the tricolour" people mean the French flag.'

The awkwardness of such a sentence as '"argon" means one of the inert gases' carries over to a rephrasal with 'meaning', the noun occurring for the most part only as a nominalization of 'mean' in its 'intransitive' use. In either case – i.e., with '*w* means . . . ', or with 'The meaning of *w* is . . . ' – we prefer the phrases which follow to be accompanied by quotes or some similar device indicating that any referential use has been suspended: 'The meaning of "A.C." is "alternating current"' rather than 'The meaning of "A.C." is alternating current.' If we wish to associate a word as subject with a referential complement we do better to invoke 'signify' rather than 'mean': 'but' signifies rather than means a certain contrast, and 'yes' signifies rather than means assent. Use 'mean' here and we are threatened with the unwanted natural meaning: '"yes" means assent' is not so much 'The meaning of "yes" is assent' as '(An utterance of) "yes" means that the speaker assents.' Similarly, 'alas' means grief or concern in the sense that utterance of the word means that the speaker is grieved or concerned. Likewise with symbols other than words: the scales in the hands of the figure of justice signify rather than mean impartiality.

The distinction between the (N) and (P) uses of 'mean' and the general restriction of referential complements to the latter have a bearing on questions of the 'ontology' of meaning, on the interpretation of such notions as those of *reference*, *existence*, and *entity* in its regard. To begin with a general observation, we note that this last is likely to provide the most prolific source of avoidable confusion: on the one hand, it is felt that talk of reference and existence goes hand in hand with applicability of 'entity; on the other hand, since the model on which use of the term is based is frequently that of a physical object, and since talk of meaning, say, does not appear to be talk about the physical, doubt comes to attach to the allied notions, and meanings come to be admitted as no more than 'postulates'. Or, while some may pride themselves on avoiding meanings altogether, others may consider themselves bold in unashamedly accepting them. But, of course, it is a mistake to think that unwelcome implications are to be avoided, uncertainties removed, by a retreat to postulation. No clarification is offered to the notions used in the scheme by moving from outright affirmation to mere postulation, but as far as meaning itself is concerned, if the notion is incoherent, then it makes no more sense to postulate meanings than to affirm their existence unreservedly, while if it is intelligible to speak of existence in this connection, then questions of existence become questions of fact.

For those who wish to bandy 'entity' about, the right procedure is first to decide how this semi-technical term is going to be interpreted, and then to see whether the grammar of 'meaning' allows of any association between the two. Compare the parallel issue concerning events. When it makes sense to speak of *x* as existing, falsity of '*x* exists' will be of some consequence, in so far as the reality of *x* has been denied. But if, as with events, it is not proper to speak in this way – events do not exist, they occur or take place – the impropriety of '*x* exists' has no such consequences; in particular, denying existence to events does not commit us to saying that nothing ever happens. Likewise with 'entity'. We have to decide whether this ill-defined term is going to embrace events, but whichever way the decision goes there is nothing to fear: accepting events into our ontology does not leave us with a welter of strange entities – but only, perhaps, with a strange sense of 'entity' – while excluding them does not make for the unreality of everything that happens. (For further discussion cf. Rundle 1979, §23, §47.)

In the case of meaning, it might be suggested that there is a harmless enough sense in which the meaning of a word could be an entity, viz. when what is meant is so characterizable. In the same vein, the meaning of a word might be a relation, an activity, or an illness. This way of speaking is perhaps at the back of our minds when we find it paradoxical to be told that meaning is always *within* language. It may indeed be harmless, though, as mentioned, it is unusual to nominalize the verb 'mean' in this use, so somewhat misleading to pass from the (P) use given with 'when what is meant is so characterizable' to the (N) use found in 'meaning'. Certainly, such a construal is not true to our use of the noun in most contexts: although sense of some sort can be made of 'The meaning of "gout" is a certain illness', we should not go on to say that a person was suffering from the meaning of the word. Again, even if it may be said that the meaning of 'parsley' is a common herb, to forget that meaning is not to forget the herb, and if the meaning of the word changes, it is once more not the herb that is affected.

The use of 'meaning' in these and similar contexts – e.g., explain, find out, discuss the meaning of *w* – is best understood in clausal terms. To know the weight or age of something is to know what it weighs or how old it is. Similarly, to forget the meaning of 'parsley' is not to forget the thing meant, the herb, but to forget what the word means – a matter of forgetting the answer to a question. The possibility of such a parsing for 'meaning' perhaps gives *some* sense, at least in this kind of case, to the idea that we remain within language: as equivalent to 'what "parsley" means', 'the meaning of "parsley"' can be said to specify – though hardly to *refer* to – a question, something patently linguistic. By contrast, when you can speak, e.g., of pointing to what is meant, the *what* is a relative pronoun, 'mean' has the sense of *meinen,* and a rephrasal with the noun 'meaning' is strained.

How does the question of meanings as entities fare when we consider the noun in this clausal use? Should we say that the meaning of a word is an abstract entity? That is hardly the conclusion to draw. What completes 'The meaning of *w* is . . . ' might, with some awkwardness, name something concrete, or it might, with appropriate elucidation, name an abstraction, but while 'the meaning of *w*' itself appears to have a designating function when a predicate such as 'is clear' completes it into a sentence, the breakdown of 'meaning' into a clause, or some other species of construction based around a verb, gives us reason to treat it as a term with a grammar that sets it apart from phrases which denote something, of whatever character. That at least is so on one way of testing for reference. The meaning of *kurt* is the same as the meaning of 'short', yet knowing, explaining, or forgetting the one is not knowing, etc., the other. A quite remarkable circumstance, if the German speaker's knowledge is of one and the same thing as the English speaker's, but of course there is nothing perplexing here: the seeming reference soon vanishes to leave us saying merely that we might know what the one word means but not the other. 'What *kurt* means is "short"' is not like 'What you are reading is confidential.' The latter uses the what-clause to refer to something which is then described; the former does not, but, as is appropriate to the interrogative pronoun, it *states* what the word means. We have alluded to the view that the meaning of a word can be considered a 'theoretical construct', justified, perhaps, by the success of the semantic theory in which it has a place. This may seem at least a *safe* supposition, given that it makes no demands on extralinguistic reality, but it fails through imposing an absurdly inappropriate grammar on the word.

I do not say that there is no sense in which reference may have application with respect to 'meaning', but because it will have to adjust to the particular clausal character of the noun, it will not be comparable with paradigmatic instances of the notion. Compare the interrogative clause in 'Why he did it is not clear.' We might pass from this to 'That is not clear' or 'Something is not clear', moves whose acceptability may legitimize *some* notion of reference on the part of the clause. At all events, our everyday propositions to the effect that such-and-such a word has a meaning, that several meanings of a word exist, are not put at risk by the failure of a philosopher's attempt to fit them into his ontological framework, and there is at least one obvious alternative to associating the notion of there being a meaning with a complementary referential use of language. As with 'Her age is 47' or 'His weight is 12 stone', so 'The meaning of *kurt* is "short"' is not an identity, nor does the notion of *describing* the meaning apply any more than it does with the clausal form, 'what *w* means is . . . '. But a meaning, like someone's age or weight, can be stated, and statability, rather than designatability, is a more appropriate semantic function with which to align the existence of meaning.

9.2 *Statements of meaning*

If the 'ontological' problem posed by meaning is largely imaginary, real enough difficulties of clarification are presented by such everyday locutions as '*auch* means "too"' or 'The meaning of "revest" is "restore"'. Here we see the grammar of 'mean' and 'meaning' at its most refractory.

The problematic sentences come in a variety of forms – '*auch* means *too*' and '*auch* means: too' are others – this variety perhaps reflecting some uncertainty as to what the word which gives the explanation is actually *doing*. The different forms serve to indicate that we are not making a standard use of the word; on the other hand, while reference does not appear to be the role enlisted, it is, as has often been observed, not a matter of the straightforward *mention* of a word or phrase that the version with quotes might suggest, for we cannot introduce 'the word' so as to give '*auch* means the word "too"', or 'The meaning of *auch* is the word "too"'. Contrast 'mean' (P), where, e.g., a speaker can mean every word he says.

One suggestion which would have us think in terms of mention rather than use is that 'means' in these contexts abbreviates 'means the same as' – and similarly with the noun 'meaning' – a suggestion which may encourage the feeling that such statements of meaning are peculiarly frustrating: if, in response to a request to explain the meaning of a word, *w*, we are merely informed, in effect, that it has the same meaning as another word, *v*, is there not a sense in which we have not as yet been told what the meaning of *w* is? This may have been one of the considerations which weighed with Wittgenstein when he proposed that we fasten on *use* in preference to *meaning* (*AWL* 44).

Consider a Frenchman who knows no English. Can it be said that by *presbyte* he means 'long-sighted'? Is it not more that he means by *presbyte* what we mean by 'long-sighted'? Perhaps this latter is all that the former involves, but the former does seem allowable, there being also a sense in which a Frenchman could be said to know that *presbyte* means 'long-sighted', given merely that he knows the meaning of the French term. Similarly, watching a child at his music lessons, might I not conclude that he knows that *piano* means *softly*, without making any assumptions about his command of English? If this is accepted, then we cannot allow the expansion of 'mean' to 'mean the same as'. Moreover, to construe the verb in this way would imply just that symmetry in the behaviour of the quoted expressions in '"*w*" means "*v*"' the absence of which gave rise to our problem: 'the word' being insertible only initially, we surely have in this feature a clue to, or at least a reflection of, the different behaviour of the second term.

Given that *mention* does not afford the right characterization, is it possible that some notion of reference is after all at work with these formulae? If so, then it should be possible to vary the form which it takes; nothing should hang on the choice of *explanans* beyond its being a synonym – unlike cases of straight mention or citation – but if a German can be said to know that *lang* means *long* then we should be able to say that he knows it means *largo* or *comprido* or *lungo* indifferently. And this is a consequence that does find some support in the use we make of the construction: the orthographic or phonetic identities of these words may be to the fore when it is a matter of direct citation, but for purposes of accuracy in stating what is known, one is as good as the other.

This hospitality shown towards different synonyms is very much like the hospitality towards alternative designations of an object displayed by referential contexts. However, reference is hardly the notion we want. Not merely is it strained even when it makes some sense with this use of 'mean', but sense itself is lacking with, e.g., '*le* means "the"' or '*Qui va là*? means "Who goes there?"' The impression of reference is explained, I suggest, not only by the formal parallel shown by substitutability, but, equally important, by the mere fact that the speaker will typically know the meaning of *v* when he says '*w* means *v*'. *w* is here paired with a term *v* whose use or application the speaker is able to bring to mind, and the ready association which he may accordingly make with the relevant property, action, relation, or whatever will account for the impression that a referential use is being made of the word. To be satisfactory as an explanation, '*w* means *v*' must display a familiar word *with* the right meaning, but the word is not in addition called upon to *refer* to that meaning, or to anything else.

How then is substitutability here justified? As I construe the claim that someone ignorant of English may none the less be said to know that *lang* means 'long', it might also be expressed by saying that he knows that *lang* has the meaning it has, where this receives its non-trivial interpretation – one in which someone may well be ignorant in this respect. Staying closer to the given words, it is a matter of knowing that *lang* has the meaning given by 'long', where it is not implied that the person knows that 'long' gives the meaning, but where 'the meaning given by "long"' is *my* way of specifying the meaning, chosen with an eye to what my audience will, I hope, find intelligible; at all events, it is a term which I am in a position to use to indicate the meaning, and without any implication that the word would be familiar to the person. It compares with a possible use of 'the one that I am holding' in 'He knows that the real diamond is the one that I am holding', where the emphasis is on knowing the identity of the diamond – he knows that it is this one - rather than that the person knows that I am *holding* the diamond in question. The rejected reading, or at least the reading that is not suited to our present purpose, would be: he knows that 'long' gives the meaning of *lang,* which clearly does demand knowledge of a fact about the English word 'long'.

I mentioned above the possible frustration which may be induced by explanations of meaning in terms of synonyms: we ask for the meaning of a word and all we are given is another word with the same meaning. What, we might wonder, does our dissatisfied enquirer expect? It is trivial to observe that you can be *told* the meaning of *w* only by being given other words, but while verbs like 'tell' and 'state' make that demand, it in no way follows that knowing or having a meaning is knowing or having a synonym. However, further comment on the equivalences, '*w* means *v*', which give rise to the dissatisfaction may be helpful, and for this we may go back to the comparison which 'mean' and 'meaning' allow with other middle verbs and their cognate nouns.

As already noted, there are numerous nouns which, like 'meaning', are formed from a verb or adjective, and which paraphrase in such a way that the latter, or some related form, comes to feature explicitly. Terms in this class are 'weight', 'age' and 'price', and typical contexts are given by such phrases as 'look up the weight', 'calculate its age', and 'know the price', with clausal expansions as 'look up how much it weighs', 'calculate how old it is', and 'know what it costs'. 'Mean' comes close to 'weigh' and 'measure' in its grammar, and the contrast which 'The jar weighed 3 lb' offers to 'He weighed the jar' throws into relief the absence of the pattern of doer-and-thing-done-to in the former that we also exclude with '*rien* means "nothing"'. Note too how the passive is possible with the latter use of 'weigh' only: 'The jar was weighed by him', but not '3 lb was weighed by the jar', which would require that the 'by' be agentive.

Such a sentence as 'The weight of the jar is 3 lb' offers useful points of comparison with 'The meaning of *rien* is "nothing"'. There is some strain in saying that the phrase '3 lb' *designates* a weight, but the weight is certainly not the actual expression, '3 lb'. Rather, this serves to *give* the weight, much as '3 miles' may specify a distance, or, of course, as the word 'nothing' can be said to give the meaning of *rien.* It would be wrong to insist that 'The weight of the jar is 3 lb' should be read as 'The weight of the jar is the same as the weight of 3 lb.' Not because this would have to be false; rather, as a standard measure of weight, '3 lb' gives the weight directly, whereas the form with 'same' is appropriate to the case where the object weighed is being measured, not against a standard, but against something that is considered just some other object that might be weighed. Similarly with 'The meaning of *w* is *v*.' The rationale behind this construction is not that the meaning is the *word v*, nor that *v* designates the meaning, but simply that *v* purportedly *has* the meaning, and, being familiar in that capacity, can serve as a standard. In view of the contrast with 'The meaning of *w* is the same as the meaning of *v*', it would seem fitting to speak of 'The meaning of *w* is *v*' as giving a *direct* specification of meaning. It may appear to be merely a pragmatic consideration to say that the latter is appropriate to the case where the speaker knows the meaning of *v*, but – and this simply repeats the point made with respect to the verb 'mean' – there is a possible divergence in truth value between 'He knows that the meaning of *w* is the same as the meaning of *v*' and 'He knows that the meaning of *w* is *v*' which shows it to be more than this.

In saying 'The meaning of *rien* is "nothing"' we give the meaning of *rien,* but all this means is that, in line with the customary use of this form, it is supposed that the meaning of the *definiens* is *known.* It is not as if the construction were endowed with some special power not available to the form with 'same'. That is, the directness of the specification just *is* a matter of the particular way of taking the expression that is open once knowledge of meaning is presupposed. Still, this does at least show that there is *something* that counts as a direct specification of meaning, that for someone with the requisite knowledge there is no cause for complaint, that any frustration he may feel is likely to be founded on an illusion.

9.3 Meaning and the existence of a synonym

A significant part of the preceding account, and especially the analogy with weight, closely matches an analysis given by T. S. Champlin, who is insistent that, e.g., 'The meaning of "cynosure" is "centre of attention"' really does give the meaning of 'cynosure', and not just a synonym (Champlin 1983, 280–1). In Champlin's scheme, however, to speak of the meaning of 'centre of attention' is of questionable propriety, since he holds that the conditions for speaking in such terms are not fulfilled with respect to the general run of familiar words and phrases. A French child learns the meaning of 'cheese' if he learns that it means *fromage,* but while an

English child learns what 'cheese' is the name of, he does not learn the meaning of the word, for that would mean learning an equivalent, a word or phrase which might correctly complete the sentence frame, 'The meaning of "cheese" is . . . '. For most words no such equivalents are available, but it is only when the vocabulary of a language has become sufficiently rich that the notion of meaning can get a grip: 'Before one can learn the meaning of a word, lots of words have to be learned in ways which do not require one first to learn their meanings' (ibid. 278).

The suggestion that only words for which there exists a synonym can be said to have a meaning may take two forms. On the one hand, it may be held that a synonym for *w* simply *is* the meaning of *w*; on the other hand, the claim may be merely that the synonym *gives* the meaning of *w*. Champlin does not wish to follow the former course, and we have already rejected the supposition that the word *v* might be said to *be* the meaning of *w* in sentences of the form 'The meaning of *w* is *v*'. Still, this rejection was made without argument, and the appearance that the meaning is the word is one that runs deep. Not only with respect to such basic statements of meaning, or with others such as '"loop" is not the usual meaning of "frog"', 'The literal meaning is "How do you go?"', or 'The meaning "tail" is less common nowadays', but also with respect to the way 'meaning' links up with other terms. So, you can look up the meaning of a word in a dictionary, and we might even be asked to write down the meaning of a word. (Compare how another prejudice is confronted by the consideration that one can write down or rub out a number.)

We move in the direction of regarding one word as the meaning of another to the extent that 'meaning' approximates to 'interpretation', 'translation', 'rendering', or 'definition', yet it would seem we never reach the point where we can say that one word literally is another's meaning. You can misspell, erase, pronounce, or form a rhyme with a word, but not with its meaning, and all that the more suggestive ways of speaking do is point up the clausal character of the noun 'meaning': writing down the meaning of a word is a matter of writing down what it means, in the sense of writing down an answer to a question, something which might also be looked up in a dictionary.

The alternative espoused by Champlin stops short of an actual identity of word and meaning, requiring only that there be a synonym before we can speak of the latter. *En route* to considering this possibility we might note the more common and more restricted claim that meaning is to be denied to certain classes of word, notably words which, like 'but', 'as', and 'even', make for a problem with the Augustinian scheme through having nothing to correspond to them outside language in any clear way – a view towards which Wittgenstein is perhaps drawn when he withholds meaning from 'five' in *PI* §1. Is this a matter of philosophers' unease occasioned by imagined implications of an inappropriate kind, or are unwanted implications actually carried by the word 'meaning' in its standard use?

It is difficult to refuse the description 'meaningful' to such terms, and if it is held that this amounts to no more than saying that they have meaning, that it is the claim that such a word has *a* meaning that is questionable, we can point to the reassuringly trivial grounds for making use of the noun as a count noun: we often wish to say that a word has more than one meaning, and such a statement is often *true*. The plurality need not be a plurality of objects. But, of course, it may be a plurality of synonyms, and if Champlin is right, the reason for any disinclination to speak here of (a) meaning may simply be that the words in question are unlikely to have any exact equivalents within the language. This is not to say, however, that we are denied all talk of meaning, since it is allowed by Champlin that the verb 'mean' may have a role even when the noun does not. Let us consider this further preliminary.

It was pointed out that it is 'mean' with a word as subject that tends to nominalize as 'meaning', and that a referential complement is not customary for either noun or verb in this (N) use. So we may say, with 'mean' (P), that by 'sparrow' is meant a small plain-coloured bird, but 'The meaning of "sparrow" is a small plain-coloured bird' rings awkwardly. Perhaps Champlin's claim just takes this observation a stage further: use of the noun requires us to stay within language, leaving us with nothing to say if a synonym cannot be provided. Questions which make use of the noun, as 'What is the meaning of *moineau*?', invite presentation of something with its own identity or individuality, as it were, something that, like a definition, might be recorded, forgotten, looked up, and so forth. Consider 'He learned a meaning for the word that I had never come across', or 'One meaning of the word has gradually come to predominate', where forms with 'mean' do not come so readily. However, while we may be happier when a synonym is at hand, this would seem to hold for the verb as much as for the noun, if the verb is the corresponding 'mean' (N). Perhaps we should hesitate to say, 'I know the meaning of "sparrow".' Certainly, if asked what the meaning is we should tend not to meet the question head on, but to answer with 'A sparrow is . . . '. However, any uncertainty here would appear to extend to 'I know what "sparrow" means'.

To see whether 'meaning' is wedded to a synonym in the way Champlin avers, we might re-open the topic of proper names, since if Champlin is right we may well have been looking in the wrong direction for what is special about such terms. Perhaps the frequent inapplicability of 'meaning' has nothing to do with names, whether proper or common, but everything to do with the unavailability of a synonymous expression, whatever the category of term. Thus, doubts about the earlier treatment may arise with certain mass nouns. What is the meaning of 'mercury', of 'magnesium', of 'phenol'? Even if these are names of substances rather than of individuals, are they not names in the way that a proper name is, and is it not as difficult to associate a meaning with them as it (usually) is with the latter? Here we might make a comparison with trade names which, like 'Persil' or 'Optrex', qualify as proper names of substances: could it not be that in either case the lack of meaning is just lack of a synonym? And is this not also true for a common noun like 'sparrow'?

Champlin's view is without doubt tempting for names, explaining in the simplest way why they lack meaning, and it also looks to be a useful corrective to a preoccupation with necessary and sufficient conditions for the application of words generally. It is unreal to demand defining conditions in many instances, and if in fact we do not have to speak of meaning at all, there is *a fortiori* not a meaning to be specified in the favoured terms. However, any such conditions have to be thought of in the inexplicit way indicated with the example of 'jar', where it seemed reasonable to hold that our usage provides the material for a definition, even if none has as yet been formulated. We may not ourselves have the necessary knowledge, in which case we may feel that the word – 'phenol' say – is *just* a name, in a way parallel to the name of a person, where there is no question of a meaning to be explained by detailing characteristics of the bearer. None the less, the knowledgeable rather than the ignorant speaker is surely the relevant subject to consider, and for him there is the possibility of articulating the knowledge in a definition. Again, it is not because of an impoverishment of the language that meaning is to be denied to

'Henry'; rather, it is because there is no set of features to which the name is annexed. As it happens, 'Henry' does have a variant in 'Harry', as well as equivalents in other languages, as *Heinrich* or *Henri,* but because the equivalences are not founded on an association with a common condition on the side of the bearers, we do not speak of synonymous names.

On the other hand, the undoubted awkwardness in talk of meaning with some common nouns suggests that the comparison with proper names is not altogether misplaced. Take the word 'hyacinth'. Like many other nouns, this applies to things which present an array of features. Since these features tend to come together, we have not had to face the problem of deciding which are necessary and/or sufficient to being a hyacinth, and I suggest that this indeterminacy is responsible for any hesitation we may have in speaking of the meaning of the term (cf. Ziff 1960, 185). It is not that we have not put the relevant conditions into words; it has not been decided what those conditions are. A verb or adjective, by contrast, relates to a single act or aspect of something, not to a whole cluster, and its relative simplicity in this respect means that talk of its meaning is not infected with the same uncertainty. Of course, the contrast between the parts of speech cannot invariably be drawn in this way. There is no significant difference between 'pinch' as noun and as verb, talk of the meaning of 'pinch' occasioning qualms in neither case – whether or not we are ready with a synonym.

Confirmation of Champlin's account of meaning does not appear to be forthcoming from a consideration of names. That account, I suggest, comes closer to describing the behaviour of 'definition' than that of 'meaning'. We may happily say of 'from', 'tease', 'peanut' and a hundred-and-one other everyday words that they have a meaning, without being prepared to say that they have definitions. In the clearest sense, there is not a definition of a word until someone has defined it, a procedure which often involves a degree of stipulation–tidying up ordinary usage for the sake of greater determinacy and precision, as required by, for instance, a legal or technical use of the term. The assimilation of 'meaning' to 'definition' has one great merit for those who are dubious of the value of statements of the form, 'The meaning of *w* is *v*', seeing these as forever giving rise to the further query, 'But what is the meaning of *v*?' If a definition is what is sought, 'It does not have one' is a possible answer. On the other hand, the comparison is surely defeated by the refusal of the question with meaning to be rejected in this way. Indeed, the very search for a synonym, a word with the same meaning, appears to presuppose a meaning for the given word. True, we may soon exhaust answers which furnish another synonym or paraphrase, but other ways of explaining the meaning of the word remain.

9.4 Noun clauses

We have been concerned so far with contexts in which words rather than persons have been subjects of 'mean', and words taken individually rather than sentences. Shifting the emphasis in both respects takes us to the question of the commitments of the clausal form found in such sentences as 'By *Tempus fugit* the Romans meant that time flies.' The occurrence of 'mean' here is from (3), where a relational reading is often acceptable, and in the present instance the grammar of the construction is superficially in accord with the picture of extralinguistic items being matched to words as their meanings.

Before trying to see whether or not appearances here are deceptive, we shall find it useful to examine the indirect speech construction more generally. We begin by looking at the contribution made by the conjunction 'that' in such sentences as 'He decided that he had had enough', 'She had no idea that you were there', and 'It happens that I shall be away.' As these examples indicate, it is the construction with a that-clause generally that interests me, despite the possibly stretched use of the label, 'indirect speech', in characterizing these contexts.

Considerations of euphony aside, does it make any difference whether or not we keep the 'that'? It does, but exactly why is far from evident. One explanation, from Bolinger, is that the term remains the demonstrative it more obviously is elsewhere, as in phrases like 'that man', being appropriate when its clause relates to some matter to which 'that' can point back. One of Bolinger's more persuasive examples of the implied contrast is provided by these two exchanges (1977, 12):

(a) I didn't know that. – Know what? – That Jack's held down six jobs at the same time.

(b) You want to know something? – What? – Jack's held down six jobs at the same time.

Given the way '(That) Jack's held down six jobs at the same time' relates now to an assertion, now to a question, the significance of the presence or absence of 'that' is not easy to assess. At all events, although reference back may look to be what underlies use of the conjunction in (a), I am inclined to opt for a more general account which sees the role of 'that' as highlighting the identity of its clause. Compare 'I guessed that there'd been a row', which is suited to indicating that it is a matter of guessing as stated rather than guessing something else, with 'I guessed there'd been a row', which does not present its clause as the focus of a possible contrast. Any allusive role on the part of the clause, any suggestion of the information presented being already given rather than new, would seem more a consequence of the way 'that' sets off its clause as a contrastive unit.

Does 'that' enjoy any further role? This is again problematic, but it is plausible to hold that it also signals a withdrawal from assertoric use. The assertoric condition is plain: contrast 'He did not know that it was loaded' with 'He did not know whether it was loaded', 'that' giving way to 'if' or 'whether' ('when', 'how', etc.) when a question is embedded. The withdrawal aspect, which is less obvious, can be approached in the following way. An assertoric form of words does not allow of occurrence in either subject or object position whilst retaining its assertoric force. Thus, the quoted words occur as subject of a predication in '"Too many cooks spoil the broth" is a well-known proverb', and this is enough to exclude them from a simultaneous assertoric use – an obstacle to any conception of assertions as names of truth values, we may note. Very roughly, to the extent that a declarative form of words occurs at a place where a name may go, to that extent the sentence is to be denied a use to make an actual assertion. Similarly, we have not asked a question if we state: 'The question, "Does crime pay?", was debated.' What holds of the quoted word holds too of that-clauses, as 'He agreed that it might fail' and 'That it would happen was clear.' Examples like this last, or 'He knows that the clocks have been put back', appear, it is true, to point the other way, towards retention rather than cancellation of assertoric force. However, while certain choices of main verb can have the effect of committing the speaker to an assertion corresponding to the clause, the clause need not of itself carry that force. The same analysis is to be given with 'It is on the cards that he will lose' and 'It is certain that he will lose'; it is just the particular demands made by 'certain' that ensure the commitment. Again, we note how various 'attitudinal' verbs have the effect of restoring assertoric force, as with 'He was surprised (glad, relieved, disappointed) that she confessed', presumably because the truth of the clause is required if it is to give a reason for the surprise.

Conjunctive 'that' had its origins in a demonstrative use – 'He said that: the nights are drawing in' – and this accords with the status of the noun clause as an object of comment, rather than as part of our own assertion, even if any demonstrative character has otherwise been lost. There is no more use of 'that' as a demonstrative in 'It happens that I shall be away' than there is when it occurs as a relative pronoun, 'It is time that we left', though in either case it is not difficult to see continuity with the earlier role. Again, consider 'Not that I mind one bit' – something of a puzzle for a traditional philosophical treatment, with its conception of noun clauses as names. The neutralizing role of 'that' dissociates the words from any assertion on the part of the speaker, as 'not' patently requires, and in doing this it confers a more independent status upon them, so that they can be thought of as something that someone else has said or might say. Bolinger would presumably explain the detachment from assertion in terms of an allusion to the words as used by another, but again I should wish to make basic the role of 'that' in giving prominence to the identity of its clause, in setting it off as a contrastive unit, with such an allusion being just one of the further possibilities.

Both 'that' and quotes serve to detach the speaker from a commitment to the associated words, but there is an important difference in the way the conjunction none the less implies a certain *use* of these, or related, words. This is apparent from the consideration that, even as reporters, we are responsible for referential uses of noun phrases within a that-clause – a commonly misunderstood phenomenon – but it also arises at another point. We can happily speak of uttering, copying, or translating 'Roses are red', but we do not utter, copy, or translate *that* roses are red, the clausal form being in place only if the words are envisaged as incorporating a linguistic act. Again, we distinguish between simply writing down the words, 'I am unwell', and writing that one is unwell, where a linguistic use is implied. 'He explained (the words) "It's late"' contrasts similarly with the report, '"It's late", he explained', which purports to tell us what the person was doing in saying what he said. The quoted words are thought of as incorporating a speech act, which is then specified; they are not *what* was explained, but the verb here is intransitive.

This brings us to a further point of interest with 'that'. Whatever its demonstrative origins, these are no obstacle to its joining with an intransitive use of a verb, such a use with the direct speech form – '"No one will have the better of me", he boasted' – carrying over into the indirect version: 'He boasted that no one would have the better of him.' 'That' does not impose a different grammar on the verb, but it often makes no sense, or alters the sense, to insert a noun phrase that might make plain the supposed status of the clause as a grammatical object. We may protest, agree, complain, or boast that *p*, but we do not protest, etc. the words, or indeed anything, such as a proposition, to which the words might supposedly refer. The that-clause gives us a report or rendering of a complaint in the sense that it gives a report of words such that in uttering them the person was complaining. The words are not what was complained, but complaining that *p* is more complaining *thus*: *p*.

As objects fail, so too do subjects. Consider 'It appears that he has left.' A traditional parsing would have 'it' anticipate the true subject, as furnished by the clause. However, not only is 'That he has left appears' inadmissible, but there is no need to impose this grammar. What we have is simply a propositional use of the words of the clause complemented by a phrase which indicates how more precisely they are to be taken. That is, 'it appears' requires any suggestion of an unqualified assertion to be removed, and the conjunction prepares the words for union with 'it appears' by doing just that. The 'it' is a purely structural 'it', not an anticipatory subject. However, it is true – and this is another central facet of its use – that the conjunction does at least package its clause in a way that allows it to have the grammatical role of a subject in many cases. We do not have '"He agreed" was surprising', but we do have 'That he agreed was surprising', even if this involves only a formal manoeuvre, and not a device which depends for its sense on there being something for the clause to designate.

To combat the construal of noun clauses as names, it is natural to challenge the supposedly transitive character of the verb which governs such a clause. As just noted, such a challenge may be successful, but with some verbs a more fruitful approach is to allow transitivity, which may in any event make only easily satisfied formal demands, and to make the contrast with contexts in which the act signified by the verb is focused upon an already existent object – a special case of transitivity. Thus, whereas with 'He translated "Crime does not pay"', or 'He copied "I shall return"', we have (on one reading) an act or activity which bears upon given words, not an act with which the words took shape, with '"You have had your share", he protested', 'he protested' purports to characterize the act embodied in the words as uttered, not an act that is directed to those words.

We may say '"You have had your share", he protested', or 'He protested that they had had their share', and with the latter no more than with the former is there any call to think of the protesting as an act levelled at an object – directly specified in the former, indirectly with the latter – but the closest we get to that is with the idea of an act *issuing in* an 'object' – a matter, as indicated, of protesting *thus*, in terms thus rendered or reported. Similarly, thinking that *p* is not an activity directed to a thought that is before one's mind, but it is thinking in terms that are either directly specified – thinking: I am late – or where the terms constitutive of the thought are given a more oblique rendering – thinking that one is late. The thought is the upshot, not the pre-existent object, of the thinking; it is what is effected, rather than something affected.

The rendering, 'He protested thus: *p*', is helpful in matching the noun clause to an intransitive verb, but what follows 'thus' is most naturally a direct speech version corresponding to the clause, so a version which detaches the reporter not only from the speaker's assertion, which is desired, but also from any referential use of terms within the clause, which is not, the clausal construction licensing the former detachment only. The characterization of the construction which this implies looks to be quite unremarkable, but it is significant if it succeeds in coping with all the relevant commitments; in particular, if the sense of the original terms in which reference was made does not also have to be maintained, and if there is not an additional item, the referent of the clause, to be taken into account. That the first poses no problem has been argued elsewhere (Rundle 1979, §§19, 20), and in so far as something lies behind the clause it will be nothing more than the words or thought reported.

Whether or not we are prepared to speak of reference in this latter connection, there is nothing problematic about forms which, like, 'He protested that he had been cheated', purport to give a rendering of what was said, but with verbs like 'think, 'hope', and 'suspect' there may be no overt words in which the thought, etc., was expressed. The most likely such case is first-person, as with 'I thought he had left.' Here what is reported allows of varying degrees of determinacy: sometimes it may be that we actually said something to ourselves, but often there will be no moment at which the thought occurred; we may still speak of a report, but this will be more a matter of giving the thought a definite verbal shape for the first time. Not a report of anything that had been clearly articulated previously, even to ourselves, but adequate none the less in so far as it now gives expression to our earlier state of mind.

9.5 Mean *and its objects*

There is much more to be said about the *oratio obliqua* construction; I have simply contented myself with highlighting features of its use which are relevant to dispelling the impression that it brings a mysterious domain of entities in its train. Before considering this further with respect to 'mean', it is worth drawing attention to a doubtful use to which this verb is sometimes put.

When discussing questions we touched upon an interesting case where natural meaning and linguistic meaning may be run together. In general, the possibility of mistaking the one for the other is minimal, given that the former is confined to words in close spatio-temporal connection with what they are signs of, but when it is an aspect of speech that is signified, a linguistic sign for this will also occur in such proximity, and in saying that a rising intonation means that a question is being put, we could be thinking of meaning in either form.

The closeness of 'mean' (1) and (2) is particularly likely to lead to confusion when a sentence is subject. First, we note that if such a form as '"furze" means gorse' is strained, the clausal construction, as in '*Il fait de l'air* means that it is windy', is even more dubious. There is nothing amiss with 'By *Il fait de l'air* he means "It is windy"', or 'By *Il fait de l'air* he means that it is windy', but of the two corresponding forms, '*Il fait de l'air* means "It is windy"', and the form just given, '*Il fait de l'air* means that it is windy', the former is certainly to be preferred. The latter is perhaps allowable as a variant of it, or as an ellipsis from the form where a person is said to mean something by the sentence, but in the absence of an implied reference to a speech act, the inanimate subject attracts the totally inappropriate consequential reading which goes with such subjects generally. Thus, with 'A weaker pound means cheaper imports', we affirm an implication or entailment; with something of the form '*p*, which means that *q*' we commit ourselves to the truth of *q*, and for the most part this locution has nothing to do with anything like word meaning. The way the dust is swirling about may mean that it is windy, but the words or the utterance of *Il fait de l'air* can hardly be said to have such a consequence. For that kind of interpretation a performative utterance is the most natural candidate, as when we say that a person's utterance of 'I resign' means that he has resigned. This is not, however, very convincing, let alone the general case.

The above points are not new (cf. Rundle 1979, §53), but their disregard is sufficiently widespread to make them worth repeating for those who think the clausal construction important in giving a *direct* specification of meaning in a way that is supposedly not true when a quoted sentence replaces the clause, a specification which enables us to make an exit from language. The thought may be, for instance, that the aim of the 'radical interpreter' is not simply to set up a translation manual, but to map the native sentences directly into the world. Someone who uses the form '"*p*" means that *q*' might be prepared to settle for a rewording which shifts the meaning from words to person as subject. Well and good. This is, I suggest, the only realistic case to consider, whether for individual words or for whole sentences, but even here it is a mistake to think that there is anything more by way of reference than is afforded by the referential terms *within* the clause.

When the elucidation of meaning is given with a direct speech form, as in 'By "It's over" he meant "The match has finished"', the interpretation of the construction is clear enough: we are simply specifying what the speaker wished to say, specifying words which have the meaning desired for the words he in fact used. When the clausal form is employed, as in 'By "It's over" he meant that the match had finished', essentially the same description is in order. With thinking that *p* the account of the noun clause falls into line with that appropriate to the direct speech form; to introduce the requisite modification it suffices to say that the clause gives an oblique rendering of words which report or constitute the person's thought, complaint, etc. The pattern with 'mean' is similar. First, the verb has a use in which words already aired can be meant: when I said that I found his remark offensive, I meant his last remark. But there is no move from this to 'I meant that *p*', where *p* is the remark in question; the sense in which I meant the person's remark is not the sense in which he, the speaker, meant it. 'Meant' in the former case complements 'referred to' or 'spoke of', but the man who made the remark, and meant it, was not referring to his words. Meaning that *p* is thus like thinking that *p*, in so far as the clause does not introduce an antecedently existing object of the meaning. We are simply furnishing an oblique specification of words which make plainer what the speaker wished to say with the words he did use; this requires that we use words *with* the desired meaning, but not that the meaning be an item referred to.

However, while there need be nothing to choose between the direct and indirect renderings, use of the clausal form can bring into play a slightly different role for 'mean', the role which we find in the context of meaning what one says. To revert to an earlier example, when we ask whether someone really meant 'never', our query may be one as to whether the word has the meaning wished for, but we may also be wondering whether the speaker is prepared to stand by the accuracy of 'never', not doubting his grasp of its meaning. If, now, the liar says, 'I've never set eyes on him', he does not mean what he says, but it might still be said that, e.g., what he meant was that he had never met the person's brother. This might simply aim at clarifying the speaker's words, but it is more geared than is the direct speech version to the case where the person supposedly means what he says. Likewise, there could be a difference between 'When he said *Je m'excuse* he meant "I'm sorry"' and the less easily satisfied 'When he said *Je m'excuse* he meant that he was sorry' – i.e., 'When he said he was sorry he meant it.' This distinction may be thought fanciful, but the example of questions gives it some support. The schema 'When he said "*p*" he meant it' might be thought to amount to 'When he said "*p*" he meant "*p*"', but the equivalence fails if *p* is a question. The man who says 'Is anyone in?' may well mean 'Is anyone in?', but he can hardly be said to mean it when he says 'Is anyone in?'

There is, then, a possible difference in use between the *oratio recta* and *oratio obliqua* forms with 'mean', but it is not one that points to the noun clause as the source of a problem – as if its use were the occasion for some object of reference, more puzzling than a sentence, to make an entry. In so far as this is the issue, there is no more to 'By *Tempus fugit* is meant that time flies' than there is to 'By *Tempus fugit* is meant "Time flies"'. A method of suspending assertoric force, which is what 'that' offers as much as quotes, is not to be mistaken for a more positive use which would project words onto something else, but all we are left with is as when words are the subject of 'mean', viz. the notion of a linguistic form as endowed with meaning. Make plain what is involved here and we are well on the way to laying to rest any problems, whether for words or for sentences, that the grammar of 'meaning' may generate.

10

Defining Meaning

As was remarked in §1.1 the philosophical concept of meaning (*Bedeutung*) which regards the notion of pointing (*deuten*) as still counting for something is not dismissed out of hand by Wittgenstein: a language can be imagined for which the description given by Augustine is right (*PG* §19, *PI* §2). This, pre-eminently, is an account that treats words in a uniform way, seemingly to its disadvantage, but whatever its shortcomings, once we move away from something like this conception, problems arise. The Augustinian scheme generalizes on the basis of the relation supposedly found between 'table' and tables. It seems absurd to take this as the pattern for linguistic meaning generally, yet if there is no way of speaking in terms of sign and thing signified, it becomes uncertain whether we should then be talking of meaning at all, even though use may have an evident application. Our main concern in this chapter is to attempt a definition of meaning, but we shall first look again at this primitive picture in conjunction with Wittgenstein's alternative.

10.1 The Augustinian picture revisited

Consider greetings. On the one hand, this category is one for which use looks to be a highly serviceable notion: we explain 'hello' simply by characterizing its use within the genre. But does the word have a meaning? When, as with 'farewell' or *au revoir*, we have some message conveyed, some sentiment expressed, meaning can be extracted, but if no such content is assignable, if, say, we have just a device for catching attention, as with 'hey!', then it is doubtful whether meaning enters. Similar observations apply to expressions in other categories, as 'amen', 'tally-ho', 'bloody' and 'abracadabra': 'amen' may be understood as 'so be it', but for many it is a word with a use – as to end a prayer – but no meaning; hunters may encourage their hounds with cries of 'tally-ho!', but no meaning seems to accompany this use; as an expletive used to punctuate speech more or less indiscriminately, 'bloody' has no discernible meaning, and the use of 'abracadabra' depends on its very status as nonsense. Rather differently, we note a contrast between certain suffixes, as '-ity' and '-less'. Both have a use, in forming nouns and adjectives respectively, but only with '-less' is there now a meaning to be taken into account.

Without relying on examples such as these, we saw that any identity of meaning and use was out of the question, that we had at best a determination of the former by the latter. It may be thought pedantic to give much weight to the grammatical differences which keep the two apart, but if a relation of determination is as close as we can strictly get, the question of what meaning is remains unanswered, every bit as much as if we were to say that the meaning of a word is in some cases determined by stipulation: many things may be stipulated; what, precisely, is it that is stipulated in this instance? Given, further, that stipulation is neither employment nor application, we have here a further argument against tying meaning too closely to use.

Use has its other problems, noted at the outset, but then we are brought up against equally formidable difficulties if we turn to the Augustinian alternative. No real alternative, this, if it requires that for any meaningful word, *w*, there must always be some item which is what is meant by *w*. What item corresponds to 'which', to 'since', to 'for'? Is not the whole idea of a word-world relation perhaps an illusion, however naturally it comes to us to think in these terms? After all, much of our earlier argument was directed at just this kind of misconception – certain phrases thought to designate something in the world do no such thing. Even with the more obliging terms, such as nouns, the 'thing' to which the term supposedly relates would appear to be of a somewhat different character than may have been supposed if, as is evident with many words, what we should be talking about is a *type*. What 'cygnet' signifies is a particular creature, but only in the sense of a particular type, kind, or species of creature. Given that the association takes this form, rather than having as its second term the individual things to which words are applied, which they describe, distinguish, and so forth, should we be thinking in terms of an extralinguistic relation in any sense? If we say that 'table' is the word for an article of furniture, 'an article of furniture' has to be taken at its most general, not in reference to a single concrete item, and perhaps it is only because this is overlooked that terms like 'table' and 'chair' are thought to give unproblematic support to the Augustinian scheme. Relatedly, there is some difficulty in saying that the feature associated with a term such as 'tall' is 'in the world'. Height or tallness is a real enough feature *of* towers and steeples, but it is far from clear that locational predicates can be applied to the feature itself. We should have to *stipulate* that the height of something was somewhere. Where, similarly, is the age, value, or speed of an aircraft?

These observations tell against the Augustinian scheme taken at its crudest, but a broader conception of the word-world relation can adjust to them. First, there is no disputing the relevance of *type* in this connection. Indeed, an association with a type is, we may recall, just what is lacking with those many proper names to which meaning cannot be ascribed. To see what this involves consider the example of *action*. We readily construe 'hop', 'skip', and 'jump' as words for actions which we can point to, even when 'action' is thought of as associated with a very broad criterion of identity – one such that we can point to the same action at different times and in different places and with respect to different agents. Similarly, detaching a word like 'bicycle' from a locational criterion of identity allows us to speak of any number of people as purchasing or riding the same bicycle. To say that *w* is the word for a type merely requires us to associate *w* with an appropriately liberal criterion of identity. The dissociation from a locational criterion is found again with words like 'height' and 'selfishness', which pose essentially the same problem. Their divergence from terms for the physical does not prevent us from saying that 'height' is the word for a property, 'selfishness' the name of a character trait. These are genuinely features of objects and persons which themselves have a well-defined location; it is just that such locatability is not transferable from bearer to property. Locatability may be deemed a necessary condition for being in the world, but it is not a necessary condition for being real.

None the less, are there perhaps considerations which would show that for words quite generally it is futile to seek a relational account of meaning? Wittgenstein's conception of ostensive definition is sometimes taken to go with a denial of any connection between language and reality. There are indications of such a view early on –

e.g., *WVC* 209–10 – and it is true that he approaches a position which we might think to describe in these terms to the extent that he puts more and more on the side of language; not merely words, but also gestures, and even the samples used in ostensive definitions. A gesture, like a word, has to be interpreted, and a sample is a means of representation which we can most naturally, and with the least confusion, reckon 'among the instruments of the language' (*PI* §§16, 50). Since ostensive definition is thus made out to be a form of explanation of certain symbols in terms of others, it would appear not to offer an exit from language. A striking demonstration of this confinement is provided by the parallel between forms of definition which clearly operate within language, as '*rouge* means "red"', and a statement like 'This colour is red', understood as an ostensive definition. The latter can be thought of as licensing a rule of substitution: in place of 'red' we could invoke the complex of gesture, sample, and phrase, 'this colour' (*PG* IV). As with the 'purely verbal' definition, what this yields is a translation rule which keeps us within language, though it remains true that word and sample differ in use – copying does not apply with both in the same way (ibid. §49), and one cannot always fall back on a gesture in place of the name; e.g., when we ask whether a man who has come into the room is *N*, '*N*' known to be the name of someone who left the room earlier (ibid. 202–3).

We might well wish to add to these acknowledged differences between word and sample. For one ignorant of the meaning of 'red' and *rouge*, exposure to the two in combination will lead nowhere; replace the one by gesture plus sample, however, and understanding becomes a real possibility, the way the sample is outside language being as important as the way it may be said to be within. Indeed, while it is doubtless an illuminating move to place samples among the instruments of the language, it is noticeable that their affinities are with non-words rather than with words.

To explain, we note that there are certain quasi-linguistic phenomena to which application of 'word' is dubious. This is especially so when there is a close comparison with grunts, sighs, cries, and the like, as with natural expressions of surprise, sympathy, triumph, and disgust – 'oh!', 'ah!', 'aha!', 'ugh!'. These vocables are adequate to their purpose in so far as they mimic or reproduce the right sound; they are not called upon to have in addition any meaning, and are accordingly not ordinarily reckoned words. Their role is representational in a strong sense: 'aargh!', for instance, is a representation of a strangled cry in that it seeks to reproduce the phenomenon. Again, compare the vocable 'bzzz' with the word 'buzz'. Whereas 'buzz' stands *for* the noise, provides a means of speaking *of* the noise without reproducing it, 'bzzz' is a representation of the noise in the sense that it actually stands *in* for it. And this, surely, is where we should look for a comparison with samples: a colour sample, let us say, is not called upon to have the character of a word, since it enjoys this more directly representational function.

We may also observe that if little or no use is made of ostensive definition, then little or nothing will have the role of a sample, yet for words to have meaning will be as now, and the question of extralinguistic reference will be materially the same. Here we may recall our earlier discussion of ostensive definition, where it emerged that what was significant was not so much that this constituted a practice which we in fact engage in, but that it revealed a correlation between word and something else as what was to be communicated. The 'something else' will be at the level of a *type*, but that is no problem, and even if a sample is invoked in the explanation, it will be no more than *one* of the type which it represents. Furthermore, the scope for introducing reference to samples will in any case be restricted. Knowledge of meaning, for instance, will not in general be knowledge in which a sample is implicated.

It is not altogether clear what we are to extract from Wittgenstein on this topic. We can grant that, if ostensive definition is to work as an explanation, it must suppose the link between word and reality already set up, and in this sense it cannot be said to *forge* such a connection By the same token, however, it can hardly lead to a *denial* of the latter. We have, furthermore, the remark at *PI* §6: 'This ostensive teaching of words can be said to establish an association between the word and the thing.' This is consistent with the above point, in that the association is established for the learner, rather than being established *ab initio*, but it is noteworthy that the association is not being rejected. Rather, Wittgenstein goes on to ask what it *means*, looking for an answer in the kind of understanding that is effected by the ostensive teaching in association with a particular form of training. True, it is ostensive teaching rather than ostensive definition that is now at issue, but this does not alter the acknowledgement that words may have an extralinguistic reference. Going further back, Wittgenstein's discussion in

Philosophical Grammar of the thesis, 'The connection between words and things is set up by the teaching of language', focuses on distinguishing the right from the wrong kind of relation (§56), and no denial of a connection is suggested when *The Brown Book* makes the predictable claim that there is no one relation of name to object, implying that 'what we call the relation of name and object is characterized by the entire usage of the name' (*BB* 173).

Whatever the precise interpretation of these passages, we have no reason to impute to Wittgenstein a wholesale rejection of any connection between words and things. But we may also note that the kinds of word use which would make such a position seem most outrageous involve *applications* of language, as when objects are classified, described, or counted. To suppose the link between language and reality already set up need mean no more than that there should be determinate answers to questions of the form, 'What falls under *w*?', 'What would count as a *v*?', and so forth; it need not have been laid down that something in reality *is* the meaning of *w* or *v*. We noted in chapter 9 that while the 'meaning of *w* is . . . ' may sometimes be completed by a namelike term, *t*, this does not give us a licence to substitute *t* for 'the meaning of *w*'; we should in general misrepresent the behaviour of this phrase if we took it to designate anything. 'Meaning' does not interchange with 'definition', but in 'The meaning of "barometer" is "device for measuring atmospheric pressure"', there is no more of a referential use on the part of the definiens than there is if we put 'definition' in place of 'meaning'.

We also found reason – though it is an unhappy way of speaking – to go along with the correlative thesis that meaning is within language. More conventional backing for both moves is given through their link with the 'autonomy of grammar': our words are not answerable to reality, to the essences of things, as if the grammar of 'chair' were determined by the nature of chairs, so that we could find out more about what the word means by finding out more about the objects. If this is what such autonomy comes to, it is difficult to see a plausible alternative, though an apparently conflicting conception is to be found in Hilary Putnam's challenge to the view that sameness of intension or concept entails sameness of extension. Putnam invites us to consider a use of 'water' on Twin Earth, where it is applied to a substance the same in appearance as our water, but with a different chemical constitution, represented by 'XYZ' (Putnam 1975). Supposedly, an inhabitant of Twin Earth will be able to claim that the word 'water' means H_2O on earth, but not on Twin Earth. We have remarked on the infelicitousness of the construction in '"water" means H_2O', but the intention is evidently that 'mean' here should complement 'refer': H_2O is what is meant by 'water'. But now, given that the synonymy interpretation is not being advanced, and given that the intension of 'water' is the same in both worlds, it would be correct for an inhabitant of this planet to say with respect to Twin Earth's XYZ, 'That stuff is what is meant by "water".' In this connection, that stuff is the same stuff as our water – i.e., where sameness is determined by what is demanded for 'water' to apply. Just as, at the level of *wood*, the pine of this dresser and the oak of this beam are the same stuff. In neither case is the sameness a 'theoretical' relation, ascertainable only with the help of scientific expertise. Not that it never could be, but that it is is revealed by the way disputes over the applicability of a word are finally settled, not by the word's encompassing a range of substances whose differences *could* be the basis for a difference in meaning. So long as the two sets of criteria used in determining the application of 'water' are indistinguishable, it is incoherent to say with Putnam that the inhabitants of the two planets understand 'water' differently (ibid. 224) – though that is not to say that the extension of a term is fixed by concepts which people have 'in their heads' (ibid. 225).

Granted that words do not disclose their meanings to us in the way envisaged, this would still not seem to put an end to the possibility of a relevant link between word and world. However, I suggest that considerations of autonomy rule this out in one obvious but important way: our concepts are not required to be true to reality, but the forms which ostensibly take us from word to world are consistent with a denial that any instances of the type in question exist. If there are reasons for supposing that the world must contain something answering to a word, that will not simply be in virtue of the word's being meaningful – though we could leave it open that for certain words the only possible explanation of meaning might be by means of a sample (cf. *CV* 82). It is not the generality brought with *type* that is a problem, nor the failure of locatability, but it is the presence in the language of words like 'elf', 'ectoplasm', and 'utopia' that brings home the autonomy of meaning. To know what *w* means it suffices that we should know how someone or something *would* have to be for *w* to apply. The clausal behaviour of 'meaning' is predominantly such as to exclude directly any idea of meanings as items in the world; on the other hand, if '. . . means . . .' does not furnish the desired relation, there are other forms which do have a grammar better suited to this role, forms such as '"rubella" is another word for German measles', 'NaCl is the formula for a chemical compound', and '"saffron" signifies both a plant and a colour.' We are not faced with an exclusive choice: there is no mystery in the possibility that a word should be said to signify something outside language, but it is not that when we speak of something signified, this *has* to be outside language; that it is or is not is *further* to the matter of its being what is signified. In advancing considerations which seemingly required us to acknowledge an extralinguistic referent, we were, I suggest, simply drawing attention to the fact that we can speak in terms of a condition correlated with a word, and a condition on the side of the things to which words are applied.

Wittgenstein's concession that the Augustinian picture is sometimes applicable is puzzling. Does he really wish to allow that the meanings of some words are objects in the world? that some sentences are to be construed as no more than strings of names? Since these ideas are said only to have their *roots* in that picture (*PI* §1), both questions can perhaps be answered in the negative, but it could be that he is simply acknowledging the behaviour of *bedeuten* and *Bedeutung* from which the uncompromising view of the *Tractatus* stemmed: 'The name means the object. The object is its meaning' (*TLP* 3.203). After all, he is still prepared to use the terms in this way, as when he speaks of 'the object that [the sign] means' (*RPP* I, §207) or of learning to use a word 'in the meaning of a *feeling*' (ibid. §125), and he apparently sees a fundamental role for 'The word means *this*' (*LW* I, §332). Such an acknowledgement is admittedly difficult to square with *PI* §40, but it would give the most straightforward explanation of his reservations over meaning as use: that identification is not to be made with full generality, since in some cases the primitive picture is *right*. At all events, the possible application of a formula in keeping with that picture, as '*w* is the word for . . .', to words quite generally – more generally than he envisages – would give us something to defend at a point where the Augustinian scheme comes close to our pre-philosophical ways of thinking.

10.2 A definition of 'meaning'

We are saying, then: forget 'in the world'; the important divide is between a view which sees words as associated with some condition – relation, type, feature – and one which regards 'meaning' as having no more implications in this respect than does 'significance', and which would seek to explain the meaning of 'here', say, not by specifying any such association, but simply by indicating the role, the use, the part played by the word.

In our discussion of truth we found 'what *w* is true of' to be inadequate as a gloss on 'what *w* means'; knowing what 'however' means is, rather, knowing when it *applies*. Similarly, we observed in the last section that to know what *w* means it suffices to know how something *would* have to be for *w* to apply. Is there anything in this approach to help the more primitive conception? On that conception, having a meaning is a matter of being associated with some property, relation, etc., and the notion, *how something would have to be*, gets in the idea of such a condition. Clearly, however, we cannot leave it at that, since there are all manner of associations, as with the geographical and social circumstances noted with respect to *tone*, which lie outside linguistic meaning. We wish to admit only conditions which qualify by dint of its being *language* that is our concern, and in speaking of how a thing must be for *w* to *apply*, we are introducing a use of language which serves to exclude the unwanted correlations, to narrow them down to the association as involved in or required by such a use.

Take this to provide a necessary as well as a sufficient condition, and a simple enough definition of 'meaning' results: the meaning of *w* is a matter of how a thing has to be for *w* to apply – 'is a matter of' giving the appropriate form of identity when the terms linked behave predominantly as interrogative clauses. While there is no need that there should be anything in the world answering to a word, this definition makes it equally clear that meaning is not thereby relegated to the mind, and in reproducing the clausal character of 'meaning', it makes explicit the noun's non-referential character, at the same time showing how we may achieve what might be thought to demand a referential role. It makes sense, for instance, to speak of *showing* someone how a thing has to be for *w* to apply, so of showing him what *w* means. I rejected the view that we are not really being told what the meaning of *w* is if informed simply that it is *v*, but what is true is that we are *only* being told the meaning. In general, the possibility of indicating meaning non-linguistically is one which remains to be exploited. We may also note a likeness to the characterization of truth in terms of things being as stated. Indeed, we may likewise enlist the plural with meaning – a matter of how *things* have to be – since this has the advantage of greater generality than the singular; 'a thing' invites a specification of which thing, whereas the plural is suitably vaguer, not so closely tied to the role of stand-in for something more specific.

It is a fairly routine matter to see how the formula works out with most word classes, including not only the relatively straightforward categories of noun, verb, and adjective, but also the more troublesome parts of speech, as prepositions, conjunctions, and articles. Some of these are best considered in the company of their typical linguistic surroundings – an article with a noun, a conjunction with appropriate clausal accompaniments – but that is no limitation. Consider terms for which, as with pronouns, *use* is favoured. With 'this' and 'that', for instance, there may be some reluctance to speak of meaning, though a use – to refer, to single out – is plain. These two demonstratives belong to the important category of *indexical* expressions, as also 'here', 'I', 'soon', and 'now', a category which is usefully enlisted to show possible inadequacies in an unqualified appeal to use.

An English speaker knows where to look for what is singled out with such a term by bringing to bear knowledge of the relation that defines the indexical more generally. He knows, for instance, that the referent of 'you' will be the person to whom 'you' is addressed, that the time signified by 'now' will be the time contemporaneous with the utterance of 'now', and in general he will appreciate that an indexical, *i*, is to be defined in terms of a relation which holds between the utterance or utterer of *i* and some object, person, etc., so that knowing what that relation is, and knowing the locational facts about the speaker, he is able at least to narrow down the area in which the referent is to be found. Clearly, then, it is not the referents, individually or as a class, that matter in an explanation of meaning for an indexical, but the general relation which they are to satisfy. This is plain with 'you', 'here', and 'now', and the same holds with indications of tense, as the past-tense termination '-ed'. This comes under the indexical heading, in that the time of utterance provides the fixed point to which time of occurrence is related.

I do not wish to see a fundamental difference in the way meaning applies to 'this' and the way it applies with respect to a general term, such as 'water'. The meaning of 'this' is not what it refers to, but nor is the meaning of 'water' water, the liquid; it is a matter of how a substance has to be to count as water. Because the role of the demonstrative is so much to the fore, we readily think in terms of the use thus defined, perhaps seeing neither need nor room for an account which would associate the word with a general condition. However, if we look at the wider class of terms to which 'this' belongs, it is the particular condition associated with a given member of this class that takes on the greater significance, rather than the common use to refer, since it will be a matter of singling out in accordance with that condition – as 'the *F*' is used with respect to an *F* that is individuated in some way, either through its contextual uniqueness or through its uniqueness more generally, or 'both' is used with reference to two things, their identity being made known from the context. Similarly with 'you'. We have a use – to address someone – but this characterization is incomplete, the idea of the satisfaction of a condition – being the person addressed – furnishing a necessary elaboration. It may be objected that the notion of such a condition does not apply at all as readily with 'this' and 'that', say, as it does with a noun like 'crystal'. We might reply, as intimated, that the same holds for meaning, but I should not agree that neither is in place. There is some awkwardness with the latter, but when we think how 'this' differs from 'that' I suggest that a difference in meaning, explained as suggested, is appropriately invoked.

Imagine this objection. In speaking of how a thing must be for *w* to apply you are envisaging a particular context for *w*; you have not explained meaning as this is involved in contexts where the word is not being applied to anything, as with 'ladder' in 'Do you have a more stable ladder?' This would be a mistake. We do not have to be applying 'ladder' to anything for it to be true that the meaning of 'ladder' is a matter of how a thing must be for 'ladder' to apply. The argument is a close relation of the misconception that a word has meaning only in a sentence – as though the meaning were left behind when we moved from contexts where the word was being applied to something to contexts where it was not, perhaps that it takes nothing less than the sentence radical to bring the two contexts together.

The objection thus fails, but the impression may linger that a particular kind of use is none the less presupposed by the formula.

The range of terms with which it can cope is extensive, but its applicability to terms which occur predominantly in non-declarative contexts is still unproven, and it is less than comfortable at the level of signs of force.

Take the first difficulty. One of the stiffest tests for accounts of meaning is presented by interrogative particles such as 'who', 'when', and 'why'. Any atomistic approach which would pair these off with anything looks hopeless, and the broader framework which truth offers seems equally unavailing. How can anything like the notion of application be of assistance here? Thinking of the problem these pose, we are likely to be envisaging their use in direct questions, as 'Why did he wave?', but for full generality we should like to take in occurrences in indirect questions as well, and, if possible, their use as relative pronouns. The first extension looks to be simple, an account of 'She asked him why he waved' naturally building on an account of the direct question embedded, but the use in such contexts as ' . . . the reason why . . . ' seems a more distant relation.

What differentiates an assertion from a corresponding yes/no question is the way the verbal phrase is to be taken. With 'He will agree' the speaker expresses, in the standard case, a belief as to its applicability; with 'Will he agree?' he seeks to be told whether it applies. Interrogative particles present an analogous pair of correlative uses, as in 'Monday was when he called' and 'When did he call?' In the former, the pronoun links the following verbal phrase to the preceding noun phrase in such a way as to provide an identity condition with respect to the latter; it is, as it were, a specialized form of the relative pronoun 'which'. The notion of 'how things have to be for "when . . . " to apply' is in place with the non-interrogative use, and the interrogative use simply invites us to specify something of which the phrase is true, as with the form given: 'Monday was when he called', or simply 'Monday'. This fundamental continuity between yes/no and wh-questions is plain enough, yet the approach via the radical cannot even find room for the latter variety, let alone for this continuity.

Individual interrogative words can, then, be fitted into our scheme, but a related difficulty remains with the central category of verbal phrases. Suppose we wish to give an account of the verb 'run' in its full generality, i.e., not as confined to any one sentence type. The sense-force distinction is ill-suited to this purpose: *sense* being tied to the indicative case, we can cope with imperatival uses only by invoking something like the radical. Unfortunately, this narrowness appears to be shared by the notion of application, which does not take us sufficiently far beyond word types for which a truth-based account of meaning is congenial. What is crucial to 'run' is that it is the word for a certain action; whether it figures in a description of action or an injunction to action is secondary. It is, essentially, the *infinitive* that is our concern – though of course an account of this must be supplemented by an explanation of the further determinations to which the root form is liable. The formula with 'apply' has the merit of directing us to the principal context in which the association which defines a word can be recognized, but to appeal to this context is like appealing to some common practice of measuring in an effort to discern the system of measurement. The same system may also be discerned in a less usual one of its applications.

The formulae which seem ideally suited to cope with a verb taken in such generality are just those formulae which go with the primitive picture, as '*w* is the word for . . . ' and '*w* signifies . . . '; in detaching meaning from any particular use, they can accommodate every use. They have, moreover, a possible role in respect of the category of force. In discussing 'The word . . . signifies . . . ', we noted that its failure to take in the force of an utterance did not constitute an objection to its applicability, given that in general force is not to be assigned to individual words, but we may also note that there is no difficulty in speaking of the force *signified* by, e.g., the word order of a sentence. Certainly, this is much less awkward than a formulation in terms of how things must be for the given word order to apply.

Recourse to these ways of speaking – very much close relations of 'mean' – is one possibility, but there is also the possibility of improving upon our initial formula, generalizing it in the direction of 'how things have to be for *w* to be correctly used' – i.e., not focusing on any particular use, but taking the notion at its most general. How useful is this move? It is certainly true that the variant with use is more generally applicable, but it may be wondered whether this is an advance to be welcomed, whether the phrase 'how things have to be for *w* to be correctly used' says anything more than 'how *w* is correctly used', which simply takes us back to meaning as use. That something may be lost in this reduction was seen with the example of 'you' and the bare 'use to address someone', and we noted a similar defect earlier with respect to 'and'. A specification of the use of 'and' comes readily enough to mind – it is used to link up a range of linguistic forms – but a fuller account will relate the conjunction to a condition to be met by the conjoined terms. Attention is quite properly taken away from use to the matter of content, not merely with 'and' but with conjunctions generally. 'And' and 'but' are associated with conditions of continuity and contrast respectively; 'because' signals a relation of consequence between things said; 'while' relates to a temporal period during which something is supposed to have occurred; and so on. It was remarked in §1.2 that the appeal to use might not be as significant as it appears if the addition of a further semantic term, as in 'used to designate', is required. The present point is similar: a shift in emphasis is called for, from the bare *use* to the condition on the side of things which a use exploits.

Our earlier discussion of explanations of meaning confirms that the expanded form is needed, that the phrase 'how things must be . . . ' is not just an empty flourish. We observed that questions of meaning need not meet with immediate answers from speakers of the language, that there can be complexities in the patterns of usage which may take considerable time and thought to bring to the surface; even if we do not get around to stating them in so many words, there are conditions which have to be fulfilled by a vegetable if it is to count as a turnip, other conditions if it is to count as a parsnip, and it is just these that a definition can be called upon to formulate. Again, we may say that the article on sale is as it should be to qualify as 'cheap', having regard to the way cheap things must be. The relevant criteria do not enter into our deliberations as explicitly given definitions – 'how a thing must be' does not presuppose a verbal formulation – but we shall have had in some sense to piece together relevant items of information. True, we have seen that with some words it is unclear that determinate conditions can be specified – and not because either linguistic resources or our own resourcefulness is wanting – but these are precisely words for which application of 'meaning' is uncertain.

This brings us back to something like the more primitive formulae, formulae whose directness has other virtues. Thus, we noted earlier that 'what *w* is true of' maps *w* onto individuals, rather than onto the features, etc., which an explanation of its meaning should specify, and the account in terms of application or use is also at risk from the examples of co-extensive terms which gave rise to the difficulty. If whatever is *w* is also *v*, and conversely, then a person can be said to know how a thing has to be for *w* to be correctly used if he knows that it has to be *v*, yet he does not *ipso facto* know what *w* means. Some such unwanted cases can perhaps be excluded with a more discriminating choice of term in place of 'be correctly used', or 'apply'. So, if everything coloured is extended, a person can be said to know how something has to be for 'coloured' to apply if he knows that it has to be extended, but does this latter knowledge amount to knowing what *counts* as coloured? This perhaps points to a means of narrowing down knowledge of meaning, but to remove all uncertainty I doubt that we can stop short of introducing the following kind of consideration. To know what *w* means is to know what feature (condition, type, etc.) warrants use or application of *w in its regard*. We have, that is, to bring in reference to the character in question to ensure that it is knowledge as to how things have to be in the right respect: a matter of knowing how something has to be for *w* to apply in virtue of that thing's being *w*, and not in virtue of anything else. What we are concerned with is precisely the question of what *w* is a word *for*.

10.3 Word meaning and sentence meaning

Our parsings of 'mean' in terms of 'signifies' or 'is the word for' are hardly revelatory. Their value is, rather, as reminders that the primitive picture is not a travesty of our ordinary conception of meaning, not just a philosopher's fiction. By the 'primitive picture' I do not mean the elaboration which Wittgenstein associates with Augustine: we are not committed to assimilating all words to names, and sentences to combinations of names; we rest nothing on the possibility of completing '*w* signifies . . . ' by a designation of a worldly item. None the less, the alternative characterization in terms of how things must be for a word to be correctly used may be thought to be an advance on any refinement of this scheme, as well as on the formula with 'apply'. After all, it does at least offer an analysis of the troublesome notions. On the other hand, one of the recurrent difficulties with *use* is still with us in that the relevant connection with meaning is not guaranteed. Repeated mutterings of 'rhubarb' may be used to simulate background conversation, but this is not the kind of use of the word that concerns us. Or consider 'boo!' When used to express disapproval or dissatisfaction it has meaning, but when uttered in order to startle someone it need not be so regarded – though of course without prejudice to its having a use. True, the formula speaks of *correct* use, which is more satisfactory, but while we should normally think immediately in terms of a linguistic use, it would seem that correctness could be aligned with uses of other kinds; certainly, we do not as yet know what is distinctive of the former. Moreover, even when we can speak of a correct linguistic use, is it certain that meaning is assured? Utterance of 'chin-chin' can be a significant linguistic *act*, and we might correct the use of someone who treated it as something other than a toast or greeting, but does the 'word' have a meaning? Is it not in these terms on a par with 'eeny, meany, miney, mo' or even 'fee, fi, fo, fum'? Or, take the exclamatory 'o' in 'O for the wings of a dove!' Again, it is not at all clear that we have a meaning, but a use is undeniable, and indeed a use that may qualify as correct or incorrect. The phrase 'how things must be' is not just an empty flourish, and it does something to bring use into line with linguistic use, but it is doubtful that it does enough.

We have reached this point. The formula with 'apply' is generally apt, but it falters in some cases; these are cases which 'correct use' can handle, but the latter covers much else besides. Is there, then, any way in which use may be circumscribed? For Wittgenstein, clearly, the necessary restriction cannot come from meaning itself, and our earlier discussion of the relation between word and sentence suggests that we are reversing the true order if we characterize linguistic uses as those which meaning makes possible. The argument was the familiar one that the learner of a language cannot grasp the meaning of a word until he knows what use is made of it, and such a use cannot be understood in isolation, i.e., without an appreciation of the use of the whole unit, the sentence, in which the word is incorporated. So, if the language contained imperatives only, it might be suggested that words contributed to the meaning of sentences in that language by realizing some part of the general theme of telling someone to do something. How, it is true, is not immediately apparent. If it is said, 'Don't keep us waiting too long', then 'too' has a part to play in specifying what someone is being told to do, but it is not obvious how the force of the whole can usefully filter down to an explanation of the meaning of this intensive.

For words which occur across different sentence types to have a common core of meaning it is in no way necessary that they should enjoy a correlative general use. The meaning may be discernible in the different uses. However, with an eye to the present issue, we may still ask whether there is any use that can plausibly be enlisted to cover all sentence types, and it would seem that a candidate was glimpsed when, with the declarative sentence in view, we found it useful to speak in terms of *representing* or *making out to be*. There were reservations about the degree to which these notions kept in step with assertion, but the reservations were in fact on the side of their generality: we make things out to be a certain way if we say 'You idiot!', even if not with the explicitness that makes for an assertion. Perhaps we can turn this excessive generality to advantage in the present connection, since the characterizations fit not only close relations of assertions – including guesses and the like – but even orders and questions: if an order is given or a question put, the speaker represents himself as having a certain desire, or represents a course of action as desirable, and even with an interjection, 'Damn!', or 'Heavens!', the speaker is making out that he is in a certain state, as of annoyance or surprise. True, this description may apply without telling us anything about the meaning of the words used, as when a person makes himself out to be Irish by adopting an Irish accent, but such cases can be distinguished from linguistic meaning in the way sugggested with respect to tone: where the accent is the usual one, it has no differential value, so drops out of any account of meaning, and where it is not usual its use with a given word or words lacks the constancy required to contribute anything to the meaning of that form.

Once more, the objection is misplaced if it is said that a single characterization, a formula which covers all the major sentential uses, cannot be reconciled with the variety which language exhibits, and once more the real question is whether the formula indeed fits. There is sometimes a curious strategy behind this style of objection: if the analysis offered applies universally, the charge of vacuousness is levelled; if it fails to hold in some cases, it is faulted on that score. As I say, it is the latter that presents the real threat; despite its high level of generality, the value of the characterization is seen readily enough in the shift of perspective which it presents *vis-à-vis* an account in terms of communicative intentions. What our *aim* is in making things out to be thus and so is further to the fact that a linguistic use is made of the words. With certain forms – the imperative perhaps above all – the appeal to intention is almost irresistible. However, we saw that, natural though it may be, it is a mistake to make the basic association one between the grammatical form of the imperative and an intention to elicit action. An intentional act requires a belief by the agent that a means which he adopts may attain an end which he seeks, and the association of an imperative with a desire for action provides just such a means for an intention to exploit: by making known our desire we may stand a good chance of eliciting action. The imperative is an instrument for such a use, but its meaning explains this possibility; it does not constitute it. Given that the interrogative also follows this pattern, and given that assertion is already geared to the formula, it seems not unreasonable to think of linguistic uses in these broad terms. Conversely, it is a fault, not a virtue, to focus on diversity to the point that we lose sight of what is genuinely common.

Making out to be is intentional in the rudimentary way indicated when assertion was under discussion, and it is easy to see how an act so describable might have a communicative purpose, but this is as far as we go in the direction of the view that words mean something only if speakers intend to produce certain effects by them. In rejecting this position, with its seemingly incoherent ordering of priorities, we are siding with those who, like Chomsky, wish to give a fundamental place to the idea of language as a vehicle for expressing thought and feeling (1976, 56–7). But then it may be thought that we run afoul of the objection implicit in Wittgenstein's question:

> 'The purpose of language is to express thoughts.' – So presumably the purpose of every sentence is to express a thought. Then what thought is expressed by, for example, the sentence 'It's raining'?
>
> (*PI* §501)

In our explanation of assertion appeal was made to the notion of belief, so to a close relation of thought, but that analysis was not offered in support of a picture whereby an already articulated thought stands behind the overt utterance. It is true that to speak of the *purpose* of language as being to express thoughts may suggest the wrong priority, but the way the concept of belief enters into a *redescription* of the utterance allows for the fact that there may be no non-trivial specification of the thought or belief, no commitment to its antecedent existence.

When word meaning is said to be explicable in terms of a contribution to sentence meaning, it may be that the latter is thought of in terms of a familiar array of speech acts with their specific intentional uses, but even with an unexceptional characterization of the sentence it may be far from clear how the overall use of the latter can or need dictate the form which an explanation of meaning should take for the individual word. So what does our account of the sentence tell us about the word? The use of the former is in making things out to be a certain way, representing things as thus and so. Consonantly with this, the meaning of a word can be said to be a matter of the condition associated with the word in its use in making things out to be, this latter giving us the necessary specification of *linguistic* use. In coming to an understanding of individual words in the context of a sentential use, as 'Lead is poisonous', the learner will have come to an appreciation of words as specifying how something is made out to be – 'poisonous' – or as specifying something, or a kind of thing, which is made out to be so and so – 'lead'. The individual words specify various 'ways of being'. Again, the imperatival form has meaning in the requisite way, a desire for action being the relevant condition, while the words within have a role in specifying the particular desire which the speaker represents himself as having. In all cases the linguistic form, whether word or bearer of force, contributes to a determination of how things are made out to be, and has a meaning to be explained in such terms.

Our two approaches to defining meaning thus converge in the idea of a representational role which linguistic uses may exploit. However, while something along these lines, something more than the bare *use*, seems inescapable, it may still be thought wrong to speak of meaning in this undifferentiated way, to fail to acknowledge the very different *kinds* of meaning that words exhibit. Meaning as presented by a conjunction is surely at a great remove from meaning as this falls to a verb, which is in turn a very different phenomenon from meaning as found with clause or sentence. Or so it is said. Talk of 'kinds' of meaning is in much the same dubious category as talk of 'describing' meanings, neither fitting happily with the clausal behaviour of the noun. Furthermore, the case for speaking of 'meaning' as itself having many meanings is extremely weak: 'The meaning of . . . is . . . ' does not mean something different depending on the part of speech which fills the gaps; that is no more plausible than if we spoke instead of 'interpretation' or 'translation'. The meanings of words can be as various as you wish, but that is not to say that the words have meanings in different senses of 'meaning'. Once more the doctrine of meaning as use has something to answer for in the way it obscures this point. What is true is that the general notion of meaning as just explained is not appropriately invoked when explaining a particular word, since it is what differentiates that word from others that interests us, not what it has in common with all words by virtue of having a meaning. But acknowledging different levels of generality in this way is not acknowledging either different kinds or different senses of meaning. It was observed in §7.1 that taking into account the larger contexts of a word such as 'ladder' does not appear to add to our understanding of its meaning. That is correct in the sense that we are explaining what it is for 'ladder' to be the word for something, rather than explaining what 'ladder' is the word for.

The general account of meaning which has emerged gives support to those who see a systematic theory of meaning as a central philosophical goal, a goal which our treatment of sentence types also brings nearer. The idea of such a theory is attractive to the extent that a language makes use of recurrent patterns and principles, as much system being called for as is needed to account for our ability to form and understand new sentences. A vast amount will have to be learned and explained piecemeal, but it is surely undeniable that a large measure of what is already familiar is discernible in the new. In so far as what we have argued is relevant to this project it also verges on the trivial, but the following observations are none the less worth drawing together. First, we have defended an approach to sentence types which allows for variety and difference within general categories. Assertions can be put to many uses, but uses which exploit, rather than contradict, assertoric character. Second, we take a major simplifying step by noting that noun phrases behave in much the same way whatever their surrounding context, variations in overall force being attributable to verbal phrases. Third, if we wish to identify a common core of meaning within these variable phrases, we naturally fasten upon the infinitive. The various moods – indicative, imperative, subjunctive – along with marks of person and tense, add to the basic meaning as conveyed by the infinitive; hence our concern with this form when discussing the imperative. Finally, linguistic uses at large can be subsumed under a common description, a description which captures in the broadest terms what we are doing in using language, and which leads to an explanation of what it is for a word to have meaning.

In traditional grammatical terms some of these observations are undeniably trite, but unfortunately these terms have not been fully appreciated by those who, under the baneful influence of formal logic, have looked to concepts favoured by that discipline for their salvation. The traditional grammatical categories may well need refining, but they have the virtue of staying close to our pre-theoretical conception of the forms we use, and of being accordingly at home in a description of our knowledge of our language. What holds for sentence types holds too for other linguistic items, as adverbs, articles, demonstratives, number words, mass terms, and the rest. None of these categories is particularly difficult to handle; they are just made to look recalcitrant if it is thought that clarification will come only once we have found the 'logical form' of contexts in which they occur, where this requires squeezing them into the confines of current logical systematizations. Finally, if our analysis has taken us away from meaning as use, our aim has none the less been the Wittgensteinian one of assembling reminders of what we already know. Recognition of the familiar, not an abstruse theory, is all that is called for; it is just that the familiar is closer to the Augustinian picture than might have been thought.

11

Meaning and Verification

If meaning is anywhere near as broad as use, it is prima facie unwarranted to allow a condition as narrow as that of verifiability to dictate what is to count as meaningful; particular uses of words may make that demand, but there need be no presumption that these relate to more than a part of the language. If, on the other hand, an account of meaning along Augustinian lines is defensible, there is more obviously room for further constraints. Meaning, on this view, is a matter of a relation between word and world; if one term of that relation falls quite outside our experience, how can we know that the word means this rather than that? The position we have arrived at aims to improve upon the crude Augustinian scheme, but it retains enough of that conception to make questions of verifiability more pressing than if just *some* form of use is all that meaning is thought to require. At all events, whichever of the approaches has the greater claim on our allegiance, verification can be counted on to raise issues of importance, and we shall now explore its involvement with meaning in relation both to Wittgenstein's thought and to more recent developments.

11.1 Wittgenstein and verification

A central position for truth in an account of meaning need not detract from the importance of verification, which might well be expected to enter into the further elaboration of any condition formulated in terms of truth conditions. Knowing what *p* means is held to be a matter of knowing what it is for *p* to be true. To the extent that this is acceptable, it remains so when verifiability is also demanded, so long as what counts as such knowledge is interpreted to accord with this condition – an interpretation that is not in the least implausible. The appeal to verification is frequently represented as an alternative to a truth-conditional approach. That risks confusion. Conversely, if an account of meaning goes astray in the place it assigns to truth, it is likely that verification will be heir to its defects. Truth confines us to just one mood, the indicative, and the range of words to which it has application within sentences of the requisite type makes for a further restriction on its relevance. Both restrictions are surely shared by verification.

Although the limitations in an appeal to truth have been made apparent, it is worth pointing out that the difficulties just mentioned are in no way insuperable, since the considerations which point in the direction of verifiability as a reasonable demand need not be confined in their scope to declarative sentences. Knowing the meaning of *p* is, with certain qualifications, knowing how things are made out to be by one who propounds *p*. How is such knowledge to be understood? It is only secondarily a matter of being able to give a paraphrase of *p*; conversely, the ability to give a paraphrase is no guarantee of understanding, since it may amount merely to knowing that *p* means the same as *q*, rather than knowing that *p* means *q*, with the latter's implication that *q*, and hence *p*, are understood. The ability to give a paraphrase must proceed from an understanding of each of the two sentences, but then it is useless as a test thereof. To reach a satisfactory account of understanding, of knowledge of meaning, we must appeal to the exit from language involved in an ability to use the right words in the right circumstances. What is required, in other words, is an ability to recognize circumstances which verify *p*.

In this argument *p* is being taken to be a declarative sentence, but we have seen that we can think of *p* as going proxy for a sentence of any type and still speak of knowledge of meaning in terms of knowing how things are made out to be by one who utters *p*. Once more, if it is not essentially a matter of being able to *say*, it must surely be a matter of being able to *tell* when things are as one who says *p* makes them out to be, to recognize when conditions for correct use have been fulfilled. Such a notion is appropriately indifferent to the particular grammar of *p*, though of course in this more general case it will no longer be appropriate to speak of verification.

Although Wittgenstein's conception of what is meaningful comes to be as liberal as the equation of meaning with use dictates, at the beginning of the thirties verification reigns for him supreme: 'To understand the sense of a proposition means to know how the issue of its truth or falsity is to be decided' (*PR* 77); 'The verification is not *one* token of the truth, it is *the* sense of the proposition' (ibid. 200; cf. *WVC passim*). Over the decade, these uncompromising pronouncements give way to a less controversial conception of the link between meaning and verification. An account of how a proposition, *p*, is verified, of how one can know *p* to be true, serves to elucidate its meaning by relating *p* to other propositions, by showing what it follows from and what follows from it (*AWL* 19–20). Provided, that is, that in doing so we give the grammar of *p*, and not merely 'symptoms', grounds whose bearing on the truth of *p* is learned of only by experience (ibid. 31), though these might be said to determine meaning in a 'less important way' (ibid. 28). When the explanation is grammatical, it may look as though we have just a variation on the notion of explaining meaning by saying in other words what *p* comes to, by specifying what it is, or is like, for *p* to be true (ibid. 184). This appears to be how Wittgenstein thought of it at one point, but as he comes to place more and more emphasis on the multifariousness of use, an account of how *p* is verified is held to have the role only of a *contribution* to the grammar of *p*, and not to exhaust all questions of meaning (cf. *PI* §353).

Relatedly, verification may be called upon to displace a misguided appeal to feelings or experiences, to direct us instead to how the proposition is used (*AWL* 29). There need again be nothing dogmatic here. Not the claim that meaningfulness depends on whether or not verification is possible; only that the latter is determinative of meaning when the particular use of the proposition makes that demand; which is not to say that we do not meet with other uses. Verifiability may be an inappropriate notion to invoke with avowals of immediate experience; likewise with forms of words which serve to *make* something so. Still undogmatically, we could say: if *p* is not verifiable, do not ask of it what you would ask of a proposition that is; respect the kind of use it has. Think how, while it may not be put in so many words, the choice as presented by Wittgenstein often appears to be between interpreting a given form of words either as a grammatical or as an empirical proposition, as a rule for testing or as a proposition to be tested. If metaphysical pronouncements appear suspect through failing to qualify as either, that could be because they purport to do what it takes character as one or other to achieve, being perhaps – as with 'Sensations are private' – in essence grammatical but masquerading as empirical. It is not to be expected that Wittgenstein will be found belabouring anyone with anything as explicit as the verification principle, his point being more likely to be made more subtly, as through a question, but that does not mean that, in some contexts and for some purposes, such a principle might not fit his thought, if not his style.

The presupposition that we are concerned only with forms of words which it makes sense to speak of as being put to the test points up an awkwardness with the condemnation given by 'unverifiable hence meaningless'. Wittgenstein is emphatic that nonsensical combinations of words, as 'This is green and yellow at the same time', are no better than a series of patently meaningless vocables, as 'Ab sur ah' (ibid. 64). But if we have such patent nonsense, our grounds for calling it such would never be that it presented us with an unverifiable proposition. Even to set about seeing whether *p* can be verified we must be able to make some sense of its constituent terms; there has to be enough of the usual framework for testability to be invited. And indeed it is noticeable that the celebrated examples of contentious sentences in this area cannot usually be faulted on their individual components. 'Ab sur ah' as a standing source of controversy is of course ludicrous; not so 'The earth came into existence five minutes ago', or, to take another of Wittgenstein's examples, 'There is a white rabbit between two chairs whenever no observations or verifications are being carried out' (ibid. 26). If this is adjudged meaningless on the grounds that the existential affirmation has become detached from any criterion of its truth, we are clearly appealing to the meanings of the component words in arriving at this verdict.

There is some understandable uncertainty as regards the relation between 'meaningless' – or 'nonsense' – and 'false'. Consider, for instance, the question whether a positivist may be described as an atheist. Not at all, we might think, if his quarrel is with the very intelligibility of the words 'God exists'. This 'proposition' is not to be rejected by introducing a negation, since that will leave untouched the defect, the unintelligibility, of the original, so the positivist is not an atheist in the sense of one who maintains the falsity of what the theist affirms. On the other hand, does not the judgement that 'God exists' is unverifiable require us to attach *some* sense to the words, much as if we were to say that they expressed a falsehood? It is not as if the characterization were being applied in a vacuous way – as might be said of words which did not even begin to present a verifiable possibility, e.g., the exclamation 'Yippee!' – so how else can we arrive at this verdict if not on the basis of an understanding of the component terms?

A dismissal as nonsense because unverifiable threatens to become incoherent, but there is another model for the use of 'nonsense'. It is not uncommon for statements that are considered outrageously improbable or patently false to be thus branded; in particular, a contradiction is likely to attract this condemnation. In such cases it will be allowed that the words make some sort of sense, even – contradictions excepted – that they could express a truth in more favourable circumstances. A justified charge of nonsense here does not mean reduction to the 'Ab sur ah' variety, which would obliterate the features which led to the more specific descriptions – as wildly implausible, say – but it is because the words have the meanings they do that we reach this appraisal, an appraisal which appears to relate to the remoteness of truth, at least as viewed from the given circumstances.

If, as with Wittgenstein's examples of unverifiable propositions, the constituent words are individually meaningful and their combination grammatical, overall meaninglessness will seemingly have to result from an incongruence between the parts that is akin to a contradiction. This fits the idea of failing to make sense, which has more obvious application to a complex unit than to a single word. Typically, however, we are presented neither with outright inconsistency nor with words which can be described as meaningless; rather, it is a misuse of meaningful terms that leads to overall unintelligibility. Suppose it is said that an undetectable object is on the table. This puts the spatial term under pressure: how can the use of 'on' be justified when there is no way of setting spatial bounds to the 'object'? How can it be anything other than arbitrary to say 'on' rather than 'under' or 'beside'? The word has simply been prised off the kind of condition that gives it sense, leaving us in the realm of distinctions without a difference.

Is this a matter of meaningless because unverifiable? On the one hand, the violence done here to our concepts consists in severing them from the practices and procedures which make them the concepts they are, an abuse of language which compares with a failure to give sense, and which may be thought on that account not to license a dismissal in these terms. Similarly, a word or phrase may fail to apply because it is not determinate how it is to do so – as when we are asked how many times certain squares fit into a larger one when the scale in which we are to take the former has not been decided (*RPP* I, §67). On the other hand, if the only relevant way of giving the word a sense is to associate it with a recognizable condition for its application, failure to do so would appear to invite this style of condemnation. Consider the theological notion of transubstantiation, understood as being a genuine change in substance dissociated from anything that would normally be recognized as such a change, and without any new criterion being introduced to give content to the notion. Compare, too, the mathematical case, where such a question as 'Are there four consecutive 7s in pi?' is held to be without sense until a method has been fixed for answering it, so which might incur the judgement 'meaningless because unanswerable'.

Another example. In the mouth of the sceptic, the venerable question, 'Is grass green in the dark?', is likely to involve an abuse of the qualification, 'in the dark'. It may be true that the grass, which is in the dark, is green; whether or not that is so is to be decided in the usual way – which is not by inspecting the grass without the help of any illumination. On the other hand, the qualification could play a more substantive role in determining the sense of the question, much as with the analogous phrase 'in the winter' in the question, 'Are these trees green in the winter?' Some substances may present us with a greenish glow in the dark; whether grass was green in the dark, understood on the model of this use, would be determined by seeing how it then looked. Under neither interpretation is there anything approaching a difficulty, but the appearance of an insoluble problem can be generated by adopting an interpretation of 'green in the dark' which is not refuted by looking at the grass in the dark and not detecting green, yet not confirmed by looking at the grass in the light and seeing that it is green. There is a problem only if we have a meaningful but unanswerable question, yet all that has happened is that the intelligible interpretations have been disallowed without anything being put in their place. It is not difficult to see more than one possibility at work here: a misuse of meaningful language, a failure to give sense, and even a contradictory conception of what it is to be green in the dark.

It is then coherent to reject a putative proposition as meaningless because unverifiable if this amounts to rejecting it as a possible truth on the grounds that criteria for the use of some of its terms have not been laid down. We may prefer to stay with the latter description in giving our grounds for rejection – this appears to be Wittgenstein's preference – but if sense can be given only as suggested, it is in order to cite unverifiability as the defect.

Whether there is inconsistency in some form, or whether what is to count as an instance of the given predicate has not been determined, it is not that we have a description which misrepresents its object, but the failure is more basic, and this is captured by an application of our formula: for one reason or another there is no such thing as how things have to be for the words to apply. However, meaninglessness may be thought to be the lot of superficially less questionable forms: of, say, 'I am here', if the situation is inappropriate (*PI* §§514, 520; *OC* §10), or of 'There are physical objects' (*OC* §§35–6). Indeed, it is noteworthy that it is just such apparently trivial truths, couched in terms of formal or logical concepts, as *physical object* or *colour*, that are the most common targets of Wittgenstein's imputations of nonsense. Here we see another aspect of the doctrine of meaning as use, what looks like a meaningful combination of words being deemed of uncertain sense so long as it is unclear how it is to be used in a live context. Such sentences may have their place in a language game, but when uttered out of context be lacking in meaning, 'not because they are superfluous, but because their meaning is not determined by the situation, yet stands in need of such determination' (*OC* §348).

The rejection of such forms is least questionable when the grounds are that the words do not make sense in the given *combination*, rather than when they are said not to make sense in the given *context*, the former qualification being more obviously relevant when we are considering the status of the words within the language. To make out the latter case, Wittgenstein is prepared to read into the given form what we should normally regard as in the more variable category of speaker's meaning. Thus: 'For how a sentence is *meant* can be expressed by an expansion of it and may therefore be made part of the sentence' (ibid. §349). A remark may be found bewildering, in that its relation to the context is quite opaque, but of course it is recognizable English, or whatever, that we have in mind, and not blatant nonsense of the 'Ab sur ah' variety. The words themselves cannot be spoken of as utterly unintelligible. On the contrary, it is because the actual circumstances are not as we should expect, given the meanings of the words, that we are at a loss to know what to make of what is said.

11.2 *Verifiability and decidability*

Although use is not in general to be constrained by considerations of verifiability, a failure of that condition could mean, as implied, that certain forms of words simply fell by the way, unfit to do what we ask of them. And, of course, the 'certain' forms are the ones that matter most if they encompass words with which we purport to state a matter of fact. Conversely, to treat some propositions as requiring to be put to the test of experience may misrepresent their status, notable examples for Wittgenstein being those bedrock judgements which hold fast for us whatever happens, as 'The world existed for a long time before my birth', or even 'This is a hand' (*OC passim*). Like mathematical propositions, these have the role of fixing our concepts, not of expressing well-founded empirical beliefs: to envisage their falsity is to contemplate our very understanding – as of 'true' and 'false' – deserting us (ibid. §514). Or at least that is a role they may have. If they do not have this quasi *a priori* status, if there is an attempt to differentiate amongst states of affairs, with both truth and falsity possible, then we have the kind of role with which Wittgenstein's early explicit endorsements of verifiability are associated: 'To show what sense a statement makes requires saying how it can be verified and what can be done with it' (*AWL* 19). Propositions are seen as meaningful in so far as there is some criterion for their truth, in so far as their truth makes some discernible difference. If each and every experience agrees with *p*, if nothing different is associated with the circumstance of *p's* being true and its being false, then no use is being made of the kind of possibility which the assertoric form offers. No contrast is made by *p*, but it says nothing, is meaningless (ibid. 26). ' . . . it means nothing to say they are the same if every method of finding out is rejected' (ibid. 169). Perhaps these demands are aimed only at those propositions whose general form gives sense to a consideration of their possible verification, but that takes in a vast area of the language.

The equation of meaning with use can allow for this emphasis on verification, even if it finds no room for the notion with respect to other uses of language. Indeed, this statement is, if anything, too cautious, the inspiration behind that equation being very much what underlies the appeal to verification itself when this is apposite. However, it is true that after the forthright demands for verifiability of the thirties, the other uses attain for Wittgenstein a status that is at least equal, and possibly of greater importance, in part because he does not see certain linguistic forms – e.g., those of a theological character – as having the function which their superficial grammar would suggest. Another demonstration of his more liberal viewpoint is provided by his discussion of verification and imaginability, of knowing what it would be like to . . . (*PI* §§395-7, §§448-51). Such a condition directs us to a possible way of determining sense, but no more, since *p* can have a use without our being able to imagine anything in connection with it. Might we not even find that, without being in any way a defect, undecidability is a dominant feature of certain language games? After all, it is integral to our concept of pain that a person may be in pain yet show nothing of this in his behaviour, and Wittgenstein himself suggests just such a possibility with respect to reports of thoughts: someone guesses my thoughts and writes them down; if I confirm what he has written, how do I know that I really did think that and, influenced perhaps by the writing, am not just imagining I did? The question would be undecidable: 'And the word "undecidable" belongs to the description of the language-game' (*RPP* I, §568). After all, the lack of relation between certain concepts can be as much laid down in the grammar as relations of entailment. Again, it might be said that the evidence we may have can never do more than make the genuineness of an expression of feeling probable, though in all these cases the emphasis is on the nature of the evidential relation, rather than on the degree of confidence possible. It is not as if, for instance, everyone were hopelessly in doubt about what others feel (cf. *LW* I, §877; *RPP* II, §684); what uncertainty there is is not a shortcoming, but is constitutive of our concepts – an indefiniteness in the nature of the game, in the admissible evidence (*RPP* II, §657; *LW* I, §888). And again: 'The "uncertainty" relates not to the particular case, but to the method, to the rules of evidence' (*Z* §555).

Here we might also mention Wittgenstein's tolerance of views which would draw scorn from a hard-headed positivist, as when he states that he understands the teaching that the soul can exist when the body has disintegrated (*PI* 178). The observation offered in support – 'I can imagine plenty of things in connection with it' – is unsatisfactorily vague, as Wittgenstein might be expected to acknowledge (ibid. §395), but he does make clear that he asks of the words only that they perform a certain service, a service which we might call upon a picture to render. Perhaps this is likewise all he asks for the intelligibility of 'God', which he thinks quite clearly has a serious use (*RPP* I, §213).

It is not clear just how much Wittgenstein regards as intelligible in this area. Certainly, he recognizes a language game with a religious vocabulary, his dismissive observations being directed against attempts to make such discourse out to be something it is not; and what, in his eyes, it decidedly is not is quasi-scientific language, where we might speak in terms of hypotheses, of high probability, of beliefs based on evidence, beliefs which make a claim to be reasonable. Such pretensions strike him as ludicrous (cf. the *Lectures on Religious Belief* in *LA*). Even words like 'believe' are used quite differently from the one context to the other, with the possibility that our usual understanding deserts us in the religious domain, despite the familiarity of the individual words. Compare his attitude to mathematics. It is not for philosophy to restrict mathematical activity, but it has something to say if a mathematician should misrepresent what he is doing – as might well happen should he stray into Cantor's paradise.

Some danger of excessive tolerance may still remain. That 'God' has a serious use in some sense is undeniable, and, while more controversial, it is hard to say that the word is without meaning – leaving aside the case where it is regarded just as a proper name. We can say so much by way of explanation, it would be quite unwarranted to align it with a patently contentless vocable, such as 'aargh'. On the other hand, our explanation is bound to run up against familiar difficulties: some of the conditions, as being outside space and time, are of questionable intelligibility, and there is a risk of conflict between others, as omnipotence and benevolence. Meaningfulness looks in this instance to be a matter of degree, though since it tends to be the interesting dimensions that are suspect – statements of what God is *not* dominating the agreed cases – the residual meaning that can be claimed for 'God' may be a pretty poor thing. Compare names of subatomic particles. Here, too, we have a *picture*, and it may be to this that we appeal in making good our claim to a grasp of meaning, failing to see that it is as much an obstacle as an aid to understanding (cf. *PI* §§422–4). Even applicability of a term like 'particle' is not automatically guaranteed, but has to receive its justification in conditions more specific than would warrant the use of 'thing', say; we could raise just such a question with words whose sense might be taken for granted in connection with 'God', as, e.g., 'individual' or 'person', though with less chance of an answer than in the physical case.

The problem posed by theological propositions may, as I see it, be stated as follows: do they make enough sense to be false, or does even that assessment treat them too kindly? Putting it this way accepts that the relevant forms of words are to be taken at their face value; that, for instance, a person who says that there will be a Judgement Day, that he will survive his death, is doing what we should most naturally take him to be doing, viz. making predictions which aim to be true. For Wittgenstein, however, there is no question that such pronouncements should compare with statements of scientific belief for which evidence may be adduced; taken that way they are mere superstition. Indeed, it seems he would regard the construal I consider natural as a misrepresentation of the beliefs of the religious person, for whom such language has an all-important expressive or exhortative role, but aims at nothing beyond this. Where the emphasis is on a broadly religious/ethical way of looking at things, that may be apt, but it does not fit the interpretation either of traditional Christian apologetics or of the deist, who may think of statements about God as having a logic comparable with statements about the age of the universe. But, of course, the main point is one of what religious language *can* aspire to, and on this Wittgenstein succeeds, in my view, in drawing the lines at the right point. Cf. the following observations:

> Religion says: *Do this*! – *Think like that*! – but it cannot justify this, and once it even tries to it becomes repellent; because for every reason it offers there is a valid counter-reason. It is more convincing to say: 'Think like this! – however strangely it may strike you.' Or: 'Won't you do this? – however repugnant you find it.'
>
> (*CV* 29)

At all events, acknowledging areas where the demand for verifiability is unenforceable should not lead us to overlook those in which its absence means that our words are not equipped to do what we ask of them. As Wittgenstein asks, '. . . how can I even make the hypothesis if it transcends all possible experience? How could such a hypothesis be backed by meaning?' (*BB* 48). And much later: 'It is only apparently possible to "transcend any possible experience"; even these words only seem to make sense because they are arranged on the analogy of significant expressions' (*Z* §260). But in that case, what are we to make of the example of undecidability which Wittgenstein explicitly allows with respect to reports of one's thoughts? Simply this: that undecidability is not the same as unverifiability.

Intelligibility of p may require the possibility of recognizing, with a greater or lesser degree of finality, when p is true or false, but, whatever the degree of finality demanded, this is not to say that we must be able to engineer a situation in which that possibility is realized, that we should have some effective means of determining the truth value of p.

The usage conferred upon 'decidable' in mathematical contexts gives reason enough to adopt this reading, though for some purposes a broader interpretation might be preferred. Consider the following example (cf. Rundle 1986). We are asked to bring to mind a familiar sound – the ringing of a telephone, say, or the pips in the time signal. The question arises whether we are recalling sounds heard on a particular occasion, but if the pips have been unvarying from occasion to occasion, it would seem there is no way of telling whether we are bringing to mind the series of pips last heard rather than some earlier series – supposing that the sounds are not remembered in conjunction with circumstances which would individuate them. However, while a sceptical conclusion threatens, it can surely be warded off: it is not that we may be recalling this or that sequence of sounds, we cannot tell which; rather, it makes no *sense* to say that we are recalling this rather than that.

In such a case we should naturally say that the question of identity is undecidable, understanding this in a way that ties the notion closely to meaning: no content has been assigned to the supposed difference, so there are not two real possibilities to decide between. We might introduce 'unverifiable' on the same grounds, but this goes better with the case where, for one reason or another, it is not possible to put the hypothesis to the test, rather than where the failing is more fundamental, the necessary difference not even having been defined, so where there is nothing to decide. This in effect continues our earlier theme of the uncertainty attaching to 'meaningless because unverifiable'. However, in mathematical usage decidability requires not merely that a difference between predicates should have been defined, but that we should have a decision procedure enabling us to ascertain how things stand in point of truth. I propose to retain this connection and to associate verifiability with the broader condition which recommends itself when we venture outside mathematical contexts: for verifiability of p it is required merely that if p is true (false), then knowledge that p is true (false) should at least have been a possibility, not, as with decidability, that circumstances in which such knowledge is within our grasp can be arranged to order. At least in the non-mathematical case, it is thus possible to hold to a demand for verifiability yet allow that, for purely contingent reasons, it is excluded. This will not put at risk the intelligibility of the given form of words. Statements about the remote past are sometimes thought to discredit verificationism, but it would be a bizarre view that was troubled by the merely contingent absence of records or memories extending back to the time in question. Such a possibility rules out decidability as a tenable demand, but does nothing to upset verifiability as here understood.

We shall see more of this issue in our final chapter. For the present let us follow up the key distinction between the reasons why verification may be lacking, viz. because it makes no sense in the given context, and because, while making sense, it so happens that it is not to be had. It proves of some importance to note that, in so far as undecidability is due simply to this latter circumstance, it does not have the power to affect attributions of truth value.

With regard to a person's thoughts, there are numerous occasions when no real problem of knowledge would be considered to arise: people make it plain by their words and actions that they think the window is open, that someone is at the door, that the bus stops here, that there is a puddle there to be avoided, and so on indefinitely. Suppose we do not take the opportunity to find out at the time whether a person thinks such-and-such, but are told only subsequently. When it is a matter of current thoughts, truth reduces to truthfulness of the person's statement, but with a lapse of time it makes sense to suppose error through faulty memory, as Wittgenstein envisages. However, since earlier enquiries could have forestalled this difficulty, our ignorance cannot be regarded as inescapable in any damaging sense. It just *happens* that the person did not divulge his thoughts to us at the time he had them.

This way around such problems may be thought evasive. It is claimed that, while a person may keep his thoughts to himself, he may also disclose them, and because of this latter possibility we may say that if knowledge of a person's thoughts is denied us, this is only contingently so, hence that any difficulties here are practical rather than theoretical. But is not the worry precisely how we might verify conjectures about a person's thoughts in particular circumstances – when he gives no sign of what he is thinking – these circumstances being part of the problem, not something we are to imagine being otherwise?

Compare: how might we verify a contrary-to-fact supposition, as

'If you had been at the party you would have enjoyed yourself'? The revelation that the person addressed was in fact at the party and did indeed enjoy himself contradicts a likely assumption behind the speaker's choice of this conditional form, but can we not now think of this as verified, however unexpectedly? Likewise with falsification: the speaker is surely shown to be wrong if it turns out that the person was at the party and failed to enjoy himself. It might be objected that, if it proves that the person was at the party, then this form of conditional is no longer apt, not fittingly assigned a truth value. However, the objection that interests me is this: appealing to verification and falsification as just explained in no way dispels the original worry, since this was precisely one concerning how we could have verification when the situation was as one who used this conditional form would normally suppose.

But now, if this is how the difficulty is envisaged, then the problematic situation is correctly described as one in which verification is *logically* impossible. There may be some alternative form that verification can take, but at least as it has so far been explained it is excluded for the most emphatic of reasons. And does it make sense to lament a failure to achieve what is logically unattainable? Surely not. Similarly with 'We cannot know what is going on in the mind of another' if this presents us with a logical 'cannot': if the claim is that nothing would count as knowing what is going on in someone else's mind, a real possibility is not being denied us. And that is how it is as the problem with thoughts is envisaged. To say that one cannot tell what another is thinking is then on a par with the statement that in tennis one cannot shoot the ball into goal; if, that is, the proposition is not treated as an empirical proposition, as it would be by one who says 'Tell me what you are thinking' (*RPP* I, §§566–7). A genuine possibility is specified when it is said that we might know a person's thoughts through his words, but ruling this out as inapplicable is not to put a real alternative in its place. Similarly, '*His* pains are hidden from me' would be like saying 'These sounds are hidden from my eyes' (*LW* I, §885).

The dismissal given with these analogies is very much to the point, but the positive account of how knowledge is possible is by far the more important element in the argument. If it is simply senseless to suggest that we might know that *p*, then the lack of such knowledge is assuredly nothing to lament, but senselessness in this regard can be granted without impugning the possibility which is held to lie beyond our knowledge. That is, it could still be maintained that it makes good sense to suppose that a person may be engrossed in thought, only that we can never really know that this is so, let alone exactly what he is thinking, and this is not unproblematic, since it prises apart what can be and what can be known to be. Wittgenstein considers that we can indeed have the knowledge in question, the thinker's word, along with the circumstances, providing a basis for deciding whether we have guessed his thoughts rightly, even if the verification which this provides is quite different from what is to be found in other language games (*RPP* I, §566) – the question of how it differs being just what it is at issue in the debate over the proper interpretation of the term 'criterion'. We note that, while knowledge that a person has had certain thoughts may be granted, what we cannot do is to have these thoughts in a way that would require us to think the thoughts for him. That, like smiling a person's smiles for him, is the absurd case.

The same point can be made in connection with the problem of verifying propositions about the unobserved. It may be that, on one conception of verification, the very idea that we should know of the existence of the room's furniture once we turn our backs on it is an idea to be dismissed out of hand. We might counter by contending that the lack of knowledge is, on the given conception, nothing to lament, but again we should be wary of simply accepting the consequent gulf between what can be and what can be known to be. Suppose it is logically impossible to find out that there is a white rabbit between two chairs whenever no observations or verifications are being carried out. Still, is there not enough for a problem if we as much as grant that there could none the less *be* such a creature?

Clearly, the difficulty here is much less acute than in the case of thoughts and feelings. With thoughts that go unexpressed we point to the merely contingent lack of verification, but to say that we could have had knowledge, that the person might have given voice to his thoughts, is not without difficulties in relation to the supposition of verifiability – in particular, difficulties presented by the possibility of insincerity. With the unobserved rabbit, by contrast, the verification that happens to be excluded is verification at its most straightforward. The claim that we have verifiability in the relevant sense is the claim that what went unobserved might have been observed. It is not the nonsensical claim that we should have observed a rabbit which all the while went unobserved. Moreover, given the lifting of any threat to the intelligibility of hypotheses about what has gone unobserved, there is the possibility of speaking of knowledge of how things are, even if this is based only on indirect considerations. As, of course, a contrary-to-fact proposition might provide. Verification is indeed ruled out if the situation is as one who used this form would normally suppose, but we should expect that use to be untouched by this circumstance. And this is what we find, 'would', rather like 'must', requiring compelling evidence, but evidence which falls short of conclusive verification, when we are provided not so much with evidence for a phenomenon, but with the phenomenon itself.

Wittgenstein's discussions of the inner and the outer are subtle and intricate, not to be oversimplified by reading in a concern with verification at every turn. Right to the last, however, there is a recurrent verificationist theme: the mental lives of others are sources of uncertainty for us, uncertainty of different kinds as well as in differing degrees, but our psychological concepts are none the less firmly anchored in unshakeable cases. Cf. the following observations from MS 171:

> A man groans under anaesthetic or in his sleep. I am asked, 'Is he in pain?' I shrug my shoulders or say 'I don't know if he is in pain.' Sometimes I recognize something as a criterion for this, but sometimes I do not.
>
> Now, do I then mean nothing by this? Not at all: I make a move in an existing game. But this game would not exist if there were not criteria in other cases.

> Something proves to be pain or pretence. And that is essential to the concepts 'pain' and 'pretence', even if it doesn't turn out that way in every one of their applications.

Again, an expression of joy or its opposite may be *unmistakable* (MS 169); we may give a *direct* description of a face as sad, bored, or radiating happiness, and not have to make inferences as to grief, boredom, or joy (Z §225).

Perhaps the main problem we are left with is the following. A person's behaviour may leave it open whether or not he is in pain. On the current argument, that is of no great consequence if it remains true that his behaviour *could* have furnished us with a telling indication of his state. However, this looks to be unsatisfying, in that there appears to be too great a gulf between what we learn of when verification is to be had, and what we can merely surmise when it is not – the gulf between behaviour and sensation, no less.

What is needed is a demonstration of the unity of our concept of pain, making it clear that one and the same phenomenon is at issue in the two cases, that an explanation of what it is to be in pain fits them both. Knowledge is a much more tractable example in this respect. You do not know whether I know your address. Untroubling, because you could have found out by asking me, and if knowledge is a species of ability, no further difficulty is furnished by the two forms – expressed and unexpressed – that my knowledge takes, since what we say or do can give proof of the very same ability as had hitherto gone unexercised. With respect to sensations we should hope to make use of a connection with desire, and therewith a tendency, disposition, or preparedness to act; there is no difficulty in understanding desire in a constant sense, whether a creature is able to do what it wants or is prevented from doing so, and since we might explain the notion of an unpleasant sensation in terms of a desire to be free, or to steer clear of, certain kinds of stimuli, there is accordingly the possibility of making sense in these terms of pain which may or may not be evidenced in behaviour.

Other complications remain, some of which we shall tackle shortly, but even at this point it appears plausible to hold that if fact-stating language is to do what we ask of it, then verifiability is not a condition we can take or leave as we please. Certainly, the case in its favour is strong enough to make it reasonable that we should aim at overcoming its undoubted difficulties, rather than simply accept these as proof that the demand cannot be sustained. This is not to say that we must be able to arrange for verifying or falsifying circumstances to come about, such a power being clearly further to the possession of understanding which we may manifest in a correct use of language when the relevant circumstances happen to present themselves. That is, it is verifiability rather than decidability that lays claim to our support.

12

Realism and Infinity

Verification is at the centre of the debate between realist and anti-realist. For the realist, it makes sense to say that *p* has a truth value even if it does not depict a state of affairs that might fall within our knowledge; it is reality that determines a statement as true or false, irrespective of whether that reality is knowable by us. The anti-realist, by contrast, holds that a statement can be true only in virtue of some state of affairs of which we could have knowledge, which we should count as evidence for its truth. Prima facie, the latter position is in keeping with the preceding train of thought, but this impression is to some extent illusory. As yet we have only a glimmering of what is involved in the two positions, and we shall find that, paradoxically, what is thought of as realism may be helped rather than hindered by association with a moderate form of verificationism.

12.1 Verification and anti-realism

The unexpected development just alluded to stems from the anti-realist's appeal to the stronger notion of effective decidability. In some connections it is not important to press the distinction between decidability and the weaker condition of verifiability, but it is clear that Dummett's anti-realist makes the former his key notion. Cf. Dummett 1981, 469, and the following passage from 'Truth':

> We are entitled to say that a statement *P* must be either true or false, that there must be something in virtue of which either it is true or it is false, only when *P* is a statement of such a kind that we could in a finite time bring ourselves into a position in which we were justified

> either in asserting or in denying *P*; that is, when *P* is an effectively decidable statement.
>
> (1978, 16–17)

While the case for verifiability is a case to be reckoned with, it is hard to say the same for decidability. Propositions about another's thoughts are not effectively decidable – there is no sure-fire method of extracting information about what is going on in a person's head – but what matters is that we should be able to *find* ourselves in a situation in which we can tell what another is thinking, even though we have no reliable recipe for bringing this about. That possibility just is the possibility that the state of affairs should come within the scope of our knowledge – in conformity with the considerations which argue the need for verifiability. There is no further difficulty with the principles of bivalence or excluded middle – the relevant contradictories are no more problematic than the propositions they contradict – but the real problem rests with verifiability: is there really such a thing as being able to tell what another is thinking?

For the realist, understanding *p* is a matter of knowing its truth conditions – knowing what must be the case if it is true, what must be the case if it is false. A verificationist opponent may hold that such knowledge is to be had only when we can be justified in asserting or denying *p*, that without such warrant the intelligibility of *p* is not to be granted. For the anti-realist, however, the stigma of undecidability may be not so much *nonsense*, as simply: *p* is without truth value. He might hold that 'either true or false' is a condition we can insist upon for verifiable statements only, yet not wish to condemn as meaningless statements which do not meet this condition. This would set him apart from the positivist, who sees in verifiability a criterion for meaningfulness, though if the anti-realist accuses the realist of ascribing to certain forms of words a meaning they cannot have, the overall effect may be much the same as a denunciation as nonsense, there being just as much a failure of the words to be as desired or required on either approach. Certainly, it is not simply that, for the anti-realist, there is no sense to an attribution of truth value so long as his preconditions go unfulfilled; since he also claims that the realist's attempts at assigning meaning cannot be reckoned successful in the disputed cases, there is ample scope for him to accuse the realist of talking nonsense.

In what follows we shall make our primary concern the intelligibility of the forms of words on which the dispute between realist and anti-realist is centred. If, as will be argued, certain purported readings simply leave us with specimens of nonsense, a refusal to regard these as suitable subjects for 'either true or false' will hardly constitute an adequate acknowledgement of their more seriously defective character. Dummett's example, (1) A city will never be built on this spot, is a case in point, and other sentences in similar vein are: (2) Britain will never again have an empire; (3) There will never be a better time than the present for investing in oil; (4) Vesuvius will never again erupt. These might be joined by spatial analogues, as 'There is no life outside this planet', but we shall consider only the explicitly temporal statements.

The 'general propositional form' of such statements is not: This is how things will turn out. We do not, in affirming them, envisage a temporal perspective from which we shall eventually be able to proclaim: 'I told you so; things have come to pass just as I predicted.' There is, of course, no point in time which would afford such a perspective, and we can rightly dismiss as nonsense any interpretation which would require that there should be; that there is no such date, no such perspective, is a grammatical, not an empirical, truth. There can, it is true, be some uncertainty about the interpretation of future-tense statements with 'never'. In some cases we shall be happy to agree to a further qualification at this point: with 'He will never go along with that proposal' it is superfluous to add 'in his lifetime', but this is what is intended, and with this reading what we have can be treated as a simple prediction, in the sense that the speaker looks forward to a time when he will be seen to have spoken truly. Not so with (1) to (4). However, this is not to say that such pronouncements do not have a use, nor in some cases a justification. It may be asking a lot of any findings to date to warrant the emphatic exclusion of an imperial future, as made by (2), but appropriate considerations can be imagined. And, knowing that reserves of oil are rapidly becoming depleted, we may be entitled to affirm (3). With such knowledge we may consider ourselves in a position to reject any claim of the form 't will be a better time than the present for investing in oil', where t is some future date. Indeed, it gives a fair restatement of (3) to say that it serves to rule out any such proposition.

What we are now condemning as incoherent is the attempt at stating how things will have come to pass when the time span to be considered is open-ended, open-endedness simply contradicting the conditions necessary for 'will have come to pass' to apply. Hence the reading proposed for (3), viz. 'Any time beyond the present can be ruled out as a better time for investing in oil.' This, surely, is all we *can* mean if we are not prepared to specify a temporal bound for 'never'.

It is here that the main point of contention arises. All will agree that each of (1) to (4) excludes a possibility, but on my reading we are denying that something is a possibility rather than simply denying that a certain possibility will be realized on any of an indefinite number of relevant occasions. Does not the former reading involve a confusion between meaning and grounds? Consider the comparison with conditional forms. The statement, 'The fabric will fade if left in the sun', may be countered by 'Not necessarily. The light may not be strong enough', a form of negation which amounts to challenging the speaker's warrant for saying what he says. It would seem that the challenge given by 'Not necessarily' ('It need not', 'It may not') does not amount to a contradiction of what is affirmed, and we may wonder how it can be any different with the pair 'Vesuvius will never again erupt' and 'It may'. Surely the latter is not the former's contradictory, but that role falls to (5) 'Vesuvius will erupt again some day.'

We shall not have an adequate answer to this objection until we have taken a closer look at the auxiliary 'will'. This defines the locus of the problem quite generally, not the further complication presented by an if-clause. For the present I simply state that while (5) is inconsistent with (4) 'Vesuvius will never again erupt', it is too strong to constitute its contradictory, to be assured of application when (4) fails. We do not, that is, have 'Either Vesuvius will erupt again some day, or a future eruption is ruled out'. If this analysis remains counter-intuitive, it is because we are persisting in seeing sense where there is no more than an illusion of intelligibility. There is an air of paradox here, yet it is surely clear that the 'interpretation' which is being dismissed is not one which we have to take into account in any way. This being so, it is at best misleading to say that, for instance, we may be unable to determine whether the conditions which justify assertion of (4) on this interpretation obtain or not; that we are accordingly not entitled to say that the proposition is either true or false. Likewise, it is a mistake to allow that a being with greater observational powers could take in the relevant reality, then exclude this as an explanation on the grounds that it does not connect with *our* use of language. This is to suppose that a genuine possibility has been specified, if only for a being with superhuman powers, but since nothing has been specified as a possibility for grammar, nothing has been specified as a possibility for any being, however powerful. The proposition is not suspect because it 'transcends our recognitional capacities', any more than is 'Ab sur ah'. It is even misleading to reject (4) on the grounds that an understanding of it could not be manifested; certainly, this is a secondary consideration, in that we shall allow that a person has displayed an understanding of p only if we consider that p presents us with something to be understood.

But, turning now to (2), suppose that Britain becomes an imperial power once more. Does this not show (2) to be false in the way that the truth of an atomic proposition Fa falsifies a generalization $\forall x \neg Fx$? No. We cannot have a counter-example to a general proposition in a reading in which the latter makes no sense – e.g., when we represent the generalization as an infinite conjunction. A proposition has the role of a counter-example to (2) through justifying the claim, 'The possibility cannot be ruled out.' This is the strict contradictory of a proposition of the form 'There will never be an *F*.' Disjoining the two – 'Either there will never be an *F* or the possibility of an *F* cannot be ruled out' – leaves us with a statement that is correct provided that for 'cannot be ruled out' it is sufficient that we have so far failed to exclude the possibility. On that interpretation we have an empty tautology, but 'cannot be ruled out' may not be applied so readily. As an analogous case, consider 'The conjecture is provable or it is not.' If by 'it is not provable' is meant no more than that we have as yet no proof, then this disjunction is similarly trivial, but of course 'can' and phrases which involve the concept may reproduce the very uncertainties with which we began. When it is said that *T* is not provable, unprovability of *T* cannot be arrived at by enumerating all possible proofs and finding them wanting. There is no such procedure. So, if it is not simply that we have no proof, we can take it to mean – what else is there for it to mean? – that a proof of *T* is known to be impossible. On this reading we do not have 'Either *T* is provable or it is not', since this means 'Either there is a proof, or that is a possibility that is excluded.' This is not, however, to advance an exception to the law of excluded middle, since the form which merits the description, 'a proposition and its contradictory disjoined', is 'Either the possibility of a proof is ruled out or there may be one.'

What, then, is the contradictory of 'Vesuvius will erupt one day'? If 'Vesuvius will never erupt' receives the interpretation here proposed, it is not the proposition we seek: we are not obliged to accept that either a future eruption can be ruled out, or else Vesuvius will erupt one day. On the other hand, while we can accept 'Either a future eruption of Vesuvius can be ruled out, or it cannot', on one interpretation, and while this reveals the latter disjunct as the contradictory of 'Vesuvius will never erupt', the form, 'A future eruption of Vesuvius cannot be ruled out', does not give an alternative rendering of 'Vesuvius will erupt one day.'

So what is it we are supposing when we suppose 'Vesuvius will erupt one day' to be false? The day will dawn when Vesuvius will erupt, or . . . .; or what, exactly? If we are confining consideration to possible developments within a specified period, there is no problem: we envisage the period coming to an end with no eruption having occurred. Take away such a restriction and we take away all applicability of this scheme, there being no such thing as: an eruption will be found not to have occurred on any of an endless number of days. We can consider how things might fall out within a finite, closed, period, but the alternative which remains when the finite case fails us – 'A future eruption can be ruled out' – is not acceptable as a contradictory. The conclusion, then, is plain: 'Vesuvius will erupt one day' simply has no contradictory. That, of course, is not to say that we are obliged to go along with someone who makes such a prediction. We can dissent in the belief that the statement is unfounded; we can have an even stronger basis for dissent if we can show the impossibility of a future eruption. Destroy the volcano, for instance, and the proposition can never be true. But such forms of disagreement do not rest on advancing a strict contradictory.

It will not have escaped notice that I am assuming that for a proposition *q* to qualify as the contradictory of *p*, the disjunction of the two must be exhaustive. But surely this is simply to accept the major principle here in contention, namely, the law of excluded middle? Yes indeed, but it is not to accept that anything that qualifies as a negation of *p* is *ipso facto* its contradictory, or even that every proposition has a contradictory. Something has to give in these cases, but it is not that law.

Consider how we might seek to justify '*p* or not-*p*'. What exactly is not-*p*? It is not just a negation of *p*, but it is required to represent a contradictory; that is, a proposition (if such there is) that is true when *p* is not true. The qualification, 'if such there is', points to an assumption written into '*p* or not-*p*' that is absent from 'Either *p* is true or it is not.' This latter simply amounts to: the alternative to being true is not being true; whence, if *p* is not true then *p* is not true. Totally trivial. Not so the transition from '*p* is not true' to 'not-*p* is true', since this requires the existence of a particular form in a particular interpretation. We need, that is, an assurance that not-*p* is a genuine contradictory to make the further move to 'If *p* is not true then not-*p* is true.' Without, then, an explanation of what counts as the negation of *p*, we do not want a putative logical principle to affirm that the disjunction of a proposition *p* with its negation is a law; even in unproblematic cases it cannot be said that anything that counts as a negation is a contradictory; it might be a contrary. But if the contradictory is, in a given case, genuinely what we have, then the instance of the law is quite trivial. What would not be trivial, but an error, would be to say that every meaningful proposition has a contradictory.

There are, of course, occasions when, for reasons that are largely uninteresting, we cannot affirm 'Either *p* or not-*p*', but these are not occasions where anyone would wish to urge that what is represented as not-*p* is the contradictory of *p*. Among the more familiar are propositions in which we have a namelike term which lacks reference, as could be the case with each of 'His son lives abroad' and 'His son does not live abroad.' Because of the presupposition common to each – that the person in question has a son – we may refuse to assent to their disjunction, in which this presupposition is retained. A less familiar illustration has been seen with unnegatable conjunctions. The sentence, 'He left because it was late', has the contradictory, 'He did not leave because it was late' – supposing the negation to be directed at the conjunction; not, that is, as in 'Because it was late he did not leave.' However, there is no matching contradictory for 'He left although it was early', the clause 'although it was early' remaining as a contestable presupposition within the negative form, 'He did not leave although it was early.' What can be considered refuted by such examples is the principle of bivalence, rather than the law of excluded middle. We have seen how the latter is protected, but the former, which holds that propositions are true or false without exception, is not in the same way provided with a saving clause, to be invoked when a contradictory is not forthcoming.

The claim that every declarative sentence has a contradictory is not something that can be affirmed *a priori*. On the other hand, have we not shown merely that the obvious way of constructing a contradictory is not always successful? After all, it does seem possible to offer 'It is not true that his son is abroad' as a presuppositionless contradictory of 'His son is abroad.' More generally, could we not suppose that the language had a negation which behaved in such a way that not-*p* was true when and only when *p* was not true? We might wish to require that *p* at least be propositional, since, as described, the proposal would appear to leave the combination in not-*p* making sense whatever the character of *p* – it might be a question or a greeting, for instance. At all events, '*p* or not-*p*' could now be affirmed without risk, without committing oneself to the kind of presupposition that may be common to each of *p* and not-*p* as negation currently operates.

However, to require of not-*p* that it be true when *p* is not true does nothing to make clear what is involved in the latter possibility. Let *p* be 'Vesuvius will erupt one day.' Knowing what it is for this to prove true, we might expect that an interpretation of 'It is not true that Vesuvius will erupt one day' should be easy to supply. However, while truth is a matter of fulfilment at some future date, and while we also have a corresponding possibility of unfulfilment whenever we have fulfilment, this possibility is not the basis for an appropriate reading of not-*p*, but all that is suggested for this is 'One day Vesuvius will not erupt.' It is not a matter of: in the only sense in which we can conceive of *p* proving true it can prove false. Not, that is, if we wish at the same time to regard the proposition which specifies the falsifying possibility as the contradictory of *p*.

12.2 Tense and mood

It will no doubt still be felt that the interpretation I have placed upon (2) and kindred forms is hard to reconcile with the words as they stand. To speak in terms of ruling out a possibility is surely to read in more than is strictly warranted – much as when 'true' is interpreted as 'assertible'. To help dispel this impression, and to develop the general topic in other directions, it is useful to give closer attention to the behaviour of the auxiliary 'will'. Dummett maintains that the realist notion of truth – as distinguished from justifiability – has its genesis in the use of certain sentential operators, and in particular the conditional (1981, 468–9). We shall focus upon this context and the distinctions which take shape within it, dealing in this section with the future case and passing to the more problematic past-tense variant in the next chapter.

Dummett suggests that, if all we wanted to do with a sentence was to use it on its own to make an assertion, then we might need no distinction between the concept of truth and that of correct assertibility; it is when sentences are linked together in truth-functional combinations with other sentences that the distinction needs to be grasped (1978, 365). I take this to mean that correct use of a prediction, say, as 'There will be a storm', would tie this to the availability of present evidence for an impending event, whereas with the same words occurring as antecedent of a conditional, 'If there will be a storm, . . . ', any ensuing inference should proceed merely on the supposition that the future happening comes about, the question of the existence of evidence in advance thereof having no bearing on the interpretation of the antecedent or the inferences that might be based upon it.

There is certainly the possibility of a distinction of this general kind, but if this is a correct reading of Dummett it is not a correct account of the terms in which that distinction is to be made. Rather, the situation is the following: either we retain the future tense in the two contexts, in which case the same words may be accorded the same treatment, or we shift to the present tense in the conditional, in which case the appropriate analyses are indeed different, but different in a way that corresponds to the shift in tense. This calls for qualification, in that there is some variability within the future tense, but the pattern which can then be discerned tends to be the opposite of that suggested by Dummett.

Before defence of these claims can get under way, there is an obvious objection to meet, viz. that the future tense simply has no place in contexts of the second type, that English requires this tense to give way to the present in the antecedent of a conditional. The reply to this common claim may be that the present as thus used is logically a future, despite its superficial grammatical form. However, both objection and reply are in error. We should certainly favour 'If he wins he will be lucky' over 'If he will win he will be lucky', and it is true that 'If there is a storm . . . ' is a more likely beginning to a conditional than is 'If there will be a storm . . . '. However, that this is less than the full picture can be readily seen from such examples as 'If he will be 66 next birthday, then he is already eligible for retirement', and 'If the tide will be in by midnight, we had better not take the coastal road.' With the former the future is as acceptable as the present, with the latter it is the preferred form. Why should this be?

When the present is used, as with 'If the tide is in by midnight, these rocks will be under water when we return', our concern is to project ourselves in thought to a future state of affairs, drawing out consequences of the occurrence then contemplated. When, on the other hand, we employ the future, as with 'If the tide will be in by midnight, we had better not take the coastal road', we remain in the present, the predictability of the occurrence being advanced as the hypothesis from which the inference is drawn. Likewise with the pair, 'Suppose Vesuvius erupts before the end of the decade' and 'Suppose Vesuvius will erupt before the end of the decade.' With the former we place ourselves in thought at some future time when the prediction has, we imagine, proven true, whereas with the latter we hypothesize a present fact about the future. This aspect – a supposed factual character in advance of the time of fulfilment – can again figure in the inferences drawn from the supposition, as with 'If Vesuvius will erupt before the end of the decade, then you would be advised to take your holidays elsewhere', whereas 'If Vesuvius erupts before the end of the decade, . . . ' presents us with a basis for conclusions which follow on the eventual eruption, rather than on its advance assertibility. Note that a conditional which maintains the future tense can itself figure as the protasis of a conditional, as with 'If he will be late if he catches the 10.30, it must be one of those trains that stops at every station *en route*.' Not a frequently used form, but again it is clear that the supposed truth from a present perspective of the contained conditional is the basis for the consequence drawn.

The present-tense form found in the antecedent of a conditional is plainly not just an idiomatic variant into which the future transforms under the influence of 'if'. It might be said that the future tense gives way to the present, but even if the future is less common at this point, it is more accurate to think in terms of a different form appropriate to a different concern. Our interest is more often in drawing consequences from the supposition of the eventual occurrence than from the supposition of advance knowledge that it will take place – knowledge which is in general difficult to come by – but it is no more correct to say that the future tense becomes the present than it would be to say that it could become past, on the strength of examples such as 'If he turned up tomorrow he would surprise us all.'

That something may hang on the choice of future over present is clear enough, though the nature and scale of the difference cannot be appreciated until the topic of tense has been pursued in some detail. The comprehensive and perceptive study in Dudman 1984 is a model for what is required, and if the analysis presented there is correct, the gulf between the two forms is far greater than has so far emerged. To compare like with like, a present-tense conditional should be seen alongside variants in which past and pluperfect figure. Consider 'If he breaks his promise, they will ignore him.' Here the speaker's concern is to develop a possibility in the light of present circumstances, accepting the world in its current state. With a shift to the past, on the other hand, as with 'If he broke his promise, they would ignore him', the imagined promise-breaking is envisaged against the backdrop of a lesser slice of history – all that has happened up to a point anterior to the present point of speech. Analogously, 'If he had broken his promise, . . . ' accepts the historical course of events up to a time that is past with respect to some past point of time. What is important is that choice of tense is dictated by considerations relating to the extent of the historical background against which consequences of the supposition are unfolded, rather than by the time of its imagined fulfilment. The tense in the if-clause locates the starting point of the fantasy developed in the principal clause. So we can have 'If he broke his promise tomorrow, . . . ', and even 'If he had broken his promise tomorrow, . . . '. The form, 'If he will break his promise, . . . ', by contrast, compares with other hypotheticals in which the time of *fulfilment* is specified, as with 'If he broke his promise, he is not to be trusted.' This Dudman regards as containing words in the scope of 'if' which can be treated as a genuine sentence, whereas 'If he broke his promise, they would ignore him' does not. That is, as they are understood in the latter, the words 'he broke his promise' do not allow of independent occurrence. Likewise with the present and future-tense protases which are our main concern: far from 'is' being a variant of 'will', the significance of the tense is quite different in the two cases. Note, incidentally, that the relevant distinctions are not confined to if-clauses. Compare 'I should like a dog that barks' with 'I should like a dog that barked.'

Consider now the use of 'will' in 'They will be sitting down to breakfast right now', and 'You will have noticed that I am wearing a tie.' A simple association of 'will' with futurity might have us regard these as grammatical sports: what is the auxiliary doing when the reference is to a current situation, or even to an event that has supposedly already taken place? An adequate answer would again require a variety of uses to be taken into account, but I suggest that the value here of 'will' lies in what it carries over from the straightforwardly future case as regards the degree of support implied for the affirmation. We may not be able to say 'They are sitting down to breakfast right now', the form appropriate when we are reporting a matter ascertained. However, the speaker could have evidence of much the same strength for this state of affairs as he might have had earlier, when the prediction, 'They will be sitting down to breakfast at 8.00 a.m. tomorrow', would have been in order. Use of 'will' acknowledges this evidential likeness, having a categorical character which matches our assurance, yet distancing us from the event in the way the future implies. Similarly, it may be presumptuous to say 'You have noticed that I am wearing a tie', yet the evidence could warrant the form with 'will'. We cannot make the same demands as regards knowledge with respect to the future as we can with past and present, so the future recommends itself when our grounds are less than conclusive, even though we are talking about a present situation. A similar distancing with respect to the past is offered with 'would': with the passage of time we might shift from 'They will be sitting down to breakfast right now' to 'They would have been sitting down to breakfast right then.' Once again, if we come to this straight from the contexts usually considered, as 'It would break if you dropped it', this use is going to seem hard to fathom.

The simplest reading of future-tense statements would be one for which truth came out simply as a matter of eventual fulfilment, leaving little to be said about 'will' beyond noting its contribution to tense. However, we have seen that there is also 'is true' to account for, and we note complications with others of the forms mentioned, as 'You will have noticed that I am wearing a tie.' It might be claimed that, in terms of truth conditions, there is no distinguishing this from 'You have noticed that I am wearing a tie', but since the latter may be reasonably asserted when the former is not, there is clearly more to be said. Uncertainty in relation to truth is a mark of modal auxiliaries, as 'should', 'may' and 'must', so could it be that we have been touching upon features of 'will' in which it compares with terms from this category?

Syntactically, 'will' bears the marks of a modal, and it can be aligned with 'must' semantically when it implies a backing in present evidence. This feature is not to the fore with a straight prediction, though it recurs with certain uses of concern to us. Consider 'Vesuvius will erupt before the end of the decade.' An invitation to suppose this true may be taken in more than one way; not only as 'Suppose Vesuvius erupts before the end of the decade', but also as 'Suppose Vesuvius will erupt before the end of the decade', where a present fact about the future is being hypothesized, and where the modal character of the auxiliary makes itself felt: we are to suppose that an eruption is *predictable*. It is clearly this latter that is the model for 'Vesuvius will never erupt', whether this occurs in isolation or within a conditional, as 'If Vesuvius will never erupt, you can venture near it with impunity.' In either case the supposition of its truth has only one coherent interpretation, viz. as a supposition of truth at the time of utterance. This can be granted only on the basis of present grounds, grounds that enable us to rule out an eruption at any future date. There is nothing special about this case, in so far as the interpretation offered is of a piece with one possible for less controversial contexts, but since there is no such time as a time of eventual fulfilment, there is no place for the form 'If Vesuvius never erupts, . . . ', where this is thought of not as featuring 'erupts' in a frequentative use – the possibility advanced in opposition to 'If Vesuvius sometimes erupts, . . . ' – but as envisaging a future state of affairs, something that will have come to pass. It is worth stressing that I am not redefining the form 'If Vesuvius will never erupt, . . . ', not claiming that it must be rejected in its usual interpretation. It is also worth stressing that, notwithstanding the way the choices have been presented, truth itself is not to be understood in two ways, any variability being not in truth *simpliciter*, but either in *what* we are supposing true or in the two notions, 'is true now' and 'will come true'.

12.3 Mathematical propositions and bivalence

The issues presented by future-tense statements are to some extent mirrored in propositions of mathematics. There are complications, in that the closer mathematical propositions approach to rules in their behaviour, the less readily we can transfer such notions as those of evidence, certainty, and verification from their empirical applications, but a clear parallel remains between such propositions as 'Vesuvius will never again erupt' and mathematical pronouncements about the infinite; to such a point that we can expect the relevant conclusions to repeat those for the empirical case, where a putative interpretation of propositions of unlimited generality was to be rejected as simply nonsensical. We meet with incoherence of a fairly straightforward variety when an infinite series is treated as if it had properties which arise only with finite series. Since such misrepresentation can also be regarded as a failure to prescribe an interpretation for the words or symbols, we may speak in terms either of nonsense or of a failure to give sense. In either case Wittgenstein would not wish to say that we had a proposition which lacked a truth value. 'Something that is either true or false' is definitive of a proposition, so this is the description that is more appropriately faulted. In the face of meaninglessness we deny that we have a genuine proposition (*AWL* 140).

This at least gives one facet of Wittgenstein's views. Various refinements can be expected. For instance, in *RPP* I, §272 he acknowledges, somewhat belatedly, that there is nothing compelling about making the law of excluded middle definitive of a proposition. More important, he insists all along that this law says nothing at all, but gives us a picture, a picture which seems to determine what we are to look for, but fails to do so, because we do not know how it is to be applied (*PI* §352). To say 'Either it is or it isn't – there is no third possibility' appears to guarantee a definite sense for a proposition, whereas it presupposes a sense, and does nothing to tell us what we have to do to determine whether that proposition is true or not.

The realist believes that our well-formed statements are endowed with a meaning which ensures that they are either true or false, independently of any means available to us whereby we might recognize their truth value. If he reveals a misconception of the infinite, to the extent of ascribing properties to infinite series which make sense only in the finite case, it would be a lame response to claim that the meaning of his statements in this area does not secure their bivalence; whether the defect is outright inconsistency or a failure to give sense, the more robust condemnation given by 'Nonsense' is more to the point. In similar vein, it is surely wrong to maintain that, e.g., consideration of quantification over infinite totalities in mathematics obliges us to take verification and falsification, rather than truth and falsity, as the central notions in a theory of meaning. That retains too much of the inapposite picture – as if there were *totalities* which could meaningfully be described as 'infinite', but which posed problems for truth – the conception of 'infinite' as a determinate measure of number, only a *very* large number, a magnitude remarkable for its unimaginable size, but a genuine totality none the less. Nor, more generally, do we have a different logic. Apart from the consideration just advanced, there are more specific objections to driving a wedge between the members of such pairs as 'not for all' and 'for some not'. Our understanding of these leaves no room for a difference, and even if the principle of bivalence is not affirmed, such equivalences could be secured definitionally. It has to be a new grammar, a new understanding of the terms, that is being proposed. That is quite trivially possible, and a departure acknowledged by those who defend intuitionist logic. What is to be challenged is the idea that there are considerations which oblige us to abandon the old grammar.

The closest we come to this latter position is in denying, as before, that certain propositions have a contradictory. Consider the pair: (6) There is an odd perfect number; (7) There is no odd perfect number. In any serious use (6) will purport to present an established fact, but it does not amount to an announcement that the speaker is in possession of a proof of existence in such a way that without this backing what he says will stand no chance of truth. On the contrary, production of an odd perfect number will verify (6), however ill-founded its assertion. In this it is like (5) 'Vesuvius will erupt again some day', which is proven true by an eventual eruption even if it has been advanced on the flimsiest of grounds. And, just as (5) has no contradictory, so too with (6). We may be able to rule out the existence of an odd perfect number, but a proposition to this effect, which is indeed how (7) is to be understood, does not function as a contradictory, despite its superficial grammar. To say that no odd number is perfect is not to report what might be established case by case for each and every odd number; far from having a subject matter of maximum extent, it has the minimum possible, relating merely to a concept, that of *odd perfect number*, and affirming its inapplicability (because contradictory). (7) is thus like (4) 'Vesuvius will never again erupt.' We are not obliged to accept that either a future eruption can be ruled out, or else Vesuvius will erupt again some day; likewise, we do not have to grant that either there is an odd perfect number, or the supposition of the existence of such is contradictory. Nor would the relationship between (6) and (7) change if (6) should prove effectively decidable. We should then be saying that we had a means of 'constructing' an odd perfect number, or else of showing the impossibility of such a construction, but that would not give sense to the missing contradictory.

Although we are entitled to deny bivalence in this instance, I do not regard this outcome as imposing a 'revisionary' conception on a theory of meaning, viz. one that rejects certain classically valid forms of argument. The idea that a principle may allow of exceptions goes ill with character as a logical law. The principle of bivalence – every proposition is either true or false – has something of the air of a vulnerable generalization, and indeed it falls to relatively non-controversial counter-examples – unless, rather arbitrarily, it is held to be definitive of 'proposition'. The form whose correctness has the triviality befitting a law of logic – the law of excluded middle – is not confounded by these counter-examples, but they are seen not to be suitable subject matter for an application of this law. It is not undecidability, but its lack of a contradictory form that takes (6) out of the scope of certain classical principles. This is not to say, however, that intuitionist logic is an irrelevance. When not-*p* is taken as a negation of *p* that is not assumed to be its contradictory, the appropriate logic will have the shape of the intuitionist system. It is just that the intuitionist's description of that logic will not apply; in particular, it is wrong to say that the 'not' which appears in the problematic forms has a meaning different from the one it receives when not-*p* is the contradictory of *p*. The differences are to be found in the character of the propositions negated, the arguments which locate the differences in 'not' itself being no better than the arguments which purport to show that the verb 'to be' has a number of meanings.

A third possibility, also different from the anti-realist's, is to be found in one of Wittgenstein's explicit dissociations from intuitionism: 'I need hardly say that where the law of the excluded middle doesn't apply, no other law of logic applies either, because in that case we aren't dealing with propositions of mathematics. (*Per contra* Weyl and Brouwer.)' (*PR* 176). For Wittgenstein, a proposition (or question) lacks a sense until a method of proof has been specified, rather than that we can say that it has a sense, only we just cannot claim that it must be either true or false: 'if the question of the truth or falsity of a proposition is *a priori* undecidable, the consequence is that the proposition loses its sense and the consequence of this is precisely that the propositions of logic lose their validity for it' (ibid. 210). The possibility I wish to stress is less extreme: not that, because of a general failure of sense, all logical laws should be inapplicable, but only those which depend on the availability of a contradictory.

A plausible form of verificationism is expressed in the thesis that a statement cannot be true unless it is in principle possible that it should be known to be true. Dummett holds that this is unacceptable to the realist unless 'in principle' is interpreted generously, requiring only that truth be knowable to *some* being, suitably placed and endowed (1981, 465). In terms of this liberal requirement the realist hopes to vindicate his picture of the infinite: God could be aware that a building will never be built here, that no odd number is perfect, even though, as far as we are concerned, these matters are beyond the scope of proof or verification. As already indicated, going over the heads of logic and grammar to make direct appeal to what is possible for a superior being does not transform nonsense into sense, and if we wish to hold out against the realist we shall seek something better than what the anti-realist has to offer. The anti-realist's reaction to the realist's inappropriate picture is to follow the intuitionist in recasting statements of existence in such a way that they lay claim to proof of existence, where this is thought of as involved in their actual content. We do not have to tamper with the language in this way, but need simply dissociate ourselves from the nonsensical interpretation put upon statements like (4) and (7) by the realist, at the same time acknowledging that these do not behave as contradictories of (5) and (6).

12.4 Verifiability and falsifiability

Is it perhaps through falsification, rather than verification, that the important connections with meaning are to be made? Consider the indicative conditional, 'If you change your mind you will regret it.' This brings with it no commitment to the actual occurrence of an event; nothing need happen to allow us to stand by the claim, but the present situation can continue quite unchanged without threat to what was said. It might then seem that the speaker's aim is primarily to *rule out* a certain development – one in which the person changes his mind without regrets. This kind of example has led Dummett to shift the emphasis from verification to falsification, to argue that, 'in the order of explanation, the notion of the incorrectness of an assertion is prior to that of its correctness' (1976, 125).

Because 'if' is introduced precisely to cancel any commitment to the future happening specified in the main clause, and in doing so to leave us with a form which goes contrary to the general run of future-tense statements, the support thus offered for the proposed general account is severely limited. It is true that an adequate analysis must find room for this case, but we should hope to do so without taking it as a model for declarative sentences as a class. 'I am not committing myself to anything; merely ruling out something' captures something of the force of the if-statement, but in a host of other cases we commit ourselves to a specific happening, as well as thereby ruling out other developments.

By themselves conditionals offer little support to the supposed priority of falsification, but perhaps there is a stronger case when they are joined by universal propositions, the more usual basis for an argument to this end. Thus, whereas it takes only one counter-example to falsify the statement, 'All *F*s are *G*', the totality of *F*s must be found to be *G* before we have verification – something which, in any interesting case, is simply not attainable. This thesis runs the risk of being purely verbal. There is a familiar sense in which a universal statement may be said to be verified by a favourable finding in the particular case; in that sense Pasteur's theory that micro-organisms cause fermentation and disease is constantly being verified. So, read 'verify' as 'find true in at least one case' – a reading which it allows, even though it is not the only one possible – and we restore symmetry: finding true in one case is no more problematic than finding false.

But surely a more fundamental difference remains, as indeed talk in terms of 'true' and 'false' soon makes plain. So, 'Her colleagues all jog' might be said to be verified in a given case by finding that colleague *A* jogs, just as it may be falsified by a single case. But whereas the latter leads to an appraisal as false, the former does not establish the proposition as true. And that is correct. Truth requires truth in all cases, falsity requires falsity in one case only. However, this is not so much an asymmetry between *true* and *false*; rather, it results from the interaction between these two terms and the particular proposition considered. That is, we have a claim that some condition holds in all cases, whence truth requires that it does, while falsity needs a breakdown in one case only. But suppose we had a proposition which required truth in one case only. Then the position would be reversed, falsity demanding falsity in all cases. And, as has been observed often enough, this is just what we have with such a form as 'One of her colleagues jogs.'

Is there perhaps a single pattern underlying this behaviour of *true* and *false*? This may be important for the following reason. Suppose we lay down a condition in terms of verifiability, but that this proves to exclude something we wish to retain. We then shift to falsifiability to express a comparable restriction, only to find that we have lost touch with what it was that made verifiability a plausible demand in the first instance, thus leaving the revised position without a clear rationale. Conversely, the shift to falsifiability may make for no advance, the same difficulties turning up to vitiate this requirement. And indeed it does appear that unverifiability and unfalsifiability can be traced to a common source – though not one that makes for the priority of either – each being problematic in so far as there is no known limit to the objects, regions, or whatever, that we are required to take into account. We seemingly have an infinite number of cases to consider, or at least no means of setting an upper bound in advance, no means of knowing when we have finished.

But should we be thinking in these terms? Have we not left behind the interpretation of universal statements as these are argued for, appealed to in explanations, and so forth? Mesmerized by the universal quantifier, we adopt an over-rigid picture of such statements, ignoring the spatio-temporal restrictions taken for granted in any realistic use of these forms. Compare our proposition (2) 'Britain will never again have an empire.' I set aside a reading of (2) which looked forward to a time when it might be seen to be true, but perhaps that would be the pattern for any realistic use of this form: we suppose that in time the country itself will cease to exist, and when that happens we shall be able to pronounce (2) either true or false. Likewise in the present case. Generality is commonly expressed in terms of an unquantified plural, as in 'Swallows migrate in the winter', a form that certainly does not elude possible verification or falsification, and does not automatically meet with the latter if some of the individuals in question fail the condition stated. If we were to make serious use of the generalization, 'All swallows migrate in the winter', it is still unlikely that such a failure would upset its truth, since the *all* would most readily be taken to embrace all *varieties*, not each and every individual swallow of whatever variety that has existed or will exist at any time. None the less, might we not wish to make a pronouncement about literally each and every swallow that has ever been or ever will be? But there is no such totality. The swallow population is in flux, presenting us with an ever-varying number of individuals; we can make hypotheses about swallows up to any future date we care to specify, but there is no such thing as the class of all swallows that will ever have been unless their eventual extinction can be assigned a date. This is simply to give another variation on the earlier argument about *never*, and while the more realistic interpretation of (2) and its fellows received only passing acknowledgement, it is the reading which assumes no bound on the period of time that presents the interesting issues.

It would appear that we do not have to give falsification priority over verification, but if any notion has that as its due it is one according to which truth values themselves are seen as secondary, i.e., some such notion as that of learnability. Even allowing for this qualification, it is plain that a concern with meaning cannot be coupled with a disregard for questions of verification. There are, of course, difficulties with any insistence that verification should always be in principle possible, e.g., difficulties relating to the degree of conclusiveness required, but, as we shall see further in the final chapter, these are in no way exacerbated by the defects particular to anti-realism.

13

Anti-Realism and the Past

To combat the realist requires us to do little more than set sober paraphrase against his metaphorical excess. That at least is so when infinity, either temporal or mathematical, is the issue. Here we find ourselves in some sympathy with the anti-realist – in his diagnosis of the malady afflicting the realist's thought, if not in his cure. How do matters stand when we shift from future to past? The question is not one that takes us directly to themes which engaged Wittgenstein, but it is important to see that his own views on use, truth, and verification do not follow the peculiar twists and turns which characterize the anti-realist's argument in this domain.

13.1 Evidence and the past

Dummett suggests that if we are to discover the flaw in the anti-realist's conception of truth, it is most likely to come to light when statements about the past are under scrutiny (1978, xxxviii). We shall have good reason to endorse this suggestion, but before taking up the question, consider a reading of 'will' prompted by its behaviour in such contexts as 'Suppose that Vesuvius will erupt before the end of the decade.' If the present perspective here adopted can be read into 'Vesuvius will erupt before the end of the decade', it would appear unwarranted to insist that this must be either true or false. Why should available evidence offer support to either evaluation? With this modal reading, truth value links may come apart in an untroubling fashion: next year brings an eruption, and therewith the truth of a present-tense report of it, but because it lacked adequate grounds when uttered, the future-tense form is not to be considered proven true.

I mention this approach, not only because of its undoubted

appeal, but because it describes a pattern to which our usage could be expected to conform if the reading of 'will' which best suits the anti-realist's purpose were consistently adopted. I do not suggest, however, that it is true to actual usage, since there would appear to be no ground for a denial that one who made the prediction spoke truly, however poor his evidence, so long as the eruption takes place in the designated period. We may not be in a position to assert either the proposition or its negation, but we can happily say, with the anti-realist's blessing, that one must be true in the sense that one is bound to prove true.

If this approach does not work for 'will', it stands even less chance of success with 'was'. The anti-realist holds quite generally that neither truth nor falsity is to be had in advance of evidence justifying assertion or denial – unless such evidence can be reliably anticipated – and this looks hard to take with a statement such as 'There was a mouse in the larder yesterday.' Surely that is true or false, irrespective of there being evidence for either alternative? On the other hand, the proper use of these words would be very much as a report or an inference, backed by memory or evidence, and we might be tempted to go along with the claim that neither this form nor its negation merits 'true' if its assertion is unfounded. This would be the correct conclusion if a basis in present evidence could be read into the content of 'was', since 'There was not a mouse in the larder yesterday' would not then be the contradictory of 'There was a mouse in the larder yesterday', but a proposition having that role would have to mount a challenge to the evidential basis implied for the latter, rather than swing to the extreme of saying that the contradictory possibility is assured. However, granted that proper use of the past tense requires a suitable backing in memories or evidence, the requirement for a justified use is not written into 'was' in such a way that what is said fails of truth if its assertion is gratuitous, but the comparison is more with predictions thought of as true by dint of fulfilment only. Compare the suggestion that *p* means 'I believe that *p*'. Whatever the involvement of belief, it cannot be as part of the content – truth is not guaranteed by possession of the belief, nor is it threatened by its absence. The case of implied knowledge is similar. Someone may assert *p* without justification. If part of the content of what he said was that his assertion was warranted – a circular notion, surely – then we could not say that he had spoken truly, which of course we can.

It would also be correct to conclude that a past-tense proposition *p* could not be pronounced either true or false without taking current evidence into account if, as the anti-realist fancies, 'true' had the meaning of 'assertible'. Such a reading is at odds with the observation, implicit in the redundancy theory, that an ascription of truth takes its character from the proposition to which it is made, so that if assertibility is not extractable from *p*, there is no way for it to be passed on to 'It is true that *p*.' To suppose it true that Australia was once joined to Antarctica is simply to suppose that Australia was once joined to Antarctica; it is not to suppose that this is something that is now known to be so. That is, the way we invariably interpret such a form puts us in the company of the realist, who will say that, despite the present tense, the supposition that *p is* true is purely a supposition about how things *were* at the time, without the intrusion of any of the circumstances which would in fact be necessary for knowledge of this remote period from a present perspective. We have, perhaps, to suppose a state of affairs as we could have become apprised of it then, but we do not have to conceive of it as known through the modes of access we have to the past now.

Because of the present in 'is true', the form 'Suppose it is true that Australia was once joined to Antarctica' is certainly more congenial to the idea that a basis in present evidence is implied than is the version without this phrase. Indeed, we may well consider that it is only by misinterpreting the significance of the 'is' that we can get any sympathy for anti-realism in this area, sympathy which is unlikely to survive reflection on the genuine rationale for the use of the present, viz. as geared to the time of the *stating*. The anti-realist expounds 'It is true that *p*' in accordance with his intuition that present truth must somehow answer to present reality. Our counter-proposal is that the verbal phrase is the focus of temporal contrasts relating to the time at which *p* is being thought of as advanced. Consider 'It has never been true that pacifists have been in a majority.' This may say no more than 'Pacifists have never been in a majority', but it is suited, in a way the simpler form is not, to envisaging the making of a claim – 'Pacifists are in a majority' – at various times in the past. Of course, the linguistic use contemplated is one for which correctness, in one sense, requires an adequate backing in evidence, but, whether we take 'It is true that *p*' or the simple *p*, the notion of a warrant for what is said is no part of what is said.

There is, then, a strong suspicion that the anti-realist's position rests on nothing deeper than a misreading of 'is true' engendered by the superficial grammar of this phrase. That, and perhaps a mistaken reaction to the errors of a crude redundancy theory. In leaving us without the means for saying what we can say so long as 'true', and not just the redundancy theory's paraphrase, is still at our disposal, that theory rules itself out, but the anti-realist appears to see its defeat as his own victory, as vindicating a 'substantial' account of truth; not merely one which insists that there be something in the world in virtue of which a true proposition is true, but an account that is substantial to the point of replacing 'true' by 'assertible'. Hence the importance of staying with the minimal elaboration of the theory endorsed earlier.

But what of the argument based on our training in the use of 'true'? According to Dummett's anti-realist, the 'only notion of truth for past-tense statements which we could have acquired from our training in their use is that which coincides with the justifiability of assertions of such statements' (1978, 363). In another formulation: 'the process by which we came to grasp the sense of statements of the disputed class, and the use which is subsequently made of these statements, are such that we could not derive from it any notion of what it would be for such a statement to be true independently of the sort of thing we have learned to recognise as establishing the truth of such statements' (ibid. 362).

We may note first that this argument takes in not only 'true', but also the propositions to which it is applied. If the anti-realist were merely asserting an equivalence of 'true' with 'assertible', we might let him have the word in this sense and make do without it in advancing instances of the law of excluded middle, propositions about the past, and so forth, allowing, e.g., that 'Australia was once joined to Antarctica' need be neither true nor false in his sense of these terms, but holding to the invulnerability of the form 'Either Australia was once joined to Antarctica or it was not.' However, while we could still say what we wished to say, this would not be the end of the anti-realist's difficulties. It is often held that 'true' is insertible before a noun clause without materially affecting what is said. Consider the pair, 'He suspects that a stream once ran here' and 'He suspects it is true that a stream once ran here.' For reasons already given, the two are not completely interchangeable, but the divergence does not amount to one in possible truth value. Not on our ordinary understanding of 'true', that is, though with the reading which the anti-realist espouses, the transition to the latter may be a transition to outright falsity. I suspect that a stream once ran here. Do I therefore suspect that I have established this to be so? What nonsense! Do I suspect that this is known to someone else? Conceivably, but that would be another matter altogether. There is no question of taking the anti-realist seriously if he is wedded to this kind of distortion, but the only question of possible interest is the residual one of seeing where the reasoning that has led to his untenable position has gone astray.

In fact, it would seem that the anti-realist cannot avoid applying the acquisition argument directly to the bearers of truth themselves. Nor would he wish to. After all, we learn to use such a form as 'There was a crowd' in circumstances which justify its assertion no more and no less than with 'It is true that there was a crowd.' Accordingly, a disjunction is, for him, still to be rejected if the possibilities it presents are envisaged in total detachment from present evidence. Likewise, since we shall of necessity advert to present findings or circumstances – memories, records, testimony – in establishing a past-tense assertion, it must on his view be a mistake to imagine that we can contemplate even a past possibility except as (hypothetically) grounded in present memories or evidence.

So long as the anti-realist insists on reading the notion of assertibility into the declarative form, whether via 'true' or independently, he is saddled with unacceptable readings of 'supposing that *p*', 'suspecting it is true that *p*', and the rest. Still, if he is right, this is all we legitimately *could* mean. Is the acquisition argument sufficiently compelling to have us adopt these readings?

First, we may well wish to query the significance of the training alluded to in that argument. The child is not going to be taught to declare that *p* is true when it has the appropriate memories, if, as may happen, it is only by saying *p* that it shows that it remembers the incident, but what training it receives is likely to be negative – it is corrected when it makes a rash or unwarranted inference or declaration. But in any event it is plainly of no real consequence whether or not training takes place at all. It could well be that no one ever troubled to help the learner along – various pressures will no doubt act to bring the child's usage into line with standard practice, but they need not have a pedagogical source.

A related objection is to question the anti-realist's dependence on genetic considerations. It might be argued that, in the light of our training, the only interpretation we are *justified* in placing upon 'true' is one according to which it equates with 'assertible'. What is actually claimed is that this is the only interpretation that we could have *acquired*, yet there is no logical reason why training in the use of words should not be the occasion for us to form all manner of conceptions about their meaning. Setting aside the genetic formulation, but adopting the narrow perspective afforded by the argument – attending only to uses of 'true' in which it correlates with categorical assertions – it is in fact not obvious that the learner has been given enough to warrant an interpretation in terms of assertibility, enough to take him beyond a stage at which he interprets 'true' simply as a sign that the speaker endorses or confirms the proposition in question – the redundancy theory in one of its cruder forms. If we are taught the word 'cat' with reference to the small domesticated variety only, it will be consistent for us to hold that lions and tigers do not count as cats, though with a broader range of examples this exclusion may not be warranted. Likewise, if we confine our consideration of the declarative form to its assertoric occurrences, we may come to regard as necessary factors which a more comprehensive account would show to be dispensable. With just this much of the usage exposed, there is nothing at variance with the supposition that 'It is true that *p*' can interchange with 'I confirm that *p*', but to exclude this interpretation we have to take in more than a fragment of the usage; in particular, we have to look to the way the form with 'true' is further circumscribed by specifying what consequences it has, and what it follows from. And not only that. We have already noted that correct use is not exhaustively characterized in terms of assertibility conditions, but, as with truth conditions, these are limited by their presupposition of a certain grammar. Witness again the subtleties that dictate choice of tense in conditionals, or in such forms as 'I wish it was Saturday tomorrow.'

Dummett's anti-realist appeals not only to the 'process by which we came to grasp the sense of statements of the disputed class', but also to the 'use which is subsequently made of these statements', so he should not be averse to assembling the materials for a more comprehensive account. Needless to say, however, it is the realist picture that then takes shape, and it soon becomes clear that the impression given of a proper respect for actual linguistic practice is highly misleading. The anti-realist maintains that, in the disputed areas of usage, we do not use past-tense statements consistently with the meanings which we are said to have conferred upon them, that we are dominated by an incorrect picture of their meanings (ibid. 362). What exactly is our error? It would appear that we are one and all persistently guilty of refusing to construe past-tense forms as embodying, through their very meaning, a claim to be justified. We accept that assertions about the past require a backing in memories or evidence, a requirement which extends, of course, to uses of 'true', but we do not regard the existence of that backing as part of what is asserted.

Dummett does not present a diagnosis in quite these terms, but it is clear that this has to be the point at which we supposedly go wrong. In effect, the anti-realist is calling upon us to explain how we can disregard the need for evidence in the problematic contexts, how the implication of such a backing, present with the categorical form – 'Australia was once joined to Antarctica' – can simply be dropped when we move to 'If Australia was once joined to Antarctica, . . . '. The realist's answer simply repeats the point already made. Perhaps there would be a problem if something *new* were introduced with this transition, but that is not being claimed. But nor is anything inexplicably or unjustifiably omitted when reference to a warrant is absent; the relevant implication can be said to be carried by the *stating*, in the sense that one who states 'Australia was once joined to Antarctica' will normally thereby give his audience to understand that he has the requisite backing for what he says, but the claim that adequate evidence has been gathered is not an implication of *what* is asserted, of what may be true despite the lack of grounds.

It might seem unfair to saddle the anti-realist with this construal of past-tense assertions. His claim is that, in the light of our training, the only legitimate understanding we can have of p is as a report of established fact; he is not saying, surely, that such character is written into the meaning of p, as a part of what is asserted, but only that we cease to respect this character when we pass to the use of p as antecedent of a conditional. However, it is not clear that he has any alternative to re-interpreting p in the way indicated if he is to counter the obvious objection that the change in status of p is simply what comes with the shift from the assertoric to the suppositional use, the demands which an unqualified assertion must meet, if it is to be acceptable, not being those appropriate to a mere hypothesis. It is only if the assertion of 'Australia was once joined to Antarctica' implies the existence of an evidential backing through the very sense of its words that there is something whose absence is in need of explanation when what was asserted is now hypothesized.

With present-tense judgements likewise, it is obvious that not every condition that must be satisfied before we are entitled to make a judgement merits recognition in an explanation of the meaning of that judgement. To be justified in stating 'The oven is on', it may be necessary that we should have examined the oven carefully from close to, and not simply given it a casual glance from afar, but while this defines the kind of condition which has a place in an account of the circumstances in which we are trained to make such a judgement, it has no place in an account of what we are judging. Though how the acquisition argument can leave room for its omission is far from clear.

Consider now the matter of truth value links. The statement, 'I am writing', is now true. Accordingly, someone who says of me in years hence, 'He was then writing', will have spoken truly, even though all knowledge, all memories, all signs of the incident may have vanished without trace, and one who says 'He was not then writing' will by the same token have spoken falsely. So that means that at this imagined later date we shall have truth even though there is then nothing in virtue of which the statement made is true? Cf. Dummett:

> . . . for if there were, as it were, nothing whatever left of the past, then there would be nothing to make a true statement about the past true, nothing in virtue of which it would be true.
>
> (1976, 98–9)

The notion of 'what makes *p* true' to be enlisted in formulating what is supposedly correct in the correspondence theory is one in which it is to relate to the state of affairs that *answers* to *p*. So, what makes 'Trevor is bored' true is Trevor's being bored, and what makes '3 is odd' true is 3's being odd. We depart from this position if we say that what makes a mathematical proposition true is a proof, or our possession of a proof, of that proposition – as with Dummett 1978, 361 – and the departure is even greater if we hold that what makes 'I was then writing' true is my remembering I was writing at the time in question. This – if you will excuse the triviality – is to give the answering state of affairs, not for this proposition, but for 'I remember I was then writing.' It is not that there is no sense of 'what makes *p* true' that can sustain the latter style of interpretation, but it would clearly be wrong to represent this as a reading of 'what makes *p* true' that is geared to the notion of what the truth of *p consists* in, this being the same circumstance whether it is remembered by me or by another. On this reading, moreover, it would be impossible for me to suppose that I was writing at the time but now had no recollection of the incident.

The anti-realist's distortion of 'true' consistently features as the chief source of his confusion. Of course it is unintelligible to suppose *p* true in the total absence of present evidence, if 'true' bears the (relevant) sense of 'assertible'. On the other hand, if, e.g., in supposing *p* true we do not even pretend to be supposing ourselves in possession of such evidence, where is the problem? What moves do we make that are unwarranted in the light of our conception of the past?

Dummett holds that the antecedent of a conditional provides a setting in which a realist interpretation of verbal forms comes into focus. This we found to be wrong with respect to the future tense, conditionals providing a context which actually highlights the modal aspect of 'will', its connection with warranted assertibility. However, what is of greater importance is the legitimacy of the respective readings which present and future tense here receive. We have both 'If the treatment will cure you, it is worth taking', and 'If the treatment cures you, it will have been worth taking', with no call to choose one to the exclusion of the other, but invoking whichever is suited to our purpose. When we turn to the past tense we encounter a realist reading, one geared to drawing out the implications of a hypothesized state of affairs, envisaged from a past standpoint. And why should such speculation be denied us? Surely, the only complaint anyone might conceivably have against the language is that it did not afford an equally natural means of putting the *other* alternative.

The anti-realist has not identified any moves that come into conflict with our conception of the past, but for him it is that very conception that is questionable. But how can that be? In seeing how we could have come by it? But what matters is that this *is* our conception; its allowability does not wait upon a satisfactory account of its origins. Indeed, questions of justifiability do not arise for the network of conceptual relations which it comprises, however critical they may be for the particular judgements which the general scheme makes possible. Our picture of the past is pieced together from such grammatical truths as that the very notion of getting it right applies to remembering, that it makes sense to suppose that what is remembered by you has been forgotten by me, that there were happenings which went unrecorded, that it may require an effort to recall something accurately, and so forth. It is not a picture that anyone is obliged to adopt, but there is no question of its failing to be true to the past; we are concerned not with a catalogue of discoveries about a given domain, but with relationships which define the very notion of the past.

13.2 Decidability and the manifestation argument

Anti-realism goes woefully astray if it considers the notion of justified assertibility to be part of the content of every assertion, or to be incorporated in our notion of truth. Likewise, it cannot be taken seriously if it implies that supposing or suspecting that *p* is a matter of supposing or suspecting that *p* is known to be true. Rather, it has to be that for *p* to embody a genuine supposition or suspicion, it must be something the truth value of which *could* be known. Dummett introduces the unacceptable reading with his very characterization of a verificationist approach: 'According to a theory of meaning in terms of verification, the content of an assertion is that the statement has been, or is capable of being, verified' (1976, 117). It is rather harsh on the general approach to present as a definition what would serve as a *reductio*, but while the condition, 'capable of being verified', is mislocated when assigned to the content of what is said, there would appear to be a large class of assertions whose use is such as to make this a plausible constraint. The question now is what exactly is the proper interpretation of this condition, or of 'could be known'. The anti-realist correlates these with the notion of an effectively decidable proposition, an interpretation which leaves predictions relatively unproblematic, but makes for much of the paradox in his treatment of propositions about the past.

To enlarge on the difference between the two tenses, with the future we are presented with possibilities that are not currently verifiable, but since we need only wait for time to pass to be assured of verifying one or the other, the disjunction of *p* and not-*p* is decidable, so for the anti-realist a legitimate instance of the law of excluded middle. Given, however, that there is no effective method for determining the truth value of past-tense statements, that our lack of knowledge may be irremediable rather than only temporary, we are not in their case entitled to anticipate a determinate answer to questions of truth value. It is worth noting, however, that even to speak in terms of decidability may represent a concession from the anti-realist's standpoint. If truth equates with warranted assertibility, then an instance of bivalence is strictly in order only when we are in a position to affirm one or other of the given disjuncts. This strict position would be intolerable, and indeed it seems reasonable to accept the weakening given with effective decidability. Our question is why there should not be a further weakening in the direction of verifiability.

The difference between the future and the past case is not at all readily felt to be relevant to putative instances of the law of excluded middle, but a disjunction like 'There was or there was not a mouse in the larder yesterday' looks to be the equal of the future version in its vacuousness. Certainly, we should continue to insist that, in the sense in which we have a trivial claim, an instance of a logical law, evidence which might lead to actual endorsement of one of the possibilities does not have to be sought to make good that claim, what 'makes it true' being simply the exhaustiveness of those possibilities. It is 'yesterday', not the time of utterance, that fixes the perspective, and it does not matter how distant the time is, exactly the same issue being presented by 'Either there was a full moon a thousand years ago today, or there was not.' The categorical 'was' finds its justification in the exhaustiveness of the condition that follows, not in what we can determine a thousand years on.

If there is no way of telling whether *p* holds, the verificationist will maintain that there is no sense to saying that *p is* true, and no sense to saying that its contradictory is true either, and here 'there is a way of telling' can be so understood that it is not refuted by the presence of obstacles to knowledge. It must be granted that the account in terms of exhaustiveness assumes that the individual disjuncts present significant possibilities. This raises the issue of verifiability in their regard, and, as before, general considerations about meaning and understanding make it reasonable to require that we be able to tell, in propitious circumstances, what truth value falls to either disjunct, but so long as we stay with this conception, all that the applicability of logical principles presupposes is the possibility, not the actuality, of a situation in which the truth value of *p* can be ascertained.

Consider again the elusive white rabbit. Either there was such a creature, in some unobserved locality, or there was not. In so far as verification enters, it does so with the further elaboration, viz. that is what you would have found; i.e., when the restriction which stood in the way of finding out is envisaged as lifted. (The sceptical doubt, 'But there might not have been a white rabbit there, however good the indirect evidence', surely envisages a failure of verification under just this condition.) Similarly with psychological ascriptions, as 'Either he heard what you said or he did not', or 'Either he knows your address or he does not.' If the person in question is co-operative, we may readily learn which possibility is realized, but so long as he is not we may be powerless to divine how things stand. That is no reason for refusing to affirm the disjunction, any more than with 'Either he can wiggle his ears or he cannot', when the person's reluctance to perform leaves us in the dark concerning his ability.

It is of interest to note that, with respect to the present issue, the realist may be a verificationist. True, there is no question of making out a case for such an association more generally if the realist is happy to affirm quite uncritically disjunctions which, like 'Either the castle is haunted or it is not', are problematic from a verificationist standpoint. However, such a standpoint is a natural one to adopt in defending the interpretations universally made of propositions about the past, and in this connection it would be wrong to regard him, or anyone else who takes exception to the anti-realist on the present issue, as obliged to hold to the intelligibility of propositions which transcend any form of human knowledge. Clearly, the realist is on the side of the angels in accepting the principle of bivalence as this applies to past-tense propositions, and in refusing to go along with the anti-realist's re-reading of 'true' as 'assertible'. He may come to grief on the matter of what can be known, but if his position here is defined through its opposition to the anti-realist's, this is not its inevitable fate. Both parties were represented earlier as requiring that truth should be knowable, but with the realist making the apparently more liberal claim that it should be a matter of knowable to *some* being, not necessarily to us. However, as already indicated, it is to no purpose to seek to establish that *p* specifies a genuine possibility by showing that its truth could be known to a superior being, since, however powerful our imaginary being is supposed to be, whether we shall count anything as knowledge that *p* will depend on our having already succeeded in making sense of *p*. In particular, if what can be known is to be taken to extend as far as, but no further than, what can be verified, this condition still stands when appeal is made to a being with powers beyond our own. Such an appeal is, after all, only a figurative way of talking of the bounds of sense; it does not enable us to confer a meaning on our words which they would otherwise lack. No doubt the realist thinks otherwise, but it is at least possible to interpret his more liberal claim in a way which parts it from any objectionable 'creative' role. Again, if the realist is simply one who holds out for the existence of an objective reality, independently of our knowledge, he has nothing to fear. He must abide by the semantic claim that what it makes sense to say exists is not independent of what we can meaningfully speak of knowing to be so, but that is not a sense in which anything might be said to be dependent on us for its existence – the ontological claim with which idealism is usually associated. To the extent that the anti-realist moves towards idealism, while the realist stays with this position, the truth is again on the side of realism.

At all events, whether or not we are joined by the realist on the account here offered, it is clear that the reading given of undecidable disjunctions makes explicit allowance for the lack of circumstances which would lead to verification, but does so in a way that preserves the links with the latter which considerations of meaning make plausible. Dummett presents such considerations in connection both with the manifestation and with the acquisition of knowledge of meaning. The latter we have already seen, and seen to fail. We shall now consider the former.

According to the realist, understanding *p* is a matter of knowing the condition for *p* to be true. But that, claims the anti-realist, is at variance with the thesis that use exhaustively determines meaning, that there can be no aspect of a sentence's meaning that is not made manifest in the use made of that sentence. If *p* is undecidable, it will not be possible to give a full manifestation of the knowledge of that condition, since nothing we say or do will reveal a grasp of what it is for that condition to obtain in those cases where we are incapable of recognizing that it does. The anti-realist accordingly urges that we shift from truth to verification (proof) as the key concept in our theory of meaning, construing an understanding of *p* as a capacity for recognizing a verification of *p* when presented with one, not simply as a knowledge of what it is for *p* to be true. This now meets the demand that we should be able to give a full manifestation of our understanding, since whenever we are in a position to assert *p*, this is something we can recognize to be so, and can make plain our recognition, verbally or otherwise (cf. Dummett 1978, 224–5).

There is an awkwardness in this argument, in that it has the anti-realist saying that knowledge of truth conditions cannot be fully manifested, when for him this can be neither genuine knowledge nor genuine truth, only knowledge and truth as these are understood by the realist. There is also the question whether the anti-realist has identified the only form that a manifestation of understanding can take. Wittgenstein, presumably, would regard him as having an excessively narrow conception of the use of the relevant forms, and we have already observed that verification, like truth, is not sufficiently fine-grained to accommodate all differences in understanding and meaning. Recall our pairs, 'He spoke' and 'He has spoken.' A clue to the difference between these is found in the consideration that the auxiliary 'has' makes, as a present form, similar demands as does 'has' in the meaning of 'possesses'; very roughly, use of the perfect calls for the continuing existence of the subject, whereas use of the simple past does not. However, just as replacing the one by the other does not transform truth into falsity, so too talk of verification and falsification is too crude to do justice to this nuance. There are these difficulties, but what is most noteworthy about the manifestation argument is that an ability to tell when circumstances in which we find ourselves serve to verify *p* is all that it holds to be necessary for understanding, there being no insistence that we be able to *bring about* such a situation. As of course there could not conceivably be, since the argument is specifically designed to handle the problem posed by *undecidable* propositions. There is not, then, the remotest suggestion that the manifestation argument favours decidability over verifiability as the requirement to defend.

Note, incidentally, that if *p* is such a statement as 'There was a mouse in the larder yesterday', no explanation of the past tense is offered by saying that *p* could have *then* been verified, even if *p* does indeed amount to a claim about what could have been found at the time in question. The anti-realist is concerned to ground such statements in circumstances recognizable at the time they are made. Shifting from 'was' to 'could' simply replaces one past form by another; it throws no light on what it is to say something about the past from a present perspective. To reject decidability in favour of verifiability is not to reject it in favour of verifiability in *principle*, where this is understood in terms of the possibility of verification at the earlier time. The problem of meaning is not addressed by this positivist move – but then neither does it call for the anti-realist's distinctive, and damaging, manoeuvre.

13.3 Conditionals and excluded middle

In presenting the case against the anti-realist we have for the most part not been telling him anything he does not already know. Like a religious belief, his position could hardly be held without an awareness of its paradoxical consequences, and like a religious belief it is thought to embody a greater truth which obliges us to tolerate apparent discrepancies with what is known on other grounds. So what is the dominant consideration which sustains the anti-realist's faith in the face of the contrary evidence? A certain conception of truth is one possibility, but perhaps more basic are the arguments relating to the acquisition and manifestation of understanding. Certainly, when the going gets difficult, it is natural for the anti-realist to fall back upon these considerations, and it is accordingly of the first importance to realize that we can do justice to them without having to pay the price of denying the obvious.

However, we have still to consider a major class of propositions to which the anti-realist may appear to have an appropriately critical approach. These are propositions which Dummett sees as falling foul of the law of excluded middle, everyday forms of words thought to harbour concealed conditionals, as 'Jones is brave' or '*X* is good at learning languages.' For these the law can be maintained only, it is suggested, by making questionable assumptions about the existence of something which makes them true. Consider the second of these examples. Dummett maintains that an interpretation of 'If *X* were to attempt to learn a language, he would quickly succeed' is here in order, and it is with respect to this and the opposing conditional that the realist's assumptions are exposed. Dummett contends that the equivalence is one that must be granted by anyone who understands the phrase 'good at learning languages' (1976, 91). I disagree. Even if the conditional is well supported, it is surely not correct to affirm '*X* is good at learning languages' of someone who has not even made the attempt to do so. Such an assertion would function as a report of actual success, not as a prediction. So long as *X* has not been put to the test the most we can say is that he *would* be good at learning languages. Similarly, if *X*, a brilliant cricketer, has never tried his hand at baseball, we are not justified in saying that he *is* good at baseball, however much skill at the one sport may portend skill at the other; and if Jones never acted bravely, the most we can say is that he would have been, not that he actually *was* brave. Likewise with the negations. Suppose that *X* is ill at ease with words. We might reasonably conjecture, 'He would be no good at learning languages', but even granted his evident dullness it is not in place to say '*X* is no good at learning languages.' Even when failure can be confidently expected, a report of failure is premature. The disjunction of these two cases is certainly resistible: if there is no attempt, then you cannot say that there has been either a successful or an unsuccessful attempt. But that is of no greater interest than the failure of 'Either he has stopped beating his wife or he has not.' Whether they equate to conditionals or not, Dummett's extensive range of propositions – affirming properties determined by test or by measurement – may reflect no more than the kind of grammatical peculiarity that places them in the same class as the mundane example of an unnegatable conjunction, such as 'although'. That is one possibility. 'Either he was brave or he was not' might be said of a person who never encountered danger, with 'he was not' understood as a simple contradictory, true of Jones if he never in fact displayed bravery, regardless of how he might have acted had danger arisen. Likewise, the sense of 'Jones was kind to animals' requires that, on some occasion at least, Jones displayed such kindness, but knowing that his life never took him near animals we could consider ourselves entitled to affirm the corresponding negation given with 'not' or 'never'.

The form, 'If *X* were to attempt to learn a language, then either he would quickly succeed or he would not', poses no problem; it is just an empty tautology. Certainly, the fact that we are not in a position to assert either disjunct individually has no bearing upon the assertibility of their disjunction. If it is thought otherwise, that is likely to be because a disjunction is being conceived of as too closely tied to the particular case where our grounds for affirming it can be traced back to knowledge of the truth of one of the disjuncts (cf. Dummett 1978, 6). This invites a particular application of the notion of 'making true'. If, let us say, 'Hercule is either French or Belgian', is true, then it will be the factual character of one of the disjuncts that makes it so. Likewise, it is claimed, with such a disjunction as 'If *X* were to attempt to learn a language, then either he would quickly succeed or he would not.' If this is true then there must be something in virtue of which it is true, and that is a matter of a fact in which the truth of one of the disjuncts consists. However, this reasoning uses the wrong model for the disjunction. It is true that a disjunction can often be thought of as derivative upon one of its disjuncts, but in many cases the disjuncts are on a par, especially with respect to future-tense statements, as 'Either Fred or James will win.' This we might affirm on the grounds that these are the only serious possibilities, not because one of them has everything going for it, and it is with this case that the affirmation of such an instance of '*p* or not-*p*' compares: whatever were to happen, it would be describable one way or the other. Similarly, of course, with 'Either there was a full moon a thousand years ago today or there was not.' Even if we have calculated that there must have been a full moon, we are most unlikely to make any use of this information in justifying the disjunction, but what makes the disjunction true is its comprehensive character.

But suppose *A* says, 'If Sue were to attempt to learn a language, she would quickly succeed', while *B* says, 'If Sue were to attempt to learn a language, she would not quickly succeed.' Is it not going beyond the trivial to claim that what one of them is saying must be true? Can that not be so only if something about the person determines things to be that way, and is it not gratuitous to suppose that there is in fact any such determination? If Sue is never put to the test, can we really hold that, though we shall never know who spoke truly, one of *A* and *B* did?

With such a pair of conditionals we feel strongly the pull of a modal reading of 'would', one in which its applicability is to be justified, if at all, by having regard to what can be established prior to the time at which the corresponding prediction with 'will' might be fulfilled. In so far as we have a departure from the trivial form, 'If Sue were to attempt to learn a language, then either she would quickly succeed or she would not', it is because we are envisaging such a use, or an application of 'true' based on that use. Reasons have already been given for not going along with the parallel interpretation of 'will', and while they remain of relevance to 'would', there is some reason for tying this more closely to present evidence – treating it as more like 'must' – on the grounds that its use generally presumes that circumstances rule out any developments which would verify or falsify the prediction. At all events, it is not difficult to entertain the possibility of the relevant usage. However, in that usage it is clear that the given negation is not a strict contradictory, that we accordingly have no more than an apparent instance of the law of excluded middle. Once more, then, in so far as that law is inapplicable, this circumstance will be traceable to unremarkable facts of usage, with no call either to endorse or to reject a principle of any substance: it just happens that, on one interpretation, a certain form of words is not contradicted in the way we might have presumed – a minor curiosity, no more, and of no greater significance than the familiar failure of pairs like 'Outdoor shoes must be worn' and 'Outdoor shoes must not be worn' to constitute contradictories.

We had cause to mention earlier Dummett's claim that there must be something in virtue of which a true conditional is true: a statement such as 'If Sue were to attempt to learn a language, she would quickly succeed' cannot be *barely* true. If truth is thought of in terms of eventual fulfilment, then it is this that 'makes' the conditional true. Suppose, however, that 'would' receives a modal reading. Then the demand for a basis in present evidence – this being now what makes for truth – is not, as already argued, a demand that requires the enlistment of a general principle, 'If *p* is true, there must be something that makes it true in a non-trivial way.' Rather, 'would' is on this reading like 'must': truth is not guaranteed by fulfilment, but the very sense of the word requires the existence of adequate grounds.

Our observations on conditionals and dispositional terms repeat the preceding pattern. Clarification of the terms in which the problematic utterances are couched – 'There will never be a building on this spot', 'Either Jones was brave or he was not' – leads to resolution of the difficulties raised without our having to engage in dubious metaphysical speculation, to take a stand on some conception of the 'constitution of reality'. It is not so much a matter of different realizations of two general standpoints as of a series of muddles – about infinity, the past, generality, conditional sentences – in need of individual treatment. Nor is there any call to tamper with principles of classical logic, but if these are inapplicable it is again because of the particular meaning of the propositions to which they are applied; most notably because a given proposition may have no contradictory. Perhaps it makes sense to suppose, as the anti-realist would have it, that we could be guilty of a systematic misunderstanding of our own language. However, more familiar is the philosophical failing of misrepresenting our language, systematically or otherwise, and much of what we have seen of anti-realism conforms fairly and squarely to this well-attested precedent.

Throughout this book two sharply opposed conceptions of philosophy have been in view. At one extreme we have Wittgenstein's emphasis on the differences between philosophy and the sciences: generalization and systematization are the sources of its errors, not its goals, the task of philosophy being to dispel conceptual confusion. At the other extreme is the approach which regards philosophy as continuous with the sciences; in particular, a principal aim of the philosophy of language is to provide a systematic account of language, a theory of meaning. The argument has turned up points for and against both positions. The removal of confusion has been very much to the fore in the discussion of realism and anti-realism, but the search for generality is not necessarily misguided, and we have found that some of the demands of a theory of meaning can be satisfied – though if it is not simply a matter of assembling reminders of what we already know, it is very little more than this. Certainly, we do not have to think of ourselves as putting forward a theory in any questionable sense – where a misguided comparison with scientific procedures is invoked – or for a questionable reason – profess a concern with theory and you can disregard the clamour of discordant facts. If we are anywhere near on target with our accounts of meaning, truth, and the rest, there is simply nothing for anything that counts as 'theory' in any quasi-scientific sense to *do*. The demand for philosophy to be scientific is irresistible, if this is explained in terms of a commitment to critical rigour, but no more is essential to the discipline than those principles and precepts which are inseparable from rational enquiry. That is not to say that positions of substance beyond such principles might not be defended, but philosophy, particularly philosophy of a more formal cast, is today in danger of elevating questionable positions to the status of unchallengeable starting points. The ideal of philosophy as presuppositionless is still characteristic of much analytical philosophy; it would be sad if it gave way to the scholasticism and dogma which threaten when the overriding concern is to save appearances, rather than to follow the argument wherever it leads.

Bibliography

Anscombe, G. E. M. 1957 *Intention*. Oxford, Blackwell.

Baker, G. P. and Hacker, P. M. S. 1980 *Wittgenstein: Understanding and Meaning*. Oxford, Blackwell.

Baker, G. P. and Hacker, P. M. S. 1984a *Language, Sense and Nonsense*. Oxford, Blackwell.

Baker, G. P. and Hacker, P. M. S. 1984b *Scepticism, Rules and Language*. Oxford, Blackwell.

Bolinger, D. 1977 *Meaning and Form*. London and New York, Longman.

Champlin, T. S. 1983 'The Elusiveness of Meaning', *Philosophical Investigations*, 6.

Chomsky, N. 1976 *Reflections on Language*. New York and London, Temple Smith/Fontana.

Davidson, D. 1984 *Inquiries into Truth and Interpretation*. Oxford, Clarendon Press.

Diver, W. 1964 'The Modal System of the English Verb', *Word*, 20.

Dudman, V. 1984 'Conditional Interpretations of *If*-sentences', *Australasian Journal of Linguistics*, 4.

Dummett, M. 1975 'What is a Theory of Meaning?', in *Mind and Language* ed. S. Guttenplan. Oxford, Clarendon Press.

Dummett, M. 1976 'What is a Theory of Meaning? (II)', in *Truth and Meaning: Essays in Semantics*, ed. G. Evans and J. McDowell. Oxford, Clarendon Press.

Dummett, M. 1978 *Truth and Other Enigmas*. London, Duckworth.

Dummett, M. 1981 *Frege: Philosophy of Language*. 2nd edn, London, Duckworth.

Frege, G. 1892 'On Sense and Reference', in *Translations from the Philosophical Writings of Gottlob Frege*, ed. and tr. P. T. Geach and M. Black. Oxford, Blackwell, 2nd revised edn. 1960.

Frege, G. 1918 'The Thought: A Logical Inquiry', tr. A. M. and M. Quinton, *Mind*, lxv, 1956, reprinted in Strawson 1967.

Grice, H. P. 1957 'Meaning', *Philosophical Review*, lxvi, reprinted in Strawson 1967.

Grice, H. P. 1968 'Utterer's Meaning, Sentence-meaning, and Word-meaning', *Foundations of Language*, iv; reprinted in *The Philosophy of Language*, ed. J. R. Searle. Oxford, Clarendon Press, 1971.

Hallett, G. 1967 *Wittgenstein's Definition of Meaning as Use*. New York, Fordham University Press.

Hamblin, C. L. 1973 'Questions in Montague English', *Foundations of Language*, x.

Hickman, M. 1986 'Psychosocial Aspects of Language Acquisition', in *Language Acquisition: Studies in First Language Development*, ed. P. Fletcher and M. Garman. 2nd edn, Cambridge, University Press.

Kripke, S. A. 1982 *Wittgenstein on Rules and Private Language*. Oxford, Blackwell.

Lyons, J. 1977 *Semantics*, Vol. 2. Cambridge, University Press.

Ogden, C. K. and Richards, I. A. 1923 *The Meaning of Meaning*. London, Routledge and Kegan Paul.

Putnam, H. 1975 'The Meaning of "meaning"', in *Mind, Language and Reality: Philosophical Papers*, Vol. 2. Cambridge, University Press.

Rundle, B. B. 1979 *Grammar in Philosophy*. Oxford, Clarendon Press.

Rundle, B. B. 1983 'Conjunctions: Meaning, Truth and Tone', *Mind*, xcii.

Rundle, B. B. 1986 'Memory and Causation', *Philosophical Investigations*, 9.

Russell, B. 1940 *An Inquiry into Meaning and Truth*. London, Allen and Unwin.

Ryle, G. 1949 *The Concept of Mind*. London, Hutchinson's University Library.

Stampe, D. W. 1968 'Toward a Grammar of Meaning', *Philosophical Review*, lxxvii; reprinted in *On Noam Chomsky: Critical Essays*, ed. G. Harman. New York, Doubleday Anchor, 1974.

Strawson, P. F. ed. 1967 *Philosophical Logic*. Oxford, Clarendon Press.

Tichy, P. 1978 'Questions, Answers, and Logic', *American Philosophical Quarterly*, 15.

Wittgenstein, L. 1958 *The Blue and Brown Books*. Oxford, Blackwell. [*BB*]

1958 *Philosophical Investigations*, ed. G. E. M. Anscombe and R. Rhees, 2nd edn. Oxford, Blackwell. [*PI*]

1959 'Wittgenstein's Lectures in 1930–33', in G. E. Moore, *Philosophical Papers*. London, Allen and Unwin. [*M*]

1961 *Tractatus Logico-Philosophicus*, tr. D. F. Pears and B. F. McGuiness. London, Routledge and Kegan Paul. [*TLP*]

1967 *Zettel*, ed. G. E. M. Anscombe and G. H. von Wright, tr. G. E. M. Anscombe. Oxford, Blackwell. [*Z*]

1969 *On Certainty*, ed. G. E. M. Anscombe and G. H. von Wright, tr. D. Paul and G. E. M. Anscombe. Oxford, Blackwell. [*OC*]

1970 *Lectures and Conversations on Aesthetics, Psychology and Religious Belief*, ed. C Barrett. Oxford, Blackwell. [*LA*]

1974 *Philosophical Grammar*, ed. R. Rhees, tr. A. J. P. Kenny. Oxford, Blackwell. [*PG*]

1975 *Philosophical Remarks*, ed. R. Rhees, tr. R. Hargreaves and R. White. Oxford, Blackwell. [*PR*]

1976 *Wittgenstein's Lectures on the Foundations of Mathematics, Cambridge 1939*, ed. C. Diamond. Sussex, Harvester Press. [*LFM*]

1978 *Remarks on the Foundations of Mathematics*, ed. G. H. von Wright, R. Rhees, G. E. M. Anscombe, tr. G. E. M. Anscombe, revised edn. Oxford, Blackwell. [*RFM*]

1979 *Wittgenstein's Lectures, Cambridge 1932–1935, from the notes of Alice Ambrose and Margaret MacDonald*, ed. A. Ambrose. Oxford, Blackwell. [*AWL*]

1979 *Wittgenstein and the Vienna Circle*, conversations recorded by F. Waismann, ed. B. F. McGuiness, tr. J. Schulte and B. F. McGuinness. Oxford, Blackwell. [*WVC*]

1980 *Culture and Value*, ed. G. H. von Wright in collaboration with H. Nyman, tr. P. Winch. Oxford, Blackwell. [*CV*]

1980 *Remarks on the Philosophy of Psychology*, Vol. I, ed. G. E. M. Anscombe and G. H. von Wright, tr. G. E. M. Anscombe. Oxford, Blackwell. [*RPP* I]

1980 *Remarks on the Philosophy of Psychology*, Vol. II, ed. G. H. von Wright and H. Nyman, tr. C. G. Luckhardt and M. A. E. Aue. Oxford, Blackwell. [*RPP* II]

1980 *Wittgenstein's Lectures, Cambridge 1930–1932, from the notes of John King and Desmond Lee*, ed. D. Lee. Oxford, Blackwell. [*LWL*]

1982 *Last Writings on the Philosophy of Psychology*, Vol. I, ed. G. H. von Wright and H. Nyman, tr. C. G. Luckhardt and M. A. E. Aue. Oxford, Blackwell. [*LW*I]

1982 Unpublished material cited in the von Wright catalogue (G. H. von Wright, *Wittgenstein*. Oxford, Blackwell, p. 46). [MS]

Ziff, P. 1960 *Semantic Analysis*. Ithaca, Cornell University Press.

Index